WHAT WAR DID TO US
COMBAT THROUGH THEIR EYES

By Sgt. Nicholas Laidlaw
USMC

CONTENTS

INTRODUCTION

What you are about to read is a collection of stories I have gathered from various conflicts and soldiers throughout the 20th and 21st centuries. This book does not focus on the efforts of any one individual nation. Rather, it is a montage of stories from many nations. This is my attempt to shed some light on one of the most extreme experiences human beings can endure. War. I do not claim to be a historian, a professional educational resource or even an author. I have simply gathered the stories you'd hear from your buddy who has just returned from a combat zone, or your Grandfather after a few drinks and put them all in one place for you to read them. Like any war story, they are almost impossible to verify completely but I choose to believe them. Read them, take them with a grain of salt and understand that these accounts have not been altered in any way other than major grammatical or spelling issues. This maintains their authenticity delivered by the veterans themselves. The sentence structure and paragraph format has only been altered in the smallest of ways. These are their words exactly.

You are reading these stories as if they have been sent directly to you. They are organized by war and approximate time periods, but other than that, I have included them in the order they were submitted. This is simply a collection of stories about the reality of war. The good. The bad. The hilarious and the terrifying. All of it. This is not a comprehensive list of every armed conflict since 1914, but a collection of stories I have been able to find. There are more stories from some time periods than others.

The majority of these stories were submitted anonymously. Only I know their true identity. This is to protect many of these veterans from ridicule or negative feelings from their comrades, family members, or former unit leaders. You'll see that by sharing a story anonymously, many of these veterans are able to express their true thoughts, feelings, and emotions. From their absolute exhilaration of killing an enemy, to the utter despair and mental stress of taking a human life. Many stories were submitted by the veteran's family members. They came by these stories through either written word such as diaries, letters, or stories that were passed to them verbally.

Try to keep an open mind. Too often in history the evil henchman and helpless victim have been the same man. Humans are diverse and so are their experiences and beliefs. These stories are presented to you in an unbiased, non-political manner. Any derogatory terms or language used in this book does not represent my beliefs or the beliefs of the respective branch of service the term is used in. This is simply the language used in the time and place of the story, and to remove it would deny that it happened at all. There will be language, situations, and beliefs that will not sit well in the modern world in this book. I ask that you, the reader, read these with the same respect I have presented them to you. You don't have to like it, but I ask you read them with the historical context in mind.

All of these stories were gathered by myself. Over three years of searching and talking to veterans from all nations and walks of life. A total of over 3,000 hours and almost 230 different stories. This was possible through my social media pages on Facebook and Instagram: **Battles and Beers: War Stories**.

This book is dedicated to the men, women, and children who have been witnesses to the violence of war. To my family and friends who have supported me during this endeavor, I thank you. To my mother, who let her baby boy leave home and follow his heart to join the Marines at 17 years old, I love you. Your support and encouragement helped make this book a reality. To Ricky Pollina, who encouraged me to start Battles and Beers with him; none of this would have ever happened without you. Serving with you was an honor. To my loving girlfriend Isabelle who endured countless hours of me interviewing veterans and editing word documents with me…I love you. To my dad, who sparked a love of history in me at a young age…I love you.

To the Marines: Semper Fidelis. By land, by sea. I love all of you.

Respectfully,
Nicholas Laidlaw.
Rifleman.
Sergeant, United States Marine Corps.
Charlie FAST 4th Platoon
2nd Battalion 6th Marines, Fox Co. 1st Platoon.
2nd Battalion 24th Marines, Echo Co. 2nd Platoon.
Global War on Terror.

"You don't have to like it, but you have to show up."

WORLD WAR ONE 1914-1918
WORLD WAR TWO 1939-1945

"I never blamed him"
British Soldier

In the 1970's once I was old enough, I realized my Grandfather never celebrated Christmas with us. I could tell he tried to be near us, especially us younger lads, but something was on his mind. I asked my father why he never celebrated Christmas. He was a Christian, but seemed to hate the holiday.
My father told me this story that his father told him. "During Christmas Eve in 1917, I was trapped in a deep shell hole with a German soldier. He and I were down there the entire night in the freezing cold, I held a gun on him and he held a gun on me. Both of us too afraid to shoot. It was the most terrifying and miserable night of my life."

Dad told me that later he had actually shot the German, but he didn't die right away. And that my Grandfather was too afraid and ashamed of what he had done to put the poor man out of his misery.

I never blamed my Grandfather for never celebrating Christmas with us again after that. Christmas Eve he would go into his study, and I would just leave the man be. He had earned his right to seclusion on that day.

-   Anonymous descendant of a British World War One veteran.

"Stretcher Bearers"
British Soldier

It was 1917, a year after the Somme. There had been a lot of shelling that day and consequently a lot of casualties. The British had the best of the exchanges and captured several hundred German prisoners. Lance Corporal William Laidlaw of the RAMC (Royal Army Medical Corp) had been left in charge of a group of 20 stretcher bearers by the Sergeant who being wounded in the arm, had been sent to the rear. The many wounded (German and British) were laying around waiting to be taken back to the hospitals. The situation was getting out of hand and a doctor asked Lance Corporal Laidlaw to try and get the wounded moved to the rear because if a shell landed amongst them, it would be a disaster. He responded that with only 20 men (4 per stretcher were needed because of the shell-holed ground) it was impossible to do more.

Suddenly Lance Corporal Laidlaw looked up and saw that the British Infantry were bringing the German prisoners back. Remembering something he saw at the Battle of the Somme he ran to the Colonel of the 'Yorkshires' and asked permission to use the captured prisoners to help move the wounded…the Colonel agreed. Braving the continuous shelling, he ran back, and organized the German prisoners irrespective of whether they were officers or not as stretcher bearers.

Lance Corporal Laidlaw persuaded the Germans to help move the wounded with an offer of a hot meal as soon as they had completed the mission. Some of the British Infantry were used as guards as stretcher bearers were not armed. The German gunners would not fire on their own soldiers and therefore the task of moving the wounded was safely accomplished. 'A neat job' said the Doctor afterwards – this praise meant more to Lance Corporal Laidlaw than anything else. Lance Corporal Laidlaw then continued assisting at the front as a stretcher bearer. Lance Corporal Laidlaw was awarded the Military Medal (Second highest award for bravery in the British Army) for his actions in the face of enemy fire.

-    Lance Corporal William Laidlaw. Story submitted by Neil and Ian Laidlaw

"My war in Normandy"
American Soldier

I remember sitting under a huge oak tree, wondering why we weren't running somewhere as we usually did, when I suddenly heard the sound of what I thought was a giant thunderstorm.   All I could see was wave after wave of bombers getting ready to drop their loads on the German troops ahead. It was about the most exciting and frightening sight I had ever experienced.

I saw the bombs dropping and knew that no one on the other side could possibly survive. I felt that the war must surely be over at last. But the planes kept on coming and dropping more bombs until a dust cloud as high as it was wide was created all along the front lines. Some of the planes must have turned and come back to drop a second load of bombs, because I could see what looked like bomb racks coming down, sliding back and forth in the sky like lazy kites in a breeze as they descended.

I was scared out of my mind that one or more of them would land on the tree I was sheltering under and kill me instead of the enemy. I had every right to be scared because the way it turned out, the huge cloud I described before was so dense that it confused the aim of our bombardiers to the extent that in using it as an aiming point, they began to lay their bombs on our own troops.

Many good 4th Division troops were maimed or killed that day by what was called "friendly fire". But, for whatever reason I was not to be one of them. The bombing totally flattened the town of St. Lo to the extent that you could stand on one side of it and see the other side without obstruction. I doubt that the inhabitants of St. Lo ever thought too kindly about their so- called "liberators" after that day. (If there were any survivors left to think about it.)

(Later in the Battle) We (my platoon, at least) seemed to be leaderless again, so unless we lost an officer during the bombing of St. Lo. or in the following battle, I'm at a loss to explain it. In any case, we were pretty confused about what we were expected to do next and for lack of a better idea, we decided to fall back a bit and take a well-earned rest. I remember a bunch of us standing at a crossroad smoking and joking about how few Germans were around to take a shot at, when a Lt. Colonel came up in a jeep and asked who was in command. Obviously, no one was, so he decided to take over. I do remember that he was wearing the insignia of the Armored Corps, so it must be that he had lost his command, or at least lost touch with it, during the battle, and had nothing else to do. He ordered us to deploy along a hedgerow and keep an eye out for any German troops that might turn up. Very shortly, he decided to move us to the left to join up with other units and we started what was to be a fateful move. The first thing we came to was an open gate in the hedgerow, which we soon found out was covered by a German sniper in a tree.

The first man across was shot at but missed and the Colonel decided to move us one at a time, at random intervals and on the run. This tactic worked fine until Reever (My friend) and a few more of us were left. When the colonel yelled "now", Reever took off like a rabbit, as the rest of us watched. About half way across he stopped, put his hand on the back of his belt, called out "Hey-he got me", and dropped dead. We found out later that he'd been shot in the base of his spine.

The rest of us got across without incident. Later, we came back to retrieve his body and resume the identical positions from which we had started, to the right of that gate, so I can't see for the life of me what we had done with all that maneuvering, except to get poor Reever killed. Maybe the colonel felt the same way, because I never saw him again after that. I'm not blaming him for anything- he was probably following someone else's orders all the time.
After scouts were put out at the perimeter, it turned out that a column of German tanks and infantry were "advancing" from our rear! Actually, they were retreating, but it looked like an advance to us! In any case, we were in a field right beside the road they were using and if they spotted us, they wouldn't care who owned which territory; they just plain had us dead to rights with their tanks against our rifles.

I remember the word coming down from the C.O. in whispers, "Don't panic and for Christ's sake don't shoot or make any sound whatsoever-maybe they'll miss us!" You guessed it, someone panicked and took a shot and they didn't miss us.

They clobbered us real good. One of our junior officers ran across the field during the ensuing massacre, yelling to anyone who could hear him, "Follow me!", and those of us who could, did. We went out through an opening in the back hedgerow and maybe 30-35 of us got away. He led us safely back to our own lines where we encountered a column of our own tanks.

7

After explaining our situation to the tank commander, we got behind them and returned to what was left of "L" Company. Believe me, it wasn't much. The Germans had continued their retreat, but not before they decimated our company. Everybody left was either wounded or dead and Diggins (my friend) was one of the dead ones.

He had been hit in the chest by a tank shell that must have been set for anti-tank use because it didn't even explode when it hit him, or even in the hedgerow behind him. It just went right through him like a rifle shot would, leaving a clean hole you could see right through, about 3 inches in diameter.

- Bill Reeves, US Army. 4th Infantry Division. Normandy, France. 1944.

"Opa's War"
Netherlands Partisan/Sailor

My Opa never wrote down his account of his wartime experiences, but he did pass down some stories to me before his passing. Anecdotes that seemed like a good adventure to my young self, but now with adulthood I think how lucky we are in this country to have never experienced occupation by a foreign army.

My Opa, Hans, was 13-14 when the German army occupied the Netherlands and his hometown. He recalled how shortly after, he saw his best friend and their family being hauled out of their house and loaded onto a truck. The family dog was making a general racket during this and a German soldier shot it in the street. Opa didn't clarify if his friend's family was Jewish or simply "On a list," but he did say he never again saw his friend after that.

When the Germans occupied a territory, it was standard to confiscate all civilian radios so that the populace couldn't tune into allied stations like the BBC. Through word of mouth though, Hans and some of his friends found out the confiscated radios were being stored in a basement warehouse in town. Armed with a map of the basement, a length of rope and a small flashlight, he and some friends headed out one night to steal some radios back. With a window pried open, Hans was lowered down but the basement was deeper than expected and he had not reached the bottom when the rope came up short. Assuming that he couldn't be that far from the ground, he let go only to crash down upon a pile of glass/ceramic power line insulators. Having lost his map and small flashlight, he yelled to his friends to get him out of there and with one boy holding on to another ones ankles, the rope was lowered just enough to extricate Hans from the basement and disappear into the night as the sound of hobnailed boots clattered up a nearby street towards them.

Being young boys, my Opa and his friends weren't blowing up rail lines and assassinating occupation officials, but they still found ways to poke at the occupation forces. He recalled once stealing a bag of tea towels/napkins from the laundry room where German officers were quartered, anything to inconvenience them. He also told of grabbing live rounds out of an airplane that crashed nearby

8

for making homemade "flare pots." He said they would take the powder out of the casings and mix in ground iron or copper to make red or blue colored flames, pour the mixture into cans and then place the cans on bridges in town. Upon lighting them, he and his friends would run away as fast as possible and listen to the yelling of sentries and vehicles racing about in the middle of the night, the Germans thinking it was some kind of signal for an airborne drop.

Upon the conclusion of the war, my Opa joined the Dutch Royal Navy and served on a river boat as a radio operator in Indonesia during the Netherlands attempts to maintain control of their colonies. He spoke less of this experience than growing up in occupied Holland, but I remember him saying there were a lot of holes in both sides of that boat, no doubt from multiple ambush attempts.

Surviving that, he moved from the Netherlands to Canada, then to the U.S. in the 50's, working as an engineer for Boeing, one of his projects being the struts connecting the jet engines to the wing of the 747. He passed away from cancer, surrounded by family in 2007 on his 80th birthday.

- Story of Hans Gijswijt, Submitted by his grandson Colton.

"Dieppe Raid"
Canadian Soldier

We were transferred to the assault landing-craft from the mother ship and arranged in two rows, one on the starboard side and the other row on the port side. I was second in line on the port side, carrying a Bren gun. Behind me was Private Bob Green who was carrying the spare barrel for the Bren. The assault craft pulled away and as it grew daylight, I noticed a man sitting on my right between the two rows of men, and as I had never seen him before and he was not one of our regiment, I began to study him. He was a lieutenant and although I looked for clues to his identity, I could find none, and I finally came to the conclusion that he was from an English regiment and was possibly something to do with intelligence. I mention this not because of something which occurred later.

We landed at 5:25 AM by my watch which I glanced at as the ramp went down, and as we raced up the beach, I remember thinking; how was it possible to surprise an enemy in broad daylight? Lance Corporal Johnny Crow was ahead of me and a little to the left as we jumped clear of some low barbed wire, and then directly in front of us was a wall with barbed wire entanglements on top. I saw Lance Corporal Crow thrust a Bangalore torpedo under the barb wire on the top of the wall and then drop back to wait for the explosion but the Bangalore failed to explode.

I made my way to the sight of the wall where the sea had swept a convenient incline of shale which I climbed. Glancing to the left I saw Johnny had climbed the wall in an attempt to find out why the Bangalore had not exploded when his head and shoulders were above the wall, he was thrown back as if he had been kicked and he fell on to the beach, shot through the chest.

Looking to my right I saw the pill-box I was looking for and opened fire with the Bren. On my right and left I heard the other men open fire with their rifles. On the third pom of ammo, I saw the helmet of one of our men from B Company had gone in. I slid down the shale a little, silently cursing the tracer bullets, when there was a shell burst in front of me. I ducked my head but unfortunately I left my right hand still around the trigger of the Bren and felt a sharp pain in the fingers. I withdrew my hand and found small pieces of shrapnel sticking out of two fingers which were bleeding.

Private Campbell, who was directly behind me suggested he bandage it with my field dressing, but to fire the Bren, I found it too cumbersome so I removed it later on. As my hand was being bandaged, I looked to see which of the men were there. There was no sign of Bob Green, While Sgt. Fairburn was a few yards behind Pte. Cambell, and on the Sergeant's left was Pte. Herb Prince and on his right was Pte. "Skim" Robertson. Corporal Hartnett had been wounded and was dragged from the barbed wire, where he was hung up, and was being attended to by Pte. George McRitchie. On the other side of Prince was my brother Bob.

I recommenced firing at the esplanade directly in front of me when suddenly one of our tanks appeared from the right. The tank swung left and if it has travelled another fifty yards it would have been about the same distance directly in front of me and I thought when it reaches that point I could get behind it and advance. It was not to be. A shell exploded on the front of the tank and after the smoke cleared I could see the track had been knocked off. Another tank directly to my right, appeared to have been bogged down in the shale but their gun was still firing at regular intervals.

Something clattered on my helmet and again I dropped back. After a time there was a shout from some of the men, "The Germans are going to attack with bayonets, everybody fix bayonets!" I glanced over the top and shouted back to them, "There is nobody there, you can unfix your bayonets." Where this panic idea came from I will never know.

Later we were joined by an officer, some say it was Major Currie but I still say it was Lt. Dick. His head was bandaged from just above the eyes, and covered the whole of his forehead and some hair. Sergeant Fairburn asked him if he knew what was going on and he replied that all our R.T.s had been knocked out with most of our officers and they could get no word from HQ. Something tickled my cheek and I wiped it with my hand. It was all blood and puss.

It was time to throw the smoke bombs and I threw them one by one as far as I could towards the town. When the smoke was at its thickest, I began to drop back towards the water's edge. There was a ship stranded on the beach broadside to the town and I took refuge behind it.

My hearing was returning and I could hear the sharp crack of a rifle near at hand and glancing up I saw someone using the slim mast of the ship for cover taking pot-shots at the Germans. I do not know who it was, but I think it was a

Marine Commando. Where it came from, I do not know, but an assault landing craft came to the water's edge behind me, and I decided to get on board. As I made my way towards it, a figure came running along the beach towards me and I recognized Pte. Gordon Joseph Lee (nicknamed General Lee for short). He was in front of me heading for the craft when I heard a shout from my right. I turned and saw one of our men sitting in the water with his knees up and one knee-cap had been shot off. He shouted, "Don't leave me here! Take me with you!" I shouted, "Hey, General, give me a hand!" and we lifted the man over the gunwales of the boat, then General got in followed by me.

The boat was taking in water, it was nearly knee-deep as we headed out to sea. A Naval Lieutenant who appeared to be in charge, was also steering the boat and was the only naval person on board. He told me to drop my bren-gun overboard to lighten the load, which I did very reluctantly and I felt naked without it.

The boat was taking in more water when the Lieutenant pulled up beside a ship which was partially sunk only its bow was above water level. "All able-bodied men will have to get off otherwise we will not get much further." Said the lieutenant. General and I climbed over the side and onto the sunken ship, leaving 3 wounded men half in and half out of the water, not counting the man we had put on board.

The sunken ships deck was sloping and we were forced to lie down and retain any hold. There were two other occupants on board who were F.M.R.s and were slightly wounded. Later we were joined by a naval lieutenant and a mate who swam their way to us.

When the tide came in, we were thrown into the water, the two naval personnel deciding to swim for the shore. I lost touch with "General", because of the choppy seas and having to ship off my equipment, blowing up the Mae West and swallowing a lot of salt water. Anyway, I think General could swim while I could not.

After about an hour in the water and I judged it was about ½ mile to the shore, I spotted a life-buoy floating near me. I forced myself over to it, grabbed it. This lifted me well up out of the water and prevented me from swallowing anymore. Later I saw someone nearby and I paddled my way over and caught him by the sleeve. His head was bowed over occasionally touching the water. I pulled his head back, his eyes opened and he looked at me. He tried to say something and blood came from his mouth. His head fell to one side and I figured he was dead. It was "General" Lee.

Another swimmer soon joined me. It was Pte. Walsh, who asked me how I was doing. I replied that I could not swim, but provided I was picked up I would be all right. He said, "I am going to try to make it to the beach." I wished him luck and watched him swim away. I was to be questioned after the war as to his whereabouts because they never found him, although I watched him swimming towards the shore and kept my eyes on him even when he became just a speck and I still swear he reached the beach and pulled himself out of the water. I watched him to occupy my mind, and I was interested to see if he made it.

The current swept me close to the harbor entrance of Dieppe in the late afternoon and I could plainly see the German sentry pacing back and forth. I weighed up my chances. Should I shout and attract his attention? Having attracted his attention, would he help or would he shoot me? I decided to stay quiet, there was a chance I might still get away or a British boat could pick me up.

The water was warm but sometimes cold. When it was cold I knew the current was taking me out to sea again. Three times I was taken to near the harbor entrance and then swept out to sea about 3 miles from shore.

It began to grow dusk and eventually the sight of Dieppe faded into the darkness. I heard the faint chug of engines and I peered into the darkness. A ship approached in front of me about 30 feet away. I hastily weighed up my chances for a second time. My legs at the top of my thighs were beginning to get the cramps and I knew I couldn't last much longer. Besides with any luck it may be a British ship. I could just make out 3 figures on deck doing various duties, one of which was coiling a rope. I shouted and saw all 3 stiffen and look around. I shouted again and one of the men spotted me and threw a lifebelt with a rope attached. It fell short the first time, but the second time I was able to grab it and they hauled me aboard. I could not stand, so while two of the men held me the other stripped me of all clothing and placed a blanket around my shoulders. They carried me below.

I was taken to a room with tiered bunks on either side, and a circular table in the centre and various cupboards at the far end. I was placed in one of the lower bunks. The men said something to me. I shrugged my shoulders as I didn't understand. They left me and went on deck but in about 5 minutes they were back. They placed something on the table and when I looked I realized it was the contents of my pockets. The watch my father had given me, the Waterman pen and pencil set my Mother had given me, two half-crown and my cigarette lighter.

For a minute or two they seemed to be arguing with each other, then suddenly each made a grab for the articles on the table. One had the cigarette lighter, another the watch, while the other two shared the coins and pencil set. They went to a cupboard and came back with a large slice of black bread and margarine. He spoke again, and went to another cupboard and came back with a small glass of Schnapps. While he watched, I ate the bread and drank the Schnapps, then thanked him in English. He nodded, but seemed reluctant to go. I had the feeling that something was troubling him. He spoke again, thrust his hand into his pocket, withdrew it, and tossed my cigarette lighter onto the blanket, then almost ran from the room.

I was exhausted and with the food, the Schnapps and the warmth of the ship coupled with the throb of the engines, I was soon asleep. I was awakened by someone shaking my shoulder and I observed the 4 men standing by the bunk. They indicated by sign language that I should get up, where upon they placed a blanket around my shoulders and blind folded me. I noticed the engines had stopped. I was led from the room up the gangway and across the deck. Someone placed my left hand on an iron ladder rung and patted my backside indicating that I should climb. It was a long way up that ladder, considering I was blind folded and trying to keep a blanket from slipping off. I finally reached the tip and hands guided me to lie on a stretcher.

The blind fold was immediately taken off and I was looking into the light of a torch held by a young looking German in uniform who spoke perfect English, and the questions came thick and fast. "What is your name?" "Mavin." I said. "Your rank and Regiment?" "B37485 Private" "How many men were on this raid?" I shook my head. "When is the next raid taking place?" "I don't know" I said. "Come now, we know this raid was only a feint and the big invasion is coming this morning. Where?" I shook my head. By his question I knew it was in the early morning hours of the 20th of August. I became bold and said to him, I am only allowed to give you my regiment number, rank and name. He nodded, but he became surly. He turned and said something in German where upon two soldiers stepped forward and picked up the stretcher and started to carry me away. His parting shot was, "We knew you were coming you know. We knew some weeks ago."

- Pte. Wilfred "Scotty" Mavin. Royal Hamilton Light Infantry. Dieppe Raid, 1942. Submitted by his Grandson, Mitchell Mavin.

"Grandpa's Legacy"
United States

My grandpa was an anti-aircraft gunner on the USS San Diego (CL-53) during World War II. His ship received 18 battle stars during the war and never lost a man in combat. He served at Iwo Jima, Okinawa, and the Philippines. He also shot down a Japanese Zero during combat operations.

His ship had the unique distinction of being the first to enter Tokyo Bay on 27 August 1945. He told us how he was standing on the deck of the ship as they entered the Bay. He says the city was quiet, and there was not a person in sight, except for a lone man standing on a dock looking out at the American armada approaching. This man seemed frozen in shock or fear, and finally he turned and ran into town. The sight of this lone Japanese man on the docks of Tokyo Bay stuck with my grandpa until his death.

He left the service as a Lieutenant, Junior Grade. I'm currently a Marine officer stationed in Okinawa. When I pinned on 1st Lieutenant on Oki, I used the silver bar he wore during the Battle of Okinawa

- 1stLt Cooper Strand, USMC

"War story"
American Soldier

       This is a story my father told me when he was the Sergeant of a mortar unit in WW2. He was in the 259th Infantry 65th Division Company K in charge of a 60mm mortar unit. They were in combat in the city of Neumarkt Germany, April 1945. He was on the 2nd floor of a building at the end of a street sighting targets and the mortar team was behind the building. There was a machinegun team on the first floor under him shooting down the street. He would spot a target and run to the back of the building to yell out the coordinates to the team, and then run back the front of the building to see if it was fired effectively.

       A German tiger tank that he described as "Their biggest tank" turned onto the street at the end of the lane and shot a round at the machinegun team below him. The explosion caused part of the building to collapse, and he was knocked out with a concussion. When he woke up on the 2nd floor everyone was gone so he retreated and later found his mortar team. They thought he had died in the building due to the explosion and it collapsing.

       I corroborated his story when I found an account in a 65th Division history book that told of the same incident from the surviving machine gunners view of the tank that was in the building below him. He had several other close calls with German mortar fragments killing a man standing next to him and another time he took cover under a wagon during a German artillery barrage that he described the shrapnel as "sounding like rain on a tin roof" as he hid under the wagon.

-    As told by Ed Schroeder 65th Division, 259th Infantry, Company K.

"Chinese discipline"
American Aviator

       My Pa signed up for the US Army Air Corps during the early years of WWII. He was assigned to be a radio operator aboard a C-47 in the India Burma Theater. His mission was to deliver high octane fuel to the Chinese via the Khyber Pass in Pakistan bordering Afghanistan. The US military called it "The Hump". Besides being constantly shot at by the enemy the route at the time was one of the most dangerous in the world. On one particular mission his cargo was high octane fuel and Chinese soldiers.

       After take-off they soon realized they carried to much weight to clear the mountains. If they didn't lose the weight before the mountains they would all crash and die. Eventually one of the pilots came up with a plan. Dump the high octane fuel and they'll make it to their destination. That wasn't acceptable to the Chinese officers onboard. A question loomed in the air. How much weight needs to be lost in order to clear the mountains? A figure was come up with. The highest ranked Chinese officer on board pointed out to a group of Chinese soldiers.

14

Pointing his finger towards them he said in Chinese you all out the back. My Pa couldn't believe what he was witnessing. They opened the back hatch and marched the Chinese soldiers off to their death. No parachutes no arguments, just march. They made it to their destination. They had successfully completed their mission. No one questioned a thing.

- Staff Sgt. Harry J Raye. Story submitted by Nicholas Raye

"The bravest generation"
Scottish Soldier

On D-day a shell exploded next to my grandfather's landing craft and flipped it over. The water caught on fire and he saved his commanding officer and got a medal for it. Once they got to the top of beach his best friend got killed right in front of him sadly and he said that he never took one prisoner after that. He said him and his mates would take turns 'taking care of them' and said the Americans really didn't do that because they didn't get their homes bombed by the Jerry's.

He also told me him and a few guys got selected to sneak up to German lines at night one time so they could observe and see what was going on for an attack they were going to have the next day. On the way the found a German solider in a forward listen post and only were able to see him because the guy was sneaking a smoke. The officer told my grandfather to take him out.
He said he sneaked up and stabbed him to death with his bayonet. I was shocked and said, 'What did you do then grandpa?' and he said he was like, 'Oi let's go!' to his mates like it was nothing!

I was shocked when I found out because he was such a nice guy and I never ever as much heard him raise his voice to anyone! But he was proud of his service until the day he passed. I just wish I was older then so I could have asked him more about it because he never spoke about it to my mom or grandmother really at all.

- Anonymous Descendant of Jack Nicholson Scottish Royal Marine Commando. World War Two

"Death is random"
US Soldier

You want to know about war? It's random, that's the best way I can put it. I showed up to the replacement depot for the 1st ID in France with 6 other guys who went to the same company as me. By the time we got to Belgium it was only me and one other guy. The rest had been killed on D-Day or in the hedgerow fighting after. So, we attacked and took this town from the Germans. We were held up in the cellar of a building while the Germans hit us with artillery. When it let up, my friend, the last of us from that replacement group told me he was going up top to get some air and have a smoke. Minutes later we heard one rifle crack and we ran up top. My friend was lying dead up there with one round having entered above his eye. That's what war is, random. You never know when it's your time

- Cpl. Albert Larkin, 1st Infantry Division, Western Front, World War Two.

"The way he told it"
American Soldier

Just outside Bastogne on Dec 29, 1944 they (My Grandfather) came into heavy contact with some German tigers. His tank destroyers was hit by a tiger and that blew his arm off. Everyone got out but the driver. My grandfather went back into the burning tank destroyer (at the point missing an arm) and drug the driver out and was dragging him across the road when the Germans opened up with a machine gun. My grandfather dropped the driver and laid on top of him and that's where the 7 gunshot wounds came from in his legs and hip. After that he crawled with his one good elbow to a ditch and stayed there until he was rescued.

- SSGT Bill Brock 654th Tank Destroyer Bn supporting the 35th ID. Story submitted by Tyler Blackmon

"Driving coffins"
German Tanker

On 15. January of 1945 I was put into the 1st Companie, 4th Battalion of the Panzer Ersatz und Ausbildungsregiment 4 of the Division Hermann Göring. As the Americans were advancing fast, our unit was put together with other remaining Panzer Units, forming the "Panzergruppe Grafenwöhr". On the 7th April 1945 we got our brand new Panthers at the MAN Fabric in Nürnberg. They were painted in a dark yellow tone. We only called them "driving coffins". In total we had 8 tanks, my commander was an experienced NCO, and he was part of the unit since 1942. Our company commander was Reimar Spitzbarth. South of Nürnberg, at Allersberg. We were driving on the Autobahn, a really open position looking at the situation from nowadays. Suddenly American tanks advanced out of the woods a few hundred meters to our right. To this day I don't know why they drove out of their cover. We quickly turned our tank sideways, just in time, as the first rounds were already flying our way.

For a short period of time we battled with the Americans, before we also closed the distance, as we weren't receiving any more fire from the allied tanks. I can't remember whether we lost any Panthers in the engagement itself, but as we drove onto the field separating the woods and the Autobahn, our tank sunk into the deep mud after about 30 meters, because the field was extremely wet and muddy. Our hull was laying on the earth, so we had no other chance than to bail out.

We made it to a nearby farmer's house when my commander shouted at me asking why I hadn't brought the machine gun - a very valuable weapon - with me. As Radio Operator you had to do that. I completely forgot. So I was forced to run the 100 meters over open terrain back to the tank. By now the Americans had realized what was going on, and fired at me with all infantry weapons they had.

By miracle I somehow reached the tank, and got the machine gun out of the ball mount, when a bazooka round bounced off the side of the abandoned tank. I quickly got out with the MG in my hands, running back to my comrades, still under enemy fire. We didn't place any explosives, or burn the tank. It was no use, we knew the war was lost, and we didn't want to put our lives into any more danger.

In an infantry engagement soon after I had to leave the machine gun, as we were out of ammo. We had few rounds anyway.

- 'Wolfgang' German Soldier. 1st Companie, 4th Battalion of the Panzer Ersatz und Ausbildungsregiment 4 of the Division Hermann Göring. Western Front. WW2.

"They kept coming"
German Officer

I returned to Russia in time to take part in the fierce defensive battles and to secure between Staraya Russia and Lake Ilmen. Here there were terrible mass attacks by the Red Army on the positions of the 81st Infantry Division. We lay on the bank of a frozen river as a backup. There weren't many of us - about half a company, about 50-60 men - the companies weren't any bigger. We had 3 machine guns set up on a dam and thus controlled the entire area in front of us. Nevertheless, the Russians attacked. Not once, not twice...5 times...10 times. After a short mortar attack they came across the ice with a loud hurry. They ran in lines - like Napoleon's - across the ice and our machine guns cut right through them. Hundreds of dead and wounded lay on the ice and obstructed the next wave, which immediately followed. After two days we had to give way because we had no more ammunition for the machine guns and infantry weapons. The innumerable dead piled up on the ice, we had 8 wounded by mortar fire.

- Captain Eberhardt Hawranke. German Army. Eastern Front

"Combined War Effort"
American Soldier

My dad was an infantryman in WW2 with the 8th ID. He landed on Utah Beach at about D +20 as a replacement. After a night spent at the Repo Depo he was assigned to his company, platoon, and squad. Shortly thereafter his division began marshalling for a move towards Brest, France as the plan was to seize the excellent port facilities there (that would turn SNAFU as the Germans demolished them).

His squad was given a mission to reconnoiter down a road to check for German roadblocks and mines as command wanted to push tanks down it and later more vehicles. My dad's squad was moving slowly and quietly down the road when a French farmer on a hay wagon with two huge Belgian draft horses came up from behind. Between the Frenchman, who knew a little English, and squad members who knew a little French from phrase books, they managed to converse somewhat.

The farmer asked what they were doing and whether the road was clear of Germans. My father started to reply "we're looking for mines", but before he could get it out his platoon sergeant shut him up and replied with something to the effect "We're done here and heading back. We haven't seen any Germans". Both parties bid each other goodbye and went their separate ways with the farmer, wagon, and horses proceeding in the direction that the squad was supposed to reconnoiter.

The farmer got a few hundred yards down the road when there came a huge explosion that sent bits of wagon, horseflesh, and farmer raining down. My father turned to the platoon sergeant and asked him "How could you do that"? His NCO replied, "I came all the way over here, thousands of miles to fight for him, he can do his part too"! They returned to their lines and reported that the road was spiked with anti-tank mines. Apparently the horses were heavy enough to set one off and were just unlucky enough to have stepped on one.

- Descendant of an American World War Two Veteran

"I was the only survivor"
Hungarian Soldier

I did not want to go to war, actually no one did. We just had to. We heard about what had happened to our soldiers at the Don River, and saw the amputated men, so we knew what was coming. But this was something else, now the Soviets had attacked our country, killed and raped our people and were hungry for revenge. We know that all what stood between them and our families.

We felt fear and horror, not bravery or patriotism. My company was surrounded near the city of Karcag, with no hope left. We knew that they (the Soviets) were out of food themselves, so they did not take POWs. Only some 20 of us were kept alive, the others were shot on sight when they were surrendering.

Then a long rail trip came deep inside to Siberia, and 5 years of hard labour in a forest. A lot of young people froze to death, starved to death, were beaten to death or simply they just died due to exhaustion. Somehow my family got a message that I died. When the Soviets released us from captivity, they only took us to Ukraine on train, from there we had to walk.

We had no water, food, money, or even clothes. We used sacks to make some kind of clothing, and ate frozen carrots from the ground so not to starve. When I enlisted, I was a miner at home, 197 cm tall and 90 kgs. When I arrived home again I was only 47 kgs. When the villagers saw me they did not recognize me at first, but then someone who did told the priest that a miracle happened, I got home.

Only I did from our village, the others were amputees, but none of the other prisoners survived. After I had met my family, the priest told everyone to go to the church for a mass. There I realised how lucky I am. I saw all the women in black, the widows and the mothers and daughters.

- Private Kálmán Verebélyi. Hungarian Army. 1944-1945. POW 1945-49. Eastern Front World War Two

"Only three came home…:"
Romanian Soldier

I was fourteen when I decided to join the army in 1941. Most of us wanted adventure and to avenge Romania's losses from the previous year. With the help of my older sister, I faked my birth certificate and went to the recruiters and told them I was sixteen. I did look old for my age. The sergeant there laughed and said 'Hell you're not! You're a seventeen year old man!'

Two weeks later, I found myself in Odessa, Ukraine with other boys from my town. We spent a couple weeks in Odessa before moving on to Crimea. The combat there was just crazy. Guys falling left and right but we got through it. Sevastopol ended up being where I got my orders to transfer to the Don region next to Stalingrad. It was colder than hell on that steppe. The Russians shelled us day and night as we awaited in this hole for that hell to end. Our bunker or hole, whatever you want to call it, was blown up by the Russian artillery. I was the only survivor from my squad.

I was taken prisoner of war and taken to Siberia. The train ride there was like going into an ice box. Men would freeze solid, and we'd throw them out the side of the train for the wolves. I spent a year in the Russian prisons until I was called again to fight for the Russians and go home. Most of us decided to go home and risk dying in combat. Russian veterans from Stalingrad would walk through our ranks and find out who fought at the Don. If you fought at the Don, poof, you'd get a bullet in your head.

I made it back home in 1944 at the age of seventeen and was a squad leader. Me and my childhood friend Nicu were once again thrown into war on the eastern front. We were outside Budapest at a village where Nicu found a sewing machine in a field for his mom. His mom asked him to bring one back if he ever found one. One day, we were patrolling a forest, and Nicu was carrying the stupid machine on his back by the neck when a sniper shot at him...

Nicu died instantly from the bullets ricochet that went into his neck. Every night, I can still hear their screams and see the faces of the men I killed and the guys who never made it home. Twenty five to maybe thirty boys left from my town to fight the Russians. Only three of us came home in 1945.

-Vasile Tolan. Regiment: 2nd Dorobanți, 11th Infantry division.

"For the Emperor"
Japanese Soldier

I am reminded of when I first realized I was not immortal and protected by valiant youth alone. We were approaching from the wilderness like ghosts. We were supposed to attack in the middle of the night when we could barely see the moon between the branches above, but we ran into so many distractions and obstacles, the sky was suddenly purple and then blue again with a golden sun by the time we had arrived at the barracks of the enemy.

Even now, I wonder who those men were. I believe they were Indians and Britons. Either way, we somehow had set off one of their diversions. I heard the jingle of wooden plates and spoons, it was a chime that one of our men had knocked down and it knocked through the trees like a maddened spirit striking the graves of its neighbors. I swallowed hard and remembered that we received fire first. The enemy had these nice rifles, their wood was red like blood.

They fired on and on, endlessly at us. All we had to do was keep our heads down and charge. Some of us did not have helmets, but those of us who did had stuffed them with twigs and branches. Some stuffed berries but were tormented by birds.

I remember thinking that "I have been shot! By all things, I have been shot in the head and now I am bleeding!" But it was merely my sweat running down my face. It was thick as blood and just as warm. I was so dehydrated that everything in my body felt dry. My bones grinded against each other in the joints like pegs being hammered into the earth for a tent.

Every step hurt me, I could feel it in my hips, in my stomach. I fell forward and vomited. It smelled like a campfire. I got up again and we pursued the enemy back into their own base. We hopped over their fortified wall of bags and hidden foliage. Then we approached their miserable base and I swear, every time I poked up my head from behind their weapon crates, I saw a new face staring back at me.

I would pop up again and fire, then go down and repeat the process. Eventually, we were doing this so often that we became immune to the terror of gunfire. I heard moaning up ahead, I thought "I must have killed so many of these men!"

I did not realize that I was involuntarily screaming the entire time. A bullet had cut through my cover and hit my flask. Water and blood poured out. I was badly injured. I was bleeding! It was just not on my face. When I collapsed and vomited, it was my body screaming in pain but the heat was so terrible I did not notice that a piece of bullet scraped my body. The bullet went in and out, tearing my muscle and flesh.

As I breathed, I felt pressure against my ribs. My ribs had felt like a casket for my dying organs. I was a walking dead man and suddenly, I was so terrified. So terrified that I would die. I try to reload my weapon but I am out of ammo. I scavenge the body of my friends who are beside me. Many of them are bleeding, many of them crying. I find one brother who is smiling as he holds himself together. He had been shot three times and his chest was spitting blood. His rounds that I took from him were crimson red in his blood.

He took one and put the round in his mouth, he spit it out and into his hand it was clean. Just as he did so, blood began to fill his cheeks. "If I am going to die! You better kill some for me!" He begged me and he tried to get up, he carried himself with an empty rifle and shoveled his way toward cover but collapsed and died before me.

I felt the gravity of his spirit leaving. A sudden emptiness. I was forced to stand on his corpse, among others - shooting at the enemy. I had hit at least two. I did not know until later that I killed at least three. But another man, he had shot five and killed them all. Each shot was between the heart and the head. He was an excellent shot. I always had a terrible habit, I aim for the mid-section and then my rounds aim downward. I shot many men in the pelvis. Their upper left thigh, sometimes in the groin. I eventually retreated while holding my injury but an officer stopped me. "No, you must go back!" "I need help! I need to treat my injury or I will die useless!" I argued.

The officer grabbed me, he was a young man with broken teeth and his eyes were blistering red. His whole face was sunburnt by the sun already. Even his sclera. "You misunderstand me! We are the rear soldiers! There is no one back there!"

I am terrified. I think all of us are dead now. And I am reminded of this scene when we are on the hill in Burma yet again by the river. I see my friends moving into the jungle to find a way to cross this gap and I am scared. I remember seeing this before, where all those men lead forward and were exposed into the open and died.

Back then, near that base - the officer shook sense into me and he helped me treat my wound. We ran to the positions of defense again. But as soon as we got there, the foreign enemy had suddenly dropped their rifles. I thought, "Maybe they have ran entirely out of munitions?" But I look back and see my comrades. Every single tree was occupied. Those who had not died, had surrounded the area with high positions. They used our deaths as a strategy, it was brilliant and brave! They climbed the trees and set up on branches, some jumped down onto the fortifications of the enemy. When the fighting ceased, it was because they started shooting the enemy and suddenly the enemy had no place to hide. These warriors in high trees! They did it! They made our enemy submit!

But we gave them no mercy. The enemy had given themselves to us. We aimed and we fired and from the trees, those men who laid down their weapons were shot too. Three of them survived. Their injuries were so horrible, we had to kill them mercifully. They did not let us suffer. If we were in the open and we were not capable of fighting back, as I saw a young man on his belly with holes in his back - these men wasted a bullet to put him out of his suffering. He was no threat to him, he was carving into his own wounds desperately with a knife to remove the bullets. He was going to die. He did not deserve to suffer.

It was beautiful to see. The blood and mud and then these men who so graciously surrendered now struggling to even breathe. In that moment I saw myself in them and I knew that I rather be shot too, than to be left dying here. I smiled and they smiled back, they begged me to do it. I had five rounds, licked clean from my dead comrade but I put one in my rifle and was aiming at this dying soldier's head. The officer from before stopped me and said "Let me do it. We can't waste ammo." And he personally stabbed them all through the ears with a blade. He would roll them over and as they coughed and got air in their bodies, they solemnly had to watch as the officer pinned their head to the ground and stabbed them with a blade. Ear to ear. The third man was struggling, he nearly sat up but the officer put him down and then held the man's free hand intimately. Their fingers were intertwined and both men were crying.

I felt sensations of lightning through my body and my eyes were wet. My eyes were sweating too as I watched the young officer slowly dig the blade into the man's ear and eventually through his head. Their grip lasted for what must have been an hour. We did not say any word to anyone about this. The officer got up, cleaned his face with water from a flask and urinated behind a tree. He then said "Let's wait for the rest of our people" and so we did.

Now, here I am - marching down this dry terrain in a humid jungle. The foliage from trees rope me in like a noose - I am like a fish constantly escaping lines! But I make it without any hooks in my face. My friend, Ashen, is scouting ahead due to his experience. But it is also because they expect him to be the first to be shot. He is expendable, even among those who favour him. In a rare bravery in these circumstances, I crawl down on my stomach and I am near him in the trees. He says, "Look. These men. Are they Gurkha?" We heard about the Gurkha the Brits deployed at times. And their strange blades. The men up ahead, two dark skinned Burmese men who were likely not a part of any conflict, were carving a tree with their own blade. At first, it was similar to a Katana. But it was thick and crude. But curved. I know now that it is a "dha". But I jokingly say to Ashen: "That is the sword they use to kill elephants."

- "Taro" Anonymous Imperial Japanese Soldier fighting in Burma. Story submitted by his grandson.

"A sniper killed him instantly"
German Soldier

You cannot imagine the despair of the city. For you younger people, even veterans of terrible wars, I can't imagine it being worse than Stalingrad. Bodies lay absolutely everywhere. So many killed by marksmen. So many friends and officers.

On one such occasion I remember we crossed a street. No one ever wanted to go first, but I always wanted to go first because by the time you were halfway across the street, the Russians had only just noticed you. It was the second or third man who usually got killed. I wanted to go first, but another man started running before me. He hadn't made it four or five paces when his head suddenly and violently jolted to the right. We heard a dull crunch, and then a loud snap. He had been killed by a Russian marksman at full sprint. Shot right in the head.

Many of us believed that our veteran status and experience for survival wouldn't even keep us from death. How many times can you beat the odds? Survival seemed to be a miracle only few would be rewarded with.

-   Mr. "E." German Army 6th Army. Stalingrad, 1942. Story submitted by his grandson.

"His blood, our lives"
German Soldier

During the war I was a machine gunner in the 144th Gebirgsjäger Regiment on the Russian front. During our long retreat I was often assigned to be the rear vanguard of our battalion along with a few marksman, riflemen and other machine gunners. I do not tell you this out of pride, but to convey to you true comradeship. My team and I were holding in a ditch when a large Soviet force appeared before us. Too many to handle. Our officer commanded we withdraw but one or two of us remain behind to slow the enemy down. I volunteered with my assistant gunner. The officer said the MG was too important to leave, so we were left with our self-loading rifles.

As our team ran fast as rabbits behind us away from the Soviets, myself and my assistant fired at the enemy to try to slow them. When it became clear we were running out of time ourselves to escape my assistant looked at me and told me to run. I told him no, but he kicked my leg with his and said to go and it was useless that both of us die. I got up and ran. I didn't look back. But I heard his self-loading rifle fire several more times, followed by a Russian machine gun. And then nothing. One man's sacrifice saved 14 others. Because of him, I lived to see three children and 19 grandchildren.

-   Anonymous German Soldier. 144th Gebirgsjäger Regiment, Eastern Front. Autumn of 1944.

"They weren't fearful men"
Russian Soldier

Both of my biological grandfathers on my mom and dad's side fought at Stalingrad. They knew each other before their kids got married, and fought together. When I was a kid my family immigrated to the US and I didn't meet my grandfathers until I was almost 20.

In the 90's I flew to Moscow to finally meet them. It was a tearful reunion and they were both at the airport to greet me. My dad's dad has lost his leg when a German panzer ran over it, and my mom's dad dragged him through the rubble and then helped him hobble back to safety. They both told me, "We will take you to Stalingrad. Show you where our family was born." When we got to the memorial, my grandpa with the missing leg was having trouble walking to the memorial. My other grandfather put him on his back and carried him all the way to Mamayev Kurgan.

I remember thinking, "50 years ago he was carrying him away from this spot. And today, he is carrying him again to show THEIR grandson where they fought together. This bond can't be broken." They are both passed on now. But I'll always remember that moment.

-    Anonymous descendant of the Defenders of Stalingrad.

"Granddad's Medals"
German Soldier

My grandpa was in the German army during WW2. Growing up, he never talked about it with me or my dad. After he was a POW he immigrated to the US and lived the rest of his life working in Minnesota. About ten years ago, he was heading out the door. He was at the hospital and asked me to grab a wooden box out of his basement and bring it to him.

I brought the box and laid it next to him in the hospital on the table. He asked me to open it. Inside it was full of old pictures and items from his time during the war. Medals, rank insignia...stuff like that.

Turns out my grandpa was a really good soldier on the Eastern Front. He was wounded 4 times and destroyed 12 Russian tanks and had received medals for both. I couldn't believe that this gentle old man I had known all my life was such a badass dude in his youth.

He asked me to hand him pictures so he could look at them. He smiled and started crying. 'I wanted to see their faces before I die. I'm the only one left, and I'll see them soon.'

It was a picture of him and his friends in a trench with a dog dressed up as a soldier. It had a helmet on and a cigarette in its mouth. Apparently he was the only one of his friends to survive the war. He died a few days after that and I buried him with all of his things.

-    Anonymous Descendant of a German Soldier. Eastern Front. World War Two.

24

"Humanity at its best"
Russian Soldier

My grandfather told me that hate between Russian and German troops on the very front, front lines was not always so bad. In some parts he said it was almost live and let live. Before he passed he told me they were in Hungary in a trench fort. The Germans were very, very close to them in their trenches. My grandfather said that one of his friends from the Leningrad area played the balalaika (a small guitar) in the night time in the trenches.

Both sides would be quiet for minutes at a time and listen to him. One day he was killed (the soldier with the balalaika) by a mortar shell. After a few days with no music, the Germans started yelling at them to not shoot. One German tossed over a balalaika because they thought the Russian musician had lost his. Both sides had lost their music. Both sides were sad it was gone. Humans will always be humans.

- Anonymous descendant of a Russian Soldier.

"He was driven insane"
American Corpsman

I was a Corpsman (medic) aboard a Red Cross ship at Tarawa. We had our first group of wounded Marines arrive not long after the first landings that morning. We couldn't control one of the fellas who had a wound on his bicep. He was prancing and dancing around on the deck of the ship babbling to himself. Frankly, it scared us. He kept saying, "That's Hell over there and I won't go back. You can't make me go back! I'd rather swim home!" And he tried to jump overboard.

The poor fella had lost his mind on that beach. It took five of us to get him held down good enough to treat him. The whole time he babbled about Hell, fire, and how we were all going to die. He behaved more like a beast than a man. I thought to myself, "How can this man have been perfectly fine just a few hours ago, but now completely out of his wits? Was it really that bad?" More casualties started arriving. More men started to babble. Each casualty I saw was a little more piece of hell. I didn't like being aboard that ship, but I didn't envy the men on the island.

- Story submitted by the grandson of an anonymous US Sailor. US Navy, Battle of Tarawa, 1943.

"Saving Lives"
American Soldier

I don't know how true this is, but I don't see why my Grandpa would lie. He used to tell me this story about the fighting in the hedgerows in Normandy. He said you could be right next to a German unit and basically have no idea unless someone shouted or made noise. He told me that he was sent to scout down a row

25

of hedges and literally bumped into a German soldier. My grandpa said that he was faster and raised his M1 to shoot the guy, but didn't. He had his hands up and only looked to be about 18. The same age as him at the time. He said the German tried to shake his hand and said, 'Bitte.'

My grandpa had never killed anyone up to that point and said, "I wasn't about to shoot a boy point blank who had his hands up." And he let him go. Grandpa said later that not taking him prisoner was probably a mistake but he just was focused on not murdering a boy who looked just like him. A few days later they captured several German prisoners. Among them was that German soldier he had come across. Grandpa said he looked absolutely exhausted and was filthy. His arm was in a sling but otherwise looked okay. Grandpa said he didn't react when the German saw him and smiled because he didn't want his buddies to figure out he hadn't done his duty, but he said a silent prayer that the German would see his home again one day, and that he would too.

- Anonymous descendant of an American World War Veteran.

"A one in a billion reunion"
American Soldier

My father was a medic serving in the US Army during the Second World War. He told me a story as a kid about how he treated a wounded German soldier who had lost his left eye and had horrible wounds on that side of his face, and a blown off left hand during the battle of the Bulge. He said he couldn't just let the poor guy die. So he treated him.

Years later, he had me, I grew up, and joined the Army. I was stationed in Germany and on our days off, my friends from my unit would do some tourist things. I wanted a pair of leather shoes, so we traveled to Mainz and I found a shoe store. I walked in, and was immediately greeted by an elderly male. This guy had a close cropped haircut…an eye patch over his left eye…and some deep scars on that side of his face…with a missing left hand.

I didn't say anything. He fitted me for a pair of shoes, and when I went to pay I asked him about his scars. He said, 'In the war. December 1944 at the Ardennes.' I asked him if he was treated by an American medic. He said he was, and looked at me curiously. I then told him about my medic father, and about the story he told me. The man told me that he believes it was my father who treated him.

We talked a bit about my father and what they each did after the war. He held my hand and asked me to pass on his most sincere thanks. He wouldn't let me pay for the shoes. I wish dad would have been alive to see the fruits of the goodness of his heart. I know there is no way to prove any of this story, but that's up to you to decide.

- Anonymous US Soldier. Cold War, Germany 1970's.

"I felt like a butcher"
Soviet Soldier

Our attacking soldiers ahead of our tanks had been halted at the German trenches and could move no further. My T-34 was ordered forward, and I hesitated to obey the command. I said on the radio, "Captain, our own wounded are laying in our path. We cannot move forward." We were ordered to move forward or to face punishment. Even through the closed tank hatch, I could hear the screams of agony and terror as our tank rolled over our wounded and the enemy. My driver sobbed as he continued on. I felt like a butcher.

During the fighting, our turret suffered damage from an anti-tank rifle and we returned to the rear to have it seen by the mechanics. On our way back we came across the path we took through the German trenches and found mangled, flattened, and chopped up bodies of Russian and German soldiers.
It disgusted me so, I have not eaten meat in almost 40 years.
- Anonymous Soviet Soldier. Soviet Red Army, 1943. Eastern Front.

"Two of a kind"
US Marines

My grandpa has a twin. He and his brother both served in the Marine Corps in WW2 and one served on Iwo Jima. My grandpa is the one who served on Iwo. We are a big gun family. Every year we go turkey and deer hunting. Everyone except for my grandpa. One day I asked his twin brother why I had never seen him even hold a rifle. My grandpas twin said, "Your Grandpa was a BAR man on Iwo. One night a two Japanese soldiers snuck into his hole, and your Grandpa beat one to death with that BAR, and blew the other one into spam bits as he tried to get away."

After that I looked at my grandpa different. Not in a bad way, but as a deep respect. It made sense why he never touched a gun or killed an animal. His twin served on Cape Gloucester, but he seemed to handle it differently. He didn't like going in thick brush, but I've got a feeling why after seeing pictures of that island.
- Anonymous descendants of two Marine Veterans. The Pacific Theater, World War Two.

"I was a Hunter"
US Marine

I was shipped to the Island of Guam with the 9th AAA Defense Battalion. On Guam we set up our guns, search lights, and radar on a hill just outside of Agana Guam. While at this point I was transferred to Island Command, this transfer was swift and to be temporary, to set up a sort of Government for the civilian population on the island; but instead I was put in a squad to hunt japs that refused to surrender.

Our orders were that these Japs who were considered renegades or desperadoes were to be shot on sight. I was responsible for killing 38 to 40 Japs. These Japs had to be hunted and killed because they would attack and kill small patrols of 4 to 5 men and strip them of their clothes, weapons, shoes, medical packs, and anything else that was of use to them.

These patrols that I was part of along with 9 other Marines and island police militia would go out whenever a report of Jap activity was reported to island command. On one of these patrols we were fairly deep in the jungles when a Private signaled that there were Japs ahead. We moved with caution but had passed by three Japs hiding in the trees. I was bringing up the rear when a Jap came up behind me, and that's when I heard a click and snap, I yelled and the Jap behind me struck with a bayonet that pierced my combat pack in which I carried extra ammunition.

His bayonet entered my back maybe ½ to 1 inch, the three Japs were shot and killed by the patrol. A S/SSgt patched me up and we continued the patrol. When we returned to I.Com, a corpsman checked me out, cleaned my wound and redressed it.

At Island Command, they got word that there was a band of renegades led by a Jap Major. His group of renegades they figured numbered about 35 to 40 who would not surrender. These renegades would raid Seabee camps and attack small patrols to get what supplies they could, and then would vanish into the jungles. Our group was sent out to try and make contact with these renegades. We were told that this Jap Major and his group were fairly well armed.

On one patrol we did manage to capture two lone Japs. They were unarmed, we brought them in to I.Com. We thought they may be a part of the renegade group, they were questioned by intelligence and were only two lost Japs. One told the Lieutenant that there were other Japs that wished to come in but were scared – one of these was his young son. I was asked to go out with one guide who knew the area to see if this was a fact.

The guide and I brought back four people, three old people and a young boy, this was his son. He made some Jap drawings on cloth and gave them to me as a thank you for doing this, I still have them.

After returning home I was transferred to Camp Lejeune. This was probably around Jan. 1946. At Camp Lejeune I was evaluated by a doctor there. This evaluation was because I had intentions of reenlisting in the Corps, but he said my hearing was bad and that I would never hear certain sounds again. He also said that I couldn't reenlist because of what I had to do in the islands of the Pacific, and that what I had done before the Marine Corps had faded from my memories and all I knew now was extermination.

I wanted to kill him because he scared the hell out of me when he called me an exterminator. This changed my mind about reenlisting. I was discharged March 1946. After getting home I had great difficulty being around people, including my family. I was always angry and very agitated with anyone, my boss, my co-workers, my wife and son. I was always ready to defend myself because I always felt threatened and uptight. When I would try to relax I would always get severe migraine headaches. These things and events that I am struggling to recall after trying for 60 years to forget them, even now is causing me great distress and nausea and shakes. This has taken me a long time to get it down on paper because I had to stop writing in between memories.

P.S. What affected me the most after returning to civilian life and still affects me today was the way we eliminated these Jap renegades. When we made contact with a group of Japs in the jungles, we would form a horseshoe semi-circle around them, this way we wouldn't be shooting each other. Once we were all in the right positions around the Japs, on signal we would all start firing. After the firing stopped, we had to check the bodies and camp area; the Japs that were just wounded we shot, none were left alive.

On this particular raid, I carried a Thompson machine gun. When I saw the 3 Japs that I hit that day and how broken up they were, I got sick to my stomach cause one of the Japs was hit in the left shoulder and arm, which was just barely attached to his body. His bones were showing through his flesh, he was still alive and moaning, so he was shot in the head – this ended his suffering. When I checked his pockets for any papers or regiment ID, I found he had a picture of a Jap woman and 2 children.

This made me realize I had just killed a husband and father. On all these Jap hunts, we never left any Japs alive. This has haunted me all my life because we could tell no one, never, of what we were doing on the Jap renegade hunts, till I was sent to see a Doctor at the VA hospital. 60 years have passed and every once in a while I see an oriental do a certain move or act a certain way and I still get the shakes and many bad memories return.

- Warren Lemoi. US Marines. Guam, 1945. Pacific Front

"The End"
German Officer

We learned via radio and reporting that the war was over. We were lying in a dune position right by the sea and had fought hard against the Russians the last few days. Although everyone knew it was over, the Russians competed again and tried to overrun us in early May 1945. Hundreds of the dead lay in no one's land. Then suddenly it was quiet...after a quarter of an hour I looked around and saw how German soldiers stood on the edge of their trenches and threw their weapons into foxholes or destroyed them.

I didn't see any Russians at first. We were then ordered to leave the position and only take the handguns with us. The first Russians I saw were looters who inspected themselves over German trucks. Only at the port was there something like an organization. Strangely enough, we were allowed to keep our guns for now, nobody cared much about us. That changed suddenly on the following day when NKVD troops appeared. Officers were separated from the men, the weapons were collected, and the Hiwis and the Balts were shot right behind the houses. However, they treated us Germans largely correctly.

-    Captain Eberhardt Hawranke. German Army. Eastern Front, 1945.

Eberhardt was promoted to Captain at the beginning of April and took over a mixed battalion made up of Germans and Balts.
During the last battles, this battalion melted away, so that on May 8, 1945 only 60-70 (from 5-600) were left.

KOREAN WAR 1950-1953

"Frozen Chosin lives on"
US Marine

I served in the Marines, and afterwards was a deputy sheriff in Minnesota for a while. A few years ago we had a pretty bad blizzard and I was dispatched to help a citizen stuck in a ditch on a county road. The roads were horrible. Total whiteout and absolutely freezing.

I find the vehicle and notice it has Korean War veteran plates. It's in the ditch in three feet of snow. An old man is sitting in the driver's seat with a dog in the passenger. I say, 'Hey Sir, deputy (redacted) with the (redacted) county sheriff's office. Let me call a tow truck.'

The man gets out of the car and pulls out an old corn cob pipe. I said, "Sir, it's freezing out here. Wouldn't you be more comfortable in the truck?" He looks me dead in the face and says, "Boy, I was with the 1st Marine Division at Chosin. Unless you see some Chinese troops in these fields I'll smoke my pipe out here."
I just thought, "Very well. Carry on, Sir."
They truly are a different sort of man. A hard breed of tough sons of bitches.

- Anonymous Deputy Sheriff and Marine Veteran

"As thick as grass"
US Marine

A lot of things about Korea scared me, but one thing in particular sticks out in my mind. During the retreat, well, right at the start, I was in a foxhole a few yards from the machine gun hole. This always made me both nervous and comforted. I was nervous because machine guns were the first thing the Chinese tried to knock out, but comforted because of the awesome power of a gun like that. It was devastating to the manpower and morale of the enemy.

During their charge, things were relatively quiet in our sector. Guns all up and down the line were firing, and we were firing too, but on our side of the hill we couldn't see very many Chinese in front of us. Then they all appeared out of seemingly thin air. I couldn't fire my carbine fast enough. They got right on top of us. The machine gun was firing every round in the belt. Before long a pile of bodies was about 10-15 yards in front of the gun. We couldn't hold so we had to move. Running in the dark, trying to stay as a group, we got jumped by a few Chinese.

We were bigger than them so hand to hand scraps usually were in our favor, but one of the Chinese had a bayonet stuck right in his shoulder and didn't quit until the BAR man almost cut him in half with bullets. Korea was not a thing I'd ever want to do again.

- Anonymous US Marine. 1st Marine Division. Battle of Chosin Reservoir. Korean War.

"Neither want to die"
US Army

This is a story told by my Father's best friend Syd about his time in Korea. He has since passed, and I know I am leaving out some details that only someone who served in combat can convey, but it speaks to the similarities of combat soldiers on either side...He was on a night patrol, and got separated from his platoon. As he was walking, he noticed a Korean soldier walking towards him from the opposite direction. With their rifles trained on each other, their eyes locked, and they proceeded to slowly walk in a large circle. He said it felt like an eternity.

Neither of them lowered their rifles....but neither of them wanted to die that day. He said it was like they spoke that agreement to each other through their eyes. They completed the circle, never saying a word, and both walked back in the direction they came from...alive to fight another day.

- Sydney Reyes. Korean War, 1950. Story submitted by N. Perez. JR Perez

"Migs"
US Airman

My paternal Grandfather was in the Air Force and stationed at Kimpo Air Base, the most forward airfield in South Korea. He was in a medical unit so he did some work on injured air crews but other than that I do not know if he saw IDF or any other enemy actions.

However one day he said they were hanging out, go figure Air Force just chillin', and a bird comes screaming over the treetops and at first they thought the pilot was going to be reprimanded for buzzing the field but then quickly noticed it was a Mig and soon everyone scrambled to their bunkers or AA guns to blast this Mig out of the sky.

Fortunately for the pilot he was able to land, pop the canopy and show his surrender before anyone was able to get their guns up.

- Story submitted by Bradley Thornburg

THE VIETNAM WAR 1955-1975

"A fathers tears, a promise kept"
American Soldier

After Vietnam, I left the army. I went to my best friend (redacted) home in Georgia (he was KIA) to meet his family. His father was going to offer me a job at his car dealership. At least that was the deal when his son was still alive. We were both going to work there. I met with his family at their home and had dinner. We didn't talk about their son during the meal. I met his momma, his dad, and his two younger sisters. After dinner his dad took me out to the garage, opened a few beers and we sat on the tailgate of his Ford.

After a few beers, he asked a question I hoped wasn't coming. "Tell me, boy. How did my son die? Did he die well? Was it quick?" I didn't know what to say at first. I had rehearsed it in my head before, but words couldn't come out. I just started crying. His son has died violently and painfully. He was shot twice in the stomach and had taken 3 hours to die. I cried and he held me. I choked out the words, "Your son was my best friend and my brother." I just couldn't bear to tell him the whole truth. How can you tell a father his son died crying in the jungle begging for his momma? How can you look a father in the eyes and tell him that?

I knew he understood after he saw my tears. He cried too. He was a veteran of WW2, and knew that men rarely got it quick and easy. He told me, "My wife can't take knowing he died painful. We won't say a word." After our meeting, he still offered me that job. I worked at his dealership for two decades. I feel like in a way, he adopted me as a surrogate son.

-     Anonymous US Army Veteran. 25th ID Vietnam War. 1970

"The silence was deafening"
American Soldier

The worst thing about the war for me was the silence when it was over. I left the army, came home, and I was sitting in my room I had at my parents' house. Absolute silence. No screaming. No weapons being fired or cleaned. No group of guys chatting or talking shit. Nothing. Just silence. I picked up a baseball and was bouncing it off the concrete wall in my room just to break the silence.

My dad poked his head in and asked if everything was okay. I looked at him and asked why? He said, "You've been bouncing that ball off the wall for almost 10 hours. Your mother is worried." I had completely lost track of time. I was thinking about Vietnam and my buddies. I looked at my hands and I had blisters on my fingers from bouncing that ball thousands of times. I looked at my dad again and said, "Dad, I don't know what's wrong with me." He sat beside me on my bed. "I know boy. It was the same for me after Okinawa." Thank god for my dad. He really helped me get through those first few years being home.

"I came home"
American Soldier

I own a tattoo shop in North Carolina and I tattoo a lot of guys in the military. One day this elderly gentleman walks into my shop and asks if I do walk in's. I say yes and we get him in the chair. He told me he wanted, 'I got home' on his wrist. Guys get tattoos for all sorts of reasons so I didn't question it.

Before I even put needle to skin he started crying. I said, "Hey sir this isn't even the painful part yet!" He just said, "No, I've been meaning to do this for 50 years." I asked him what he meant by that and he told me that the last words of his buddy as he loaded him onto a medical helicopter in Vietnam were: "You get home, too. You get home!" He said his friend died on the helicopter, but he kept his promise and made it home. It was a simple tattoo. But hands down one of the most meaningful ones I've ever done. I told him, "Welcome home. Your money is no good here." Bless our vets.

- Anonymous American Civilian.

"Grandpa is my hero"
US Marine

My Grandfather served in the Marine Corps from 1963-1966. He served at Da Nang AB, Vietnam. He was in charge of moving essential supplies to and from the perimeter, which was constantly under attack by ground and air forces. He worked through the night of May 21 through to the 22nd, stopping once to help 8 wounded Marines get to safety and proper medical attention.

He then returned to moving supplies, constantly under fire. On one of his many supply runs a mortar round landed near him, resulting in losing one leg immediately, and having "golf ball sized holes" in the other, which would later be amputated. He then refused evacuation until all the Marines under him knew exactly where all the supplies were to continue to reinforce the frontline. He refused an ambulance had to be transported by helicopter, he always said the ambulances where a big target and he would rather die on the ground than be blown to bits in a truck.

For his actions on May 21-22nd 1966 he would be awarded the Purple Heart and the Silver Star. He is very proud of his service. And very much a hero. But does not talk about Vietnam much. To this day he hates hospitals. Says they make his stumps hurt.

One story does stand out, while hunting with my dad, he was helping gut the deer. My dad asked him "Doesn't it bother you to see the blood and guts of a deer?" His response was "When you see you and your friends get turned into Human Hamburger, not much else can bother you."

34

- Sgt Michael F. Wojcik, USMC. Story submitted by his grandson, Tyler Heeter.

"Unfortunate Sons."
NVA Soldier

As a medic, my job was both to fight and aid my wounded soldiers. I would shoot my rifle and when someone called for me, I would then perform the job I was trained for. Many of the men I treated did not survive. Not because of my own faults, but because we did not have hospitals in the same way as the Americans. Many of ours were huts in the jungle or rooms tunneled underground.

There was one boy, I was only 21 at the time, but this soldier was a boy. Maybe 17. He was shot in the belly by a rifle. I dragged him through the brush and the whole time he was crying, "I don't want to die! Please! Help me, brother! I can't die here!" I dragged him into a hole, and began my work. It was so hard for him to sit still. I was saying, "It isn't that bad. You will live! Keep awake and it isn't that bad!"

He died in that hole. He lost too much blood and my meager kit couldn't perform the surgery he needed. We buried him and marked his body on a map for his family to come find after the war. I think about that boy many nights. I lied to him. I said he would be okay but I knew he was dying. I tried my best, and I am proud I did my best. But it was in vain. It has been many years and I still think of him.
- Anonymous North Vietnamese Soldier. Vietnam War. 1968.

"Giants among us"
American Soldier

I work at a middle school. Today we had an assembly for the school to honor the veterans on the staff. The veterans were seated in chairs in front of the bleachers and then announced by their name, branch of service, rank, and any other information.

The announcer read the name of our sanitation director. (Redacted). Corporal. US Marines. Vietnam War. Recipient of two Purple Hearts and the Silver Star. The kids couldn't comprehend what those were, but I could. I googled what he did afterwards and found out that he had basically repelled an enemy NVA attack all by himself while sustaining a gunshot wound and multiple pieces of fragments from a grenade.

And to think, I had walked past this sweet elderly man hundreds of times in the hallways and never knew what a fucking badass he was, or to even thank him for his service. He never spoke a word about it to anyone. It's safe to say that I will forever be more aware of the elderly and their sacrifices. This holiday has its uses, and I'm glad that this man was recognized for his service. Also, his 'Hold the line' tattoo on his forearm with 5 names written under it makes a lot of sense now.

- Anonymous. Veterans Day, 2021.

"Balls blown off"
Australian Soldier

There was one small event which I sometimes smile about even all these years later. Rod Lees stood on a mine and was blown up into a rubber tree. He came back down in the crater left by the mine which was only a few feet from me.

I remember seeing Rod trying to take off his green trousers and I saw his (very white) bum. He called out to me, "Skin, Skin, me balls, me balls, are they alright?" I could not see anything more than his bum, my left eye was swimming in blood but I told him it was OK. I remember he slumped down then, just like he relaxed. Rod was hit in the back of his legs in more than 100 places and all four hamstrings were severed. It took him about two years to walk unaided and to this day, still has a limp. And no, he didn't suffer any permanent damage to his manhood and went on to have children.

- John Skinner. Australia 5RAR Victnam War 1968-1969.

"Grandpa's trauma"
US Soldier

My grandfather served two tours in Vietnam, one as a crew chief on a Huey Gunship, and another the pilot of a Huey Gunship. Both tours he also served with the 1st Air Cav. One day, he was called out to support some infantry guys who were getting lit up by the Viet Cong. Prior to their arrival to give air support, napalm had been dropped on the jungle where the VC were shooting from. Once the fighting died down, my grandfather landed and began helping out and talking with the infantrymen on the ground. Due to him seemingly dismounting and helping out the infantry guys, I'm assuming this occurred during his first tour as a crew chief, but I can't say for sure.

Anyway, he gets out and notices that in the tree line there were a few infantrymen screwing around with something by a burnt down fence. As he looks closer, he realizes it's the charred body of a VC, and they had propped up a sign next to him that read, "smoking kills". It always amazes me how the darkest of humor in the darkest of situations and somehow, almost always without fail, lighten up the mood.

Years later, I and my Dad sat down one day to watch Apocalypse Now for the first time. My dad told me he had never seen it before because of my Grandfather, when I asked him why, he told me this story. One day, my dad walked in on my grandfather sitting in his recliner like usual. However, Apocalypse Now happened to be playing on the TV. He thought nothing of it until he looked a little closer at my grandfather and realized he was incredibly focused.

He was sitting straight up, crisscrossed in his chair, eyes glued to the screen. The scene that was playing was the famous beach assault scene, with the 1st Air Cav (his unit), Ride of the Valkyries and Captain Killgore. However, my grandfather wasn't paying attention to how cool or action packed the scene was, he was actually there. He was in that pilot seat, and he was reliving the war.

Apparently, my dad's stepmother walked over and tried to turn off the TV because she could see he was not in the right mental state. Upon her attempting this, my grandfather said in the most serious, and deadpan tone imaginable, "if you touch that TV, I'll kill you". She understood, and left him alone. He finished the movie and wouldn't anyone in the house watch it, and he himself never watched it again.

- John Reed Gailfoil. US Army, Vietnam War. Story submitted by his Grandson,Ben Gailfoil

"Bag of scalps"
US Marine

Native Americans were some of the fiercest warriors in history and they continue to be so. I've got a story for you. I was a Machine Gunners assistant in Nam. Deadly fucking weapons, those things. During the battle for Hue, my gunner was killed, and I was reassigned to assist a different Marine on the M-60. His name was Joseph (redacted), a Sioux Native American. We were covering a street during the battle, and when I tell you it was target rich, I mean there were VC absolutely everywhere. My 12 man squad alone must have killed 20 men in an afternoon.

Joe fired almost a whole belt into a group of them crossing the street and they lay there in front of our positions. Some of the riflemen shot some rounds into them to make sure they stayed down. We held the position well into the night.

In the dark I noticed Joe went missing. I couldn't find him. I whispered, "Joe! Joe! Where the fuck are you?" Shortly after he appeared behind me and tapped me on the shoulder, shoving something into his trouser pockets. I thought nothing of it. Later on the next day, we were taken to a rear area after being relieved and we got our packs off some trucks. As we were sitting down on our packs I noticed Joe rummaging around in his pack. I stood up behind him out of curiosity and saw what was in there.

Scalps. I shit you not, son. Three of them. To be honest, I'm not SURE if they were scalps, but he definitely had clumps of hair in there. I assume Joe had gone out in the dark with his bayonet and cut three scalps off of the dead VC he has killed with the M-60. I looked at him, as he knelt he turned to me and looked up. He had a grin and raised his pointer finger to his lips. "Shhh." He whispered. Joe was one of the craziest, bravest, and wildest men I had ever met. I'm sure glad they're on our side now.

- Anonymous US Marine. Vietnam War. Hue City. 1968.

"Night Ambush"
US Soldier

We went on ambush every night out of that place. We would wait until it got dark, then saddle up, leave our steel pots behind, go out in boonie hats, with plenty of claymores and grenades.

During the day what I remember better than anything is the anxiety, and the mounting terror. The fear of going out on ambush, the sheer fear, the hours passing, the day darkening into night, then it was time to go. Put on the web gear, the ammo, the grenades, the Claymore mines, the M-16, the weapon just cleaned, in my hands. To stand ready in spite of the fear. But I would never tell of that. It was impossible to make them understand, these people, civilians, in front of me now, how scared I was of those blind night patrols.

As soon as it was dark enough so that nobody could see us, some scout that the North Vietnamese or the VC would have watching us, we went through the wire, counting off as we went out, to make sure that we remembered how many of us there were in the patrol, so that when we came back in before it got light in the morning we could count off again and get the same number and make sure some NVA didn't sneak in with us.

One night the platoon leader let some new guy, one of those shake 'n bakes, take over the patrol, and this guy took us to the edge of some rice paddy where we had to lie down with our feet in the water. That's where this dumb motherfucker thought the ambush was supposed to be. Have you ever lain flat on your stomach, trying to be absolutely quiet, no movement, you can't move at all, you can't even fart, with your feet in smelly rice paddy water, and that water starts to get real cold real fast, and pretty soon your feet feel like they're going to fall off, but you can't move, you can't pull your feet out of the water, you can't do anything, just endure it, just suffer all night long?

Well, we did it, because that's what we had to do. We lay there all night, on the side of that rice paddy berm, where it was a little flat so that we could stretch out on it, but there wasn't enough room to stay out of the water, but it was hairy because the H & I artillery was falling near us, and the map didn't show where they were going to shoot, not that we could look at it, anyway, and, of course, I knew that dumb shake 'n bake had put us in the wrong place because the Harassment and Interdiction rounds were falling too close, but anyway we went, we were there, even if it was pitch black so that you couldn't see your hand in front of your face. Lucky for us it wasn't the thick jungle.

How much more I could tell them. Some of them knew, of course. But many didn't. I remember again that the base camp commandos really knew little about the war. How to explain to this crowd that most soldiers in Vietnam, the ones who had it easy, were safe back in the base camps, more like towns in the States. They would spend their time in the huge protected base camps drinking

38

beer, smoking dope, and screwing the whores. I always had that same thought, how they spend their time screwing the whores, lucky bastards. The guys in the rear, they never saw combat, safe in the base camps—clerks and jerks.

The night had been pitch black. But that was just a term. No one could know how black the night was who had not been in it. So black that everything was literally invisible. You were totally blind. It was a miracle that no one got lost. And how did you know where to step? You didn't, but you did it anyway, put one foot in front of the other.

We did it right, most of the time. Only the man walking in front of you, the faint clink of a sling, not muffled with tape the way it should have been, or the crunch of a boot on a twig or dry grass, or the breathing, or even just the swish of a pants leg. That was enough to keep you in the column. The silent, slow procession, the point stopping often, checking his bearings, stopping to listen, or just to feel, just to feel if that had been something unnatural, that little noise, or that feeling that seemed to come out of those darker shadows that somehow he seemed to be able to see in the darkness. And you would walk like that for one, two, even three hours. In the dark, deathly quiet.

There were other nights. Other nights when we had a real squad leader, not one of the new guys. We would find the place. A good place, not some narrow rice paddy dike, not some place where we had to lie with our feet in the water. Some place where the prey would walk. And then the lying in wait. The fat ammo pouches on the web belt getting in the way. Slowly unbuckle the belt, slowly, no noise, spread it out. Lie back down flat. The squad leader reaching over to grip the arm. No noise. The mosquitoes stinging, but no bug juice. Smelled too much. And then the terrible paralyzing swiftness of the overpowering tiredness.

You would sleep, but only in that way that you could still see and hear, even if asleep. In that way, the way I still sleep today, and I know that many combat veterans sleep that way too, only a faint and fitful sleep. And maybe, maybe, in a heart-stopping moment you would hear the soft step of the Ho Chi Minh sandals, coming closer, how slow they walked, wearing those homemade sandals cut out of truck tire inner tubes. And then you pick up the detonator, no, you had never let it out of your hand, you feel the hard squareness of the angular device. Feel it? How like a vise grip it feels, something almost normal, an ordinary tool, harmless even, but now, now you slowly push down the stiff wire safety, it's ready to blow, the squad leader's hand on your arm closing—the signal—and then ever so consciously you squeeze, ever so gently and tenderly but so firmly you squeeze the hard plastic handle, and then you shut your eyes tight. Tight against the huge brilliance of the explosion. The ugly unforgettable consciousness-penetrating forever flash of light of the Claymore mine. The cataclysmic roar. The explosion. A million steel pellets rip into the flesh of those far-wandering North Vietnamese who have dared to come to the South, and the M-16s and the M-60 machine gun explode, raking them, and then the grenades, more brilliant flashes, always throw plenty of grenades before you get up, make sure they're dead.

Maybe, maybe. If you're lucky—how could he think that?—you pop the ambush. Pop the ambush. Yes, that's what we used to say.

- Joe Barrera. Vietnam War, 1967-1968.Charlie Company, 1/27th Infantry "Wolfhounds"

"Get Doc up here"
US Soldier

I was at a firebase called Roy. It was at the top of a mountain, it was a pretty high mountain, and there was a little fishing village down at the bottom. Well a couple of mama-sans and papa-says walked all the way to the top of the mountain, basically looking for medical care. So they brought them over to where I was.

One of them was hurt. Of course they could do nothing for him in the village. It was a Papa-san, and he'd been shot. Of course I knew it right away. They tried to tell me he'd been stuck by a stick or something. Our interpreter was saying, "You know, they're lying to you." Well they were, he was shot the night before. They had a bunch of little kids with them too. So I patched him all up, gave him some penicillin, It didn't break any bones it just went straight through him. They Didi-bopped on down, went back to the village. Thanked me, gave me a little cake of rice...

That night, we were out on guard, it was about 2:00 in the morning. Right behind my Hooch was a big drop about 900 to a 1000 feet down, right down into the ocean. There was guys on perimeter guard all around me. And of course somebody started opening up. Word came that there were dinks in the wire, and that they were coming through, and then it got real quiet. So I went down to the one bunker, "Is anyone hurt?" "No doc we're all OK but we think we got somebody down there. We're going to go down and give it and bring him back up here."

So they did. 2 guys went down there and drug his body up. And it was one of those little kids that I took care of's papa-san that day. In his shirt they found an extra pocket sown into it. And there were stakes in it. Here he had been marking a path all the way up to the top of the mountain and it came RIGHT behind my Hooch. So I thought maybe that's why they were there that day to see if they could get through right there. Evidently they thought so.

They said "Doc didn't you take care of this kids papa son today?" I said oh yeah I did. "Well you're elected tomorrow morning with 3 other guys to take him back down to the village". I said oh no, no, no I'm not going to do that. And they told me oh yeah you are. So we loaded the body up into the Jeep and took him down when it was daylight, I thought those people were going to kill us. I didn't think we were going to make it out of the village alive.

40

Boy, they were upset. Their baby-san was dead. We tried to tell them what he was doing but they didn't care. They were all VC anyway. Boy they mortared us every night for a week after that. I'm taking care of them and here they're trying to find out how they can kill us all at night. Of course I don't even think about it that day....Until I saw that dead boy that night. Of course a couple guys felt bad, but not after they found out what he was doing. Those bastards would use kids to die for them a lot. It was bad.

- Ralph "Doc" Slawter 326th Med BN, 101st airborne, 1969

"The mortar almost cut him in half"
US Soldier

As a mortar man you rarely get to witness the fruits of your labor. You fire your rounds, and listen for the sound of the impacts. It's not a glamorous job, but a necessary one. We were dug in on this hill in northern South Vietnam. The hill overlooked a valley and there were about 150 of us up in this little base. We dug our mortar pit and spent most of our time waiting for fire missions from the guys in the holes lower down the hill. One night we got attacked, and the infantry in the holes requested flares and HE mortars. We fired our flares, and then 4 mortars. As each mortar dropped, I listened for the sound of the explosion. 'Boom. Boom.....boom'
"That was only three. What happened to the fourth? A dud?" Our mortars helped repel the attack and we waited the rest of the night in our pit. In the morning, a bunch of the infantry went out onto the base of the hill to check out the enemy dead and wounded the VC had left behind. As we were looking over the bodies we came to the area where we fired our mortars. I saw three little craters in a circular pattern, and next to one of the other craters was a dead VC with one of our 60mm mortars sticking out of his stomach.

The round nearly cut him in half. It had entered his right shoulder and traveled down his body and protruded out of his belly button. "Holy shit. It was a dud, but still killed the guy. Divine intervention or what?" After that some of the rifleman started calling us the Trebuchet squad.

- Anonymous Private First Class, US Army. Vietnam 1967

"Greater love hath no man"
US Soldier

When you are in extended combat your love for your comrades and fellow soldiers almost transcends the love of anything else in your life. Especially in the moment. Even above your family it seems. Let me give you an example. Two soldiers in my platoon were always bickering about absolutely anything. Anytime we had some rest, they ran their traps at each other and picked each other apart. I'll call them soldiers A and B.

41

We were on patrol, and soldier A stepped on a booby trap which initiated an ambush. Immediately heavy fire came from the village behind us and from the jungle to our left. Soldier A's foot was mangled and he couldn't move. Laying wide out in the open. The first guy to run out under fire was soldier B. Soldier B dragged his ass into cover and even took some grenade fragments in his back while doing it. We asked soldier B later why he did it; because we all sort of assumed they genuinely hated each other. "Hate him? Yeah maybe I do. But we're soldiers, ain't we?" I never forgot that.

- Anonymous. US Army. 11th Infantry Brigade. Vietnam 1967

"Vietnam, my own hell"
US Soldier

During my tour in Vietnam, I saw many horrifying events. I was in Nam from June 1966 till I was wounded on March 31st, 1967. I celebrated my 20th birthday in the jungle of Vietnam. For my birthday dinner I received a hard-boiled egg and a container of juice because our rations were dropped on the wrong LZ. I am now 57 years old and those times and experiences from Vietnam are as vivid to me now as they were then. I find that reliving these times and putting them down on paper very troublesome. I was with the First Infantry Division Second of the 28th, A Company, 1st Platoon. We were sent out all over Vietnam and we were in several fire fights. Here are just a few of the incidents that are now dreams I continue to have. We were on patrol in Vietnam, when a grenade booby-trap goes off and blows the face off of my first platoon leader, Bob Wier. Bob and I were bunked together and became friends when I first arrived with the company.

Another time, a North Vietnamese soldier ran past our position. As we went patrolling out after him we cornered him in the field and he threw a grenade at us. It landed close to me but luckily it did not go off. I returned fire at him, blowing the top of his head off. The next day as we were leaving the area we went right by where he was lying and I could look down the top of his head and see his throat.

When we flew into a hot LZ by helicopter after a short firefight, we were patrolling the area when we were called to help another squad who had been ambushed. When we arrived in the area, everyone in that squad had been shot. Some dead, some wounded. The enemy had vanished. On March 30, 1967 my whole battalion was sent out on patrol and we were to set up camp in the jungle near the Cambodian border. That night we heard off in the distance a massive firefight going on. The next morning around 5:30 AM we were hit with mortar fire. They zeroed in on our battalion CP which I was positioned directly in front of. A round hit just behind me and in front of the battalion CP. I was hit with shrapnel and a burning pain in my left leg and then it went numb. I yelled, "God, please make it stop!" When the mortar fire stopped the medic got to me and moved me to the company foxhole.

42

- Dixon Ferrin, US Army. 1st ID, 2nd of the 28th. Vietnam War. 1966-67. Story submitted by his Grandson, Timmothy Rodrigues

"Hazardous for your health"
US Soldier

We had some bad guys shooting at us while we were set up for a couple days. I was in a foxhole with another guy. He was not the 60 gunner but we need the fire power so he got on the M-60 and started shooting. He had his shirt off. A hot round off the 60 bounced off the side of the foxhole and hit him in the back. He thought he was hit and was making the noise a wounded guy makes. You know like "I don't want to die in this country!" and stuff like that.

After the shooting stopped I had time to bandage the wound. Only problem was I couldn't find the wound. Haha! After we figured out what happened he told me if I ever told anyone he would kick my ass. I believed him and didn't spill my guts until today.

- Ronald Salzer. Co C 3/8 4th ID 1970. Vietnam.

"I love the smell of napalm"
US Soldier

I loved killing because I was good at it. Not because it felt good or any conclusion most people might jump to. The feeling of besting another man who is trying to kill you is euphoric. Creeping through the jungle, hunting men. It was man's work. It's like a mutual agreement or a contest where both the fighters know only one of them is going home. I was always competitive growing up so combat and the stress of it always came naturally to me. Killing came natural. The first man I ever killed in Vietnam; I killed with a shotgun. One single slug in the chest. I walked over to him after the fighting was done and just stared at him for a while. That big ol' bloody hole in his chest. His eyes were open and I looked into those dead eyes and thought, 'That could have been me. But it was you instead.'

Now let me make this clear. I would never harm a human in the real world. I worked a normal welding job after Nam. I've got grandkids and a wife and we are all very happy. My grandkids call me Gramps. I just had fun in the war. Maybe I was crazy, but I felt the most alive when I was terrified. The only regret I have about Nam is that I never got to put all that bayonet training to use.

- Anonymous Sergeant, US Army Rangers. Vietnam War

WAR IN THE 1960's, 1970's AND 1980's

"My last cigarette."
IDF Soldier: Yom Kippur War

My dad was a fighter in the Israeli Golani unit, Unit 51 to be exact. (Same place I would end up serving 25 years after him) Yom Kippur is the biggest holiday in the Jewish religion and holiest of holiday. It's the Day of Atonement, to repent, forgive, etc. That day people fast for 25 hours, pray, and is a very somber day of the Jewish people.

My dad was home in Tel Aviv from leave from the army for the holiday. Having been praying and fasting, he and several others started hearing commotion coming from the streets, passing vehicles with people screaming and radios blasted on full volume. "Israel is being attacked on 2 fronts by Egypt and Syria, all soldiers, active and non-active, report to base immediately."

My dad grabbed his army pack and gun, kissed my grandmother goodbye, and ran out the door. He told me it was chaos with people running everywhere, all kinds of soldiers jumping into cars, army vehicles, busses, any type of transportation just to get to army pick-up checkpoints so soldiers can learn where they are being sent.

Well my dad arrived to the check point, checked in, and found out his Golani unit was sent/stationed up in the north of Israel of the Golan Heights. When he arrived, he was met by his unit. They were in a region of the Golan were the Syrians had done serious damage and advanced into Israel. He saw a lot of his fellow soldiers hurt, ripped apart, mortally wounded, or just a complete mess. Morale was low and he and his fellow soldiers all thought the end was near.

They finally arrived to the front lines with orders to hold the line and keep pushing forward no matter what, no exceptions. Things were quiet for a bit when radios started going off. Syrian forces advancing, 100s of tanks against their handful of tanks. My dad said he could feel the ground shaking and in the distance, just a handful of Syrian soldiers and tanks. He thought to himself that the information that came in was somehow misunderstood. That all changed in seconds. His cousin, who was also a in his unit, ran up to his side getting ready for what's about to come.

My dad told me that his cousin looked at him, gave him a hug, kissed him on the cheek and told him,

"ילש אחרונה הסיגריה לעשן לי תעזור ,חיוך אחי יאללה"

"Come on bro smile, and help me smoke my last cigarette"

Those were the last words my dad's cousin spoke to my father. What happened next, my dad said it felt like hours of a slow motion movie and that he felt like he saw every little detail up to the point of grenades exploding and seeing shrapnel spread everywhere across people's bodies.

44

Tank rounds started coming in and being fired on their positions. What started out as just a handful of Syrian soldiers and tanks turned into hundreds in just a few minutes when the Syrian soldiers were close enough, grenades were being thrown with one falling onto my dad's position. And without thinking, he grabbed it and threw it back with the grenade blowing up at the exact moment it left his hand, splitting his arm open from his index finger, up his arm to his elbow. My dad's cousin ripped a piece of his uniform and tied my dad's mangled arm together as to stop the bleeding, then tied this mangled arm to my dad's gun so my dad could stay in the fight. Just as he finished tying my dad's arm to his gun, my dad's cousin was shot in the head and died there instantly in front of my dad.

My dad screamed and cried, yelled, not because of his injuries, but because of his cousin that just fell in front of him. My dad continued to stay in the fight, saw a lot of death and carnage, and survived this was and the 6 day war, as well as the Lebanon war. He has seen it all and enough.

That's as far as he got into his story. My dad never left the Golan Heights. Before he just disappeared in his memories. I could see in his face, him reliving the moments, and he broke down, cried, and went quiet. Hugged me, told me he loved me.

We went outside so I can smoke a cigarette, and while I was there smoking, he looked at me and said "Let me help you finish your last cigarette". Grabbed my cig from me and threw it on the floor and stepped on it.

2 days later I was back here in Israel, in the north of the Golan Heights, in the same unit as my dad, exactly at the same location where he was during the wars (or at least I would like to think to myself that I was) doing my part and serving in the IDF (Israeli Defense Forces).

Happy to say that day was also my last cigarette.

-   Bentzi Gershon. IDF Soldier. 6 Days War, Israel. Story submitted by his son.

"Elephant vs Landrover"
Rhodesian Soldier: Rhodesian Bush War

It's Late 1970's, Rhodesian bush war and the fight against the march of communism down Africa is increasing. Operational area is the Northern border with Neighbouring Zambia in the summer's oppressively pressing heat off the Zambezi Valley. We were returning to Salisbury from Kariba, after doing an Instrumentation inspection and repair of all operating units in the area of the border town of Kariba. As the Landrover climbed the 5 to 1 gradient off the escarpment road at a snail's pace, me in the driver's seat of the fully loaded Landrover and my boss WOll, riding shotgun, when he orders me to stop so that he could take some photos of an elephant feeding in a culvert by the road. When you are a mere corporal. The breaks came on with the landy burning rubber into the tarmac and the prompt, 'Yes Sir'.

45

My boss hops out and starts to enjoy the moment, one eye shut, peering through the lens with a constant click, click lost in concentration. Well all the while I'm watching the Elephant get angrier and angrier, mock charging, trumpeting and ripping out small shrubs and trees, all because he could not run up the culvert slope and trample this human disturbing his afternoon siesta.

I had kept the engine running, just as well, as the picture was! We were stopped on a slight hill rise with the road veering to the left in the distance approximately 20 yards further on, when all of a sudden that Elephant turned left and headed up in the direction off our escape route. I realised he was going to cut off our escape as the culvert rose gradually to the road height at the bend in the road.

(Our landrovers never had any get up and go, and an even worse turning circle and turning around on a culvert with 4mtr. drop either side, no chance). I shouted out that we had to go and I started rolling the landy, my boss telling me to "GO, GO, GO!" and the landrover straining to pick up speed on the hill with my foot flat, with that Elephant almost reaching the road, my boss hanging on the back off the rover with his fingers grabbing through the back mesh screen canopy, camera flying from his neck by a safety cord and feet planted on the bumper bar, screaming "Get us the fuck out of here!"

We reach the bend at the same time as that Elephant, with us getting past only a split second before him, thus allowing him to take a swipe at the boss for disturbing him. Result, I felt the Landy launch forward a mite faster and the boss had a bruise on his back for months from that Elephants trunk, even though our "speeding" past prevented him getting the full contact and force off its power. Lucky Day.

PS. Thanks for the memories Sir

- S/Sgt. D,Uys Rhodesian Army, Services Corp, Armements and Instrumentation. Rhodesian Bush War

"I always piss"
Rhodesian Soldier: Rhodesian Bush War

I saw a few men die during the war, and they always pissed themselves when they died. I know you can't help it, but seems exceptionally degrading to me. I always, always made a point to stop and take a piss and shit whenever we had the chance in the bush. My fear was I'd be shot, you see, and I'd piss my trousers like a child. I did it so often, that my bladder has shrank to what I assume is the size of an acorn. To this day, I still piss as soon as I feel even the slightest need to, and I start to panic if I can't find a lavatory. I don't know why I get so worried. It's an old war habit that I can't seem to shove off. I feel like an old man now, and maybe I am. The war was ages ago, but I still almost piss my trousers once a day.

- Anonymous Selous Scout. Rhodesian Bush War.

"Can't turn it off"
Russian Soldier

I was a Russian soldier in the early 70's. After I left and went to Bulgaria, then Greece, Britain and then the United States. As young Soviets, we were trained to despise Americans and to dream of the day where we set our boots on the White House lawn. Even in school we were given classes on machine guns and the Kalashnikov. My grandson is a US Marine now. He often would call me during his first year of training and complain, "They have us up at 1 in the morning saying your enemy is training just has hard if not harder than you right at this moment. I just don't believe them." I say to my grandson, "I promise you, somewhere they are."

I will admit, at times I do miss parts of the army. Not so much the brainwashing to destroy Capitalism...but have you ever witnessed a full military parade? Marching in step with thousands of other men can make you feel very powerful. I went to see my grandson's graduation parade and could only smile as I heard the old Soviet anthem words in my head. Some things you can never turn off.

- Anonymous former Russian Soldier. 1970-1975

"I live in guilt"
Iraqi Soldier: Iran Iraq War

Father, I write you a few lines to let you know I am safe. I have some bruises but overall I am in good health.

I must confess to you, I have committed a heinous crime. I killed a child in uniform. I live day to day, minute to minute with this guilt. After I killed him, I held his little body and cried.

I joined the army to become a man, and now I have become a murderer. What shame! The other soldiers say, 'Better him than you!' But my guilt and shame resides. I suspect they are right, but I close my eyes and feel his small body in my arms again and again!

God, release me from this pain of guilt! I fear you will not recognize your son. I do not recognize him.
I still remain your loving and faithful son.
(Redacted)

- Anonymous Iraqi Soldier. Iran-Iraq War, 1981. - This letter was submitted to me by the brother of the soldier and has requested his identity remain anonymous.

"Playing with the big boys"
Russian Soldier/ Soviet Afghan War

Our commander (redacted) had given myself and three other Spetsnaz permission to hunt the Mujahideen North of Mandūl as one would hunt wolves. We drove two zil 131's out into the wilderness and mined one. The one we mined was to be stripped for parts, but we found better use for it.

Under the wheel we planted a mine, and positioned ourselves in a half circle several hundred meters away and waited. Half the day later we see 4 men with rifles approaching. Mujahideen. Two inspect the vehicle while two look around. We wait. One gets in the driver's side and starts the truck. Two more get in the uncovered back and sit on the seats. I don't know why the fourth didn't mount the vehicle, but he didn't. The second the vehicle moves forward they detonate the mine.

Immediately the driver and one of the passengers are killed. We open fire on the third and fourth man with our rifles. We are not conscripts. We are professional soldiers. The entire engagement lasted no longer than four or five minutes.

- Anonymous Russian ExPat. Soviet-Afghan War. 1983.

"Why did they use children?"
Surinamese Commando: Surinamese Interior War

We got our orders to raid a rebel village near the border with French-Guyana. A dozen of us commandos were to meet up with infantry in a garrison close by. A group of 4 soldiers were to come with us since they knew the area around the rapids to guide us through to our target

We drove a few hours and went further by boat. As soon as we came into enemy territory we got out and went on foot. A good few kilometers. We moved a lot by night. We came to where the village was located and saw a few men walking around with shotguns and rifles. We had to get across first. Due to dry season the water level lowered to where we could use the rocks to safely cross over. Almost lost the crossbow and my rifle.

Then I saw a boy about mid teen of age coming towards the water with a shotgun. He may just wanted to take a bath or something. But if he saw us we could all die right there.

I knew he was gonna die in the raid. And then it had to happen....he came closer. I held that crossbow pointed to the side of his head and released. The raid was successful. But why the fuck did they use kids to fight. Fucking why!

- Anonymous Surinamese Commando. Surinamese Interior War, 1980's

"Bimbi's Letters"
South African Soldier: South African Border War

In any military situation the Brass knows that letters from home are important for morale, so Executive Outcomes set up a similar system to what most of us had known in the SADF. Obviously without all the bullshit, like having to do push-ups if your letter smelt of perfume.

Every plane that came in had some mail for us. We could get stamps at the canteen and our letters would be posted from "The House" in Pretoria. My mail was mainly from Charmaine; she even sent some drawings based on what I wrote about camp life. We had been in Angola for a few months when I noticed that Bimbi never received any mail. So I watched to see if he ever sent any out; he did not. I knew he had a wife and kids living in Phalaborwa, although he was Congolese. At this stage the South African news was full of stories, some actually true, of a bunch of South African mercenaries in Angola. A few guys had been killed already and the newspapers were having a field day.

Charmaine kept a photo of three bodies; dead and half-naked, that Savimbi had sent to the South African news services as a warning to keep South African soldiers out of his country. I'm sure all the wives and girlfriends were eagerly waiting for mail.

One day I asked Bimbi why he did not write, would his wife not be worrying about him? Now, Bimbi was a really black man, not some shade of brown. If he could have, he would have blushed. The story was, he and his wife had no common written language. Although he could speak five or six languages, he could only write in French. His wife, being from Venda, probably had never even heard French before she met Bimbi. I offered to write on his behalf, and, after much cajoling, Bimbi arrived in my tent late one night. It was touching to see how embarrassed this hard-assed ex-5 Recce soldier was; so shy about his personal life. He told me to write that he was well and to ask how the kids are. That was it! When I asked if I should write that he missed his wife, he nearly crawled under the bed. I then teased him further. I asked if I should tell her how much he loved her, too. We eventually sent a letter off.

His next embarrassment came when Goodness, his wife, replied. The poor bugger couldn't read English either. So he snuck into my tent late one night again and very shamefacedly asked me if I would mind reading his letter. The cost to him must have been enormous. He was pleased that his family were all well. Bimbi was a truly brave man, in every respect, and I liked him all the more for it.

-   Wayne Bisset Mortarist in the South African Defense Force. 7 South African Infantry. Executive Outcomes.

"Ground troops hate enemy aircraft"
South African Soldier: South African Border War

In the South African Defense Force, my first experience with the Migs came as we got stuck in a river on the way to the front. We managed to extricate our Ratel (Honey Badger in English) IFV after a few hours of being stuck in the mud just before dawn, concern was starting to set in as there was always dawn MIG combat air patrol down the length of the river as it was part of our supply route. We just managed to get into the tree line as 2 Mig 21's came down the river at about 100 feet. We started to take camo'ing our vehicle seriously after this.

The Migs used to fly sorties against us every day but we could always tell the Angolan pilots because they would stay high and bomb from high so we could watch the parachute and see where the bomb was going. This changed in the New Year (1988). My first experience of this change came early on the 3rd January. We had done a pin-prick assault on the Angolan 21st Brigade the night before and then withdrew to a harbour area.

I had just got into my sleeping bag in my foxhole at dawn when I heard bombs close by followed a sonic boom then a Mig 23 went over me at tree top height. You heard the shrapnel flying through the trees so you knew it was close. A while later one of my guys came to me with a piece of shrapnel about 4in x 4in and 2 inches thick. I asked where he found it and he replied it had ricocheted off the branch above his foxhole and buried itself about a foot into the ground on the edge of his foxhole. He asked what should he do with it so I said take it home and put it on the mantelpiece so every time you see it you can thank your lucky stars it wasn't a foot over and taken your head off.

We heard rumours of East German and Russian pilots now being in the conflict not just Angolan and Cubans which was confirmed a few weeks later after we had attacked the 21st Brigade again and took them out. The battle only finished at around 9pm at night so we sent the night on their emplacements. The next day we had plenty of Mig activity and as I was stood on top of my vehicle I had two Mig 21's in a tight wing tip to wing tip formation come past me at tree top height with the pilots wearing the orange flight suit, white helmet with the red star on the side - the Russian flying uniform. We now knew we had effective pilots fighting against us.

When we arrived in Angola the guys we relieved told us that the Migs don't fly in bad weather and at night but with the Russian pilots that all changed. Night time sorties against us became a reality and the Migs would drop illumination flares and MI 25 Hinds would be scouring the bush underneath them looking for us. One night we were watching the flares which were about 10km's away when someone from the vehicle next to me lit up a cigarette. The Mig must have picked up this up on his IR because next second we had 2 air to surface missiles coming at us out of the night, they landed close by but fortunately no one was injured but we had to move our location before they came in strength in the morning to bomb us, which they subsequently did.

The sorties were becoming more frequent and we would bemoan our lack of air cover but the aging SAAF fleet of Mirages, Buccaneers and Canberra's could not operate for long so far from base and against the massive AA radar blanket set up by the enemy, the politicians also didn't want to risk the airframes but at the time we were told the pilots didn't want to fly which transpires wasn't accurate. This led the SAAF to develop a technique whereby they would lob bombs onto targets.

They would approach their target at tree top height then go rapidly gain altitude in to the radar blanket, release their bomb then turn and descend to tree top height below the radar blanket again and exfil. The bomb would then continue on its trajectory and fall on the target. It wasn't accurate but as they were aiming at the area taken up by a Brigade it didn't have to be.

The last attack we did was the indirect heaviest fire we received and Mig sorties. Our recce elements had not identified a minefield and we hit it. All the artillery and BM 21's were then brought to bear on us and the Migs came as well. They flew 59 sorties that day dropping 26 tons of bombs on us as well as over 300 BM 21 ripples and over 1000 heavy artillery shells.

During this engagement our AA was allowed to open up for the first time with their 20mm Ystervarks (Porcupine in English). I watched a Sukhoi 22 fly through the exploding 20mm shells 3 times until he determined the position of the AA battery then dropped his bombs on them. We were in Angola for 3 1/2 months before being withdrawn and replaced but none of us will forget the Migs.

- L/CPL Russell Jones, OPs Medic Platoon 2, Bravo Company, 62 Mechanised Infantry Battalion, SADF.

"Incredible courage from both sides"
British Soldier: Falklands War

After the initial landings it did not take long for the first air raid hit us, the noise, intensity, violence and ferocity of the attack gave us an indication of what it was to come. Welcome to living in a war zone without air superiority in ground zero of the primary targets. We continued to fortify our trenches combined with working parties in a race to unload stores from that rickety pier and consolidate the beachhead, thus followed days of total chaos as wave after wave of Shite Hawks and Daggers absolutely smashed us.

An acknowledgement to the bravery shown by the Argentine pilots with their low flying passes into walls of tracer, blowpipe and SeaCat. The daily attrition of "Ajax Bay Airshow" took its toll on both sides, success of the raids was evident as Battleships backs broken exploded turning night into day with casualties filling "The Red and Green life machine" aid station, it was fortunate those opportune bursts of 30m cannon into hill positions had little effect. This success came at a heavy price as the amount of aircraft I witnessed being shot down is still vividly etched in my mind, however despite the huge and obvious losses undeterred those pilots kept coming, and coming and coming.

We had all been issued small vials of morphine, for ease of use they were taped to our dog tags. Great idea, you are hit everybody knows where they are, rip it off inject the upper third of the thigh (if it is still there) paint an M on forehead and crack on.

This particular raid came from a different direction, a curious skyward observation we quizzically thought "oh look parachutes" attached to the canopies were 500lb bombs. As they floated down on realisation Eric legged it quicker than an Olympic sprinter from open ground towards his trench diving in head first. A few minutes later he stood up smiling, no wonder really as he had the morphine vial sticking out of his neck. During the tumble he had smashed the cover and injected himself. After mainlining morphine he spent the rest of the afternoon raids on Planet Mongo fending off Ming the Merciless.

There was a certain crazed euphoric hysteria at surviving those huge explosions, a wide eyed high of elation and adrenaline that suddenly turned to a massive gut wrench as the news came through.
RIP Mac and Goosey.
- Colin Adams. Royal Marines. San Carlos. Bomb Alley Falklands 1982.

"Heavy weight, Long steps"
British Soldier: Falklands War

I can still feel the straps digging in from the weight, (on the scales at 155lbs) we actually ended up burying respirators, tin helmets and other surplus kit. Yomping towards the Argentine 'Ring of Steel' Tasked to join 45 we set off catching up at Teal Inlet. On arrival we saw trees for the first time, then the Unit Padre a Welshman affectionately known as 'Taf the Cross' kneeling openly praying for his god to take his life and put an end his suffering. Meanwhile the venerable Sgt Malone was conducting a feet inspection, even this grizzled old veteran from Aden was perplexed to find one of his men barefoot, forget his name but a hill shepherd before joining up, apparently he did not wear socks when he was a child and was not going to start wearing them now as they were for poofters. Not sure how that would go down in these enlightened times, thankfully no one took offence and the war able to continue, we cracked on set bivvies, talked to oppo's, ate scran with another checking of our kit. How do you eat an elephant? The same way as Yomping with heavy weights. One piece at a time. Several miles in, the constant and seemingly unending mental torture combined with relentless physical pain has to be dealt with, best way is to break it down into stages. Pick points in the distance, once you have made one, you can do another, then another.

Unfortunately the comfort of switching off "Thumb up bum, mind in neutral" was not an option due to the threat of enemy attack, that point in the distance came down and down, for certain periods the simple effort of putting one foot in front of another took pretty much everything you had. This one was an absolute monster.

Getting the call to go firm for the night, ankle deep in a bog near Lower Malo House with muddy fetid water well over the ankles, is someone having a laugh??? We quickly started to dig up a raised level, however too tired to bother about the discomfort of sleeping wet in a marshland peat bog just collapsed into a few hours' kip. On waking I have to admit considering asking the padre for one of his thunderbolts, the decision to wrap, just sit there and let the warmth of hypothermia drift over to do its thing would be a blessed release to what lay ahead. Observing George trying to squeeze his now enormous trench foot sodden feet back into his boots, while men with open sores and huge blisters bound their feet with masking tape so as not let anyone down by dropping out jolted my mind out of its bizarre thoughts. On with wet kit, (although nothing was particularly dry by now) and Crack On. Within 20 mins it was back to another day of intense pain and discomfort but at least I was warm again.

However in something of a paradox that continuing intense pain was not wearing us down instead having quite the opposite effect. As we continued Yomping determination not to quit grew, the inner resolve of dealing with the agonising pain was benefiting us and we started growing in strength and mental fortitude. Going firm on Mount Kent a Forward Patrol Base was established less than 3k from Two Sisters, being able to see our objective and advisories we now did not just become immune from the pain but actually started to thrive on it, that night within 8 hours fighting patrols were probing positions, harassing and killing the enemy.

-    Colin Adams. Royal Marines. Falklands 1982.

"Night battle for Two Sisters"
British Soldier: Falkland War

If you ever find yourself in a proper infantry battle, with all of the supporting arms, against a force that has most of the advantages, and you survive, your perspective on life is changed completely as is your psychological state.

The morning after. Northern peak, at first light we found ourselves in a small bowl type feature, there seemed to be something of a lull with everything quiet, after securing the area now pretty much hanging our thoughts drifted towards getting a hot wet when we were told we had to cross the saddle. There was serious manking and moaning as some had just got the water boiling for that first hot drink, it would have been an easy decision for Roger to say "Ok 5 mins" but thankfully he remained resolute.

Pissed off we quickly stowed our kit, Thumper being the Troop radio Operator had managed a veritable feast of apple flakes mixed with hot chocolate while we were busy and was quite happy lording it over us. All packed ready and waiting he saw a random boot in the rocks and picked it up, unbeknown to him there was still had half an Argentine leg inside that spilled its contents out over him, then much to everybody's laughter and amusement he threw up his breakfast.

With moral raised we set about crossing the saddle. The last person was barely out of the area when a 155 shell hit directly where we were not 2 minutes ago. Luck or good judgement? A cup of coffee and the whole section would have been hit. The next round landed at 200m away setting off a secondary explosion and 'Deep Joy' dawned on us. As if being in the open getting bracketed by 155 artillery fire and 120mm mortars was not bad enough we were also in a Minefield.

Certainly had better starts to the day.

I still laugh today at what we looked like crossing the saddle, it was exactly like the end credits of benny hill show.

Now sat on the Southern peak afforded that hot wet, we sat in the snow beside one of the still hot .50 Browning gun pits that had held us up observing as clearance patrols brought in prisoners and the dead. The course of events seemed like some sort of freakish vivid dream that lasted for maybe thirty minutes, something of a shock when on checking my watch the brain scrambled trying to compute the 6 hours we had been in battle.

Our instructions to proceed onto Tumbledown Mountain if time allowed were cancelled due to the tenacity of Argentine resistance and we went firm, the rest of the day we shared artillery, mortar stomps and occasional White Phosphorus with Longdon and Harriet.

-    Colin Adams. Royal Marines. Falklands 1982.

"IRA Bomb makers"
British Soldier: Ireland

I was a young Guardsman on my first tour of Northern Ireland. My TOAR in Belfast was, Ballymurphy, Turf Lodge, and Anderson Town. Bad places in a bad country. Sometimes we would be teamed up with mobile RUC patrols, call sign Red. I was in a red call Sign driving around with the RUC when suddenly they flashed their blues and screamed off, me on top cover, didn't have a clue what was going on. We stop, jumped out in Springfield Ave, a really bad place, full of bad people.

My knees were literally knocking. There was an RUC I foot call sign trying to arrest the local bomb makers brother. I see his hand grabbing an RUC M1 and another RUC guy smacking him with a baton. One of my patrols trying to control the situation, basically craziness. My mate, a Falkland vet rifle butts the player and the RUC throw him in their wagon. We try and contain the area. Next day, I'm foot patrol, same street, probably the worst street in West Belfast, I'm carrying ECM which picks up radio stations. I'm hard targeting, whilst listening to Sam Fox, ex page 3 model, singing touch me, thinking…What the fuck.

- Anonymous British Soldier, Welsh Guards. Belfast 1986. "The Troubles"

"They were all headshots"
French Foreign Legion: New Caledonia

My Foreign Legion observer and over watch unit was mobilized to support GIGN operators hunt down Kanak militants on òveu island (New Caledonia) a French colony/ interest at the time. Island militants had entered local hotels or businesses with machetes and guns and done some serious damage to French civilians and islanders. Took a few hostages and retreated to a cave system inland on the island.

I was ordered to kit up, grab the long range rifle and spotter and tag along with these high speed GIGN guys. We took a helicopter close and went in on foot. We were told to watch the mouth of the cave and shoot anything that comes out. The GIGN guys were real pumped and a little trigger itchy.

Orders came over radio to capture if possible not kill the militants. I watched the team through my scope head into the mouth of the cave. I heard bangs and blasts and obvious gun fighting. GIGN guys took pictures and info and bounced out in the chopper. My guys and I were tasked to clean up the cave and bodies. I walked in and saw a canoe in every militants head. (Gunshots to the head) They weren't given a chance, the GIGN guys took out their anger and slayed them all. This was the first time I witnessed a war crime and immediately put in for honorable leave.

- Anonymous Legionnaire. Special Reconnaissance Company. 2nd Parachute Regiment. French foreign legion. New Caledonia, 1988

WAR IN THE 1990's

"Because I was inverted"
Swedish Peacekeeper: Lebanon

I was serving with the Swedish peace keeping forces, a part of UNIFIL, in south Lebanon in the early 90s. This was during the middle of one of the biggest Israeli operations into south Lebanon for decades. They were fighting the Hezbollah guerrilla, but at the time they shot at everything that moved, including white vehicles with UN letters on, resulting in up to 300.000 civilians fleeing from their homes.

My company of 135 men was stationed in the middle of the AO and we were locked down in our camp going up and down our shelters when we took a number of firing close grenades that dropped down around the camp. No supplies with water, food etc. could come so we were getting short of everything after about a week. One night I was alone in our TOC, tactical operation center, and my mission was to keep up the radio contact with other units, keep track of shoot reports etc. The TOC was in a closed room with no windows except for a tiny one with a plastic glass.

Around 2 am there was this huge blast in the pitch black night that shook the building and made the plastic window bulge. This was the first time I got scared for a few moments, what the hell happened, was it a bomb that blew the whole camp away? Soon guys from around the camp started calling the TOC asking what happened, I had absolutely no idea while trying to reach the duty officer for advice. It was also on my duty to call for Shelter over the speakers if needed, should I make the call or not?

After a few confusing moments/minutes I called up our watch tower to ask the guard there what happened and he/we realised after a while that it was in fact an Israeli jet fighter that passed our camp on a really low altitude while crossing the sound barrier and causing a huge sound bang right over our heads, just to scare the shit out of us, and he sure did!
So, in the end, everyone was ok and very much awake the rest of the night.
- Sgt 1st Class Engdahl, Swedish combat engineers.

"My toughest battle"
Swedish Peacekeeper: Bosnia

I was deployed to Bosnia in the late 90s with a Swedish Medevac company, our mission was to help out wounded SFOR-troops (NATO Stabilization force) from the AO with our APC ambulances and with the aid of US Dust-off Blackhawks when needed. All in all it was a pretty slow mission with not much to do.

Our company was stationed right next to the SFOR HQ with troops from many nations, among them the SFOR MP-coy. The very first day we arrived one of our guys had some errand to the MP-coy and he came back all excited telling us about this amazingly beautiful Norwegian female MP. As you all know, at least back then, there were few females in the military and good looking ones were even more rare, so I didn't really believe him at the time.
Anyway, I was in the gym a few days later and then I saw her, and damn, she was all that, and more!

We slowly got to know each other but it took a lot of patience, the whole MP-coy (all men of course) acted as her personal body guards so I had to befriend pretty much all of them first, just to have a cup of coffee with her. We had this 9 km trail around the camp that we could run or power walk along, and when we did, the MP had two guys in a car driving 10 meters behind us. Talk about being protective...

Anyway, we soon found out that we were both deployed 5 years earlier with the UN-forces in Lebanon, at different places and without meeting, and then we were both back home as civilians until we did another tour and met in Bosnia. What's the odds on that..? At the end of my deployment, we both agreed that we wanted to continue seeing each other at home, her contract in Bosnia lasted another 7-8 months so it was a long distance relationship for a start. But once she got back home we lived in Oslo and Stockholm, which is a 5 hour drive, for about a year, and since about 20 years we are still happy together and we both live in Stockholm with our two kids.

If nothing else, it's a more fun story to tell rather than meeting on Tinder, and we are both thankful for our common military experiences. And sometimes we wonder if there is something called fate!
-    Sgt 1Cl Engdahl, Swedish Med coy, Bosnia

"Could have been me"
Algerian Civilian: Algerian Civil War
I worked for a local newspaper during the Algerian civil war in the nineties, and there was a curfew obviously but I and colleagues had a pass allowing us to work late night. I just got my driving license and I was still not so good. One night a colleague offered to drive us back home along with two others and since I was new I rejected the offer, I REFUSED to drive during night with risk of snipers.

Anyway we were close to reaching a square and by the time we got there I heard a pop and windshield glass shattered. My colleague who offered me to drive got shot in the head.

By the time I realized what happened we got surrounded by soldiers fighting against the revolution party, they thought we were some fighters that they planned to ambush. It could've been me, thank god. But the sad thing is that those things, those "collateral damages" happened all the time during that period, and not only military men suffered from the atrocities of war but civilians as well, sometimes civilians suffer more.

- Anonymous Algerian Civilian. Algerian Civil War. 1995

"Bald guys, bad men"
Algerian Civilian: Algerian Civil War

During the civil war some bad people took advantage of the situation to make profit, they would create their own militia and sack villages and kill their habitants in the name of the revolted party, some of those militias were by the state as well to terrorize the people in case they considered joining the party, so what we did was putting lookouts on high ground of the village to spot the "bald guys" (nickname for terrorists) and alert everyone to evacuate the village before it was too late.

One day our lookouts spotted the lookouts of another village close to ours and started alerting us "bald guys are coming", at the same time the other village's lookouts saw ours agitating and thought they were bald guys coming so they alerted their village as well. It was mayhem in both villages, everybody was mobilizing their vehicles whatever the kind was to evacuate the women, children and elderly people, screaming and carrying precious belongings while there was no attack, no bald guys and no danger at all.

After a while the men that were left behind discovered that it was a misunderstanding and everything was just a false alert, which added to our frustration especially after seeing the aftermath of actual attacks by these militias on other villages. Today we recall this incident and laugh about it with tears, that day the day of bald guys we call it.

- Anonymous Algerian Civilian. Algerian Civil War. 1996

"Caught in the middle"
Algerian Civilian: Algerian Civil War

Back in 1994 I worked for gas Installation Company and we frequently had to work during night time, in which most clashes between army and revolted fighters happened. One night I was home and it was past midnight when dispatch called, it was my shift and I received a call to inspect and repair a pipeline that alimented an entire neighborhood in center Algiers.

I had a pass allowing me to circulate during the curfew so I could do my job at night, and so I drove to my destination before I could make it to the address I heard gunshot sounds that came far away behind me, and as soon as I looked through my side mirror it blew up to pieces and I stopped the car immediately, before I knew what happened I found mystery surrounded by soldiers.

Unfortunately that night I got caught up in the middle of a firefight, when the C.O. recognized me as a civilian he instructed me to stay with him until reinforcements arrived and evaluating could be possible, it was really quiet for a firefight so I asked the C.O. where are the enemies and he told me to 'Shut it', while we were taking cover by a building when I felt dust falling on me so looked up and saw men moving from building to another using large wooden planks to cross, that's how they displaced which was very effective.

As I looked up the soldiers with me started blasting the fighters above us and we started to move before they could surround us, I didn't see much after that as I kept my head down during the entire fight until reinforcements arrived and outnumbered the fighters I guess which made them flee.

I was too scared to go do my job and I couldn't anyway because I was escorted to my home by police, I didn't sleep that night and I had nightmares for weeks.

-    Anonymous Algerian Civilian. Algerian Civil War. 1994

"We all died in that war"
Russian Soldier: First Chechen War

All of us entered Chechnya as young, innocent boys. All of us left as dead men. Whether you physically died or not. I often thought the ones who fell in battles or ambushes were the lucky ones. I was drafted into the first Chechen war as an 18 year old boy who had never even seen or fired a rifle. I left, not as a man, but a shadow of one. I had killed men and watched friends die horribly in front of me.

Some were killed by mortars, rockets or bullets. Others burned to death or were tortured by Uncles. (Chechens) I remember a good friend of mine was riding atop a tank in Grozny. A Chechen fired an RPG and killed all 7 men riding it. Not one of those men had seen a single day of fighting yet. It was their second day in the city. The tank fired right into the building, wounding several people badly.

We stormed the building, captured the Chechen, and dragged him out into the street by his ears like a child so he could see what he had done. We shot him in the head. Senseless. All of it. If you walk the streets of any Russian town today you can almost pick out the veterans of the First War. Their eyes. There's nothing in them.

-    Anonymous Russian Soldier. First Chechen War. 1995.

"I couldn't murder a man"
Chechen Rebel: First Chechen War

Shooting started in the streets. From both our men and the Russians. My group and I had built an ambush area and began to fire upon them. It was my first fight and total chaos. I became frightened in the smoke and noise and tried to cross the road to where I thought my friends were. I just ran! Fast as I could run! It was dark and hard to see and I ran straight into a man. We crashed and fell to the ground. I felt him and climbed over him to see him better to discover if he was okay. I got closer and saw he was a Russian soldier.

We both realized this at the same time and froze. I grabbed for my knife, but he didn't move. I couldn't kill him. He couldn't kill me. We both got on our feet and ran different directions. Later we went through the bodies and I found the Russian I had collided with. I said nothing about my cowardice to my comrades. I just couldn't murder a man.

- Anonymous Chechen Rebel. First Chechen War. Grozny 1995

"His corpse was burnt to a crisp"
Russian Soldier: First Chechen War

We came across a destroyed armored troop transport vehicle in Grozny. We halted to remove the bodies from inside. I stood on top of the latch and opened it. The smell hit me immediately and immensely. It was so bad I vomited. Inside were three men in various forms of decomposition. I jumped inside and helped my comrades move them outside to be transported for burial. On the ground next to the vehicle lay three young dead Russians. One of them was badly burned. His uniform had been burnt off of him. Inside one of the pockets of one of the others I found a letter. It read:

"My darling, Igor. Come back to me. Finish this war and come back safely. It's not fair that you had to be taken to Chechnya and away from us. When you get back we will be married and forget any of this happened. My mother and I pray for your safe return. So please, my darling. Return to us."

I stood over the body and looked at his face. His eyes were closed, and they would never open again. He just have been Igor. I wanted to write to his sweetheart and tell her what the fate of her Igor had been, but I never had the courage to do it. So many sons never returned to their mothers. So many men never returned to their sweethearts.

- "Alexei", Russian Army. Second Chechen War. Chechnya, 1999

"Close Combat"
Russian Soldier: First Chechen War

I saw men die was in close combat with the Chechens in Grozny. We were occupying an apartment building on orders from our commander. I was on the second floor with one squad, and another squad was on the floor below us. A rocket sailed across the street and into the first floor window. A loud explosion was followed by screaming men below us. I ran down the stairs to find the room filled with dead and dying Russian soldiers. The one in the middle of the room was missing one of his arms and I decided to drag him back up the stairs with me.

As I dragged him on the floor, I slipped on a liquid and fell on my bum while the wounded man thrashed in my lap. It was a puddle of blood and human organs. The blood quickly soaked through my trousers and I could feel the warmth

60

against my skin. As we were sorting out the situation on the first floor, a burst of rifle fire came through the window and hit my comrade in my squad. The bullet severed an artery in his throat and he collapsed on the ground and gurgled while he rolled on dead and wounded men. I didn't know what to do. I looked around for an officer but none were there. Two Chechen fighters then rushed through the front door. Luckily one of my guys thought they may rush the door, and he shot the first one directly in the face, spraying brains on the one behind him. The second one slipped on the gore in the doorway and fell down onto the flat of his back. Another soldier quickly jumped on top of him and dispatched the Chechen a blade. The sound of a knife puncturing cloth and flesh over and over is not something I'd ever like to hear again.

Later that day a truck came to get our dead and wounded and newsman came with the vehicle. We told him to leave. Our mothers already feared for us. They didn't need videos to fuel their fear. It was the single worst day of combat I ever experienced in both wars.

-   "Alexei", Russian Army. First Chechen War. Chechnya, 1995

"Armored Storm"
Iraqi Tanker: Operation Desert Storm

I was a tank driver. I actually fought against American tanks and survived to tell you this story today. My whole crew survived, but our tanks mobility was destroyed by one of yours. We were halted in a defense behind the ridge. The ground was flat in front of us. Perfect ground for tanks to drive and shoot. Also perfect to get shot. It was a one sided fight but I firmly believe we Iraqi's fought valiantly and bravely.

I have no knowledge of if we attained any strikes on American tanks. My commander was 3 years my senior, and he ordered us to halt with the rest of our group, and fire on the Americans. Through our armor and headsets I could hear low 'pwoom. pwoom. pwoom.' noises of tank guns firing and striking each other. It was scary, but very exciting! As untested tank soldiers, it was difficult to understand what we were doing was real. An American tank struck ours on the track. I heard a sudden loud noise like a metal bar hitting a container. I realized I could not move our tank. We were useless. We could not move. Our commander ordered the rest of us outside. My memory of the battle is like observing a movie through a thin tube. I saw very little. I'm glad I made it alive. I miss my crew as I have not seen them in over 20 years. I fled Iraq before the invasion and fall of Saddam. I do not miss the army. I do not miss war. I do miss Iraq.

-   Anonymous Former Iraqi Soldier. 52nd Armoured Division. Operation Desert Storm 1991

THE IRAQ WAR 2003-2011

"Iraq's Finest"
Iraqi Soldier

I served as member of the Republican Guard. I was young and proud of it, but I never spoke of it but once to my brother and his son, who I also consider my son. I never married. My friends were in the counter attack at Jumhuriya Bridge in Baghdad in 2003. I was there too, but not near enough to the bridge to claim I fought.

My friends on the bridge during the attack said they initially chased American soldiers away, but then American planes came and killed many of our friends. He (one of the RG soldiers) said, "Our sense victory was premature. When the Americans abandoned their positions we didn't expect it to be because the planes were arriving. One of the guns cut a line right through the middle of us and cut (redacted) completely in half."

I was invited by my former friends after the dissolution of the Republican Guard to join the new insurgency amassing in Fallujah, but I thankfully declined. I said, "My war was short, but I have had enough for a lifetime." I am thankful I declined. Almost everyone who joined the insurgency in Fallujah was killed by the Marines. Today I am a friend to the United States. I don't talk much about it, but I think I'm just glad to be alive and still mourn my friends.

- Anonymous former Republican Guard. Iraqi Army. Baghdad, 2003.

"Rockets and guts"
US Marine

During the battle of Fallujah we got to fire a lot of rockets, at everything, all the time. On one such occasion, I literally blew a man into such tiny pieces that the only thing left of him could fit in my pocket. Being the boot in the squad, I got the honor of carrying the rocket for my squad. On one particularly difficult street, there was a low wall sitting in front of a two-story villa type of building. We were taking pretty effective machine gun fire from the second floor of that building. My squad leader told me to "vaporize that fuck" so I prepped my launcher, made sure my back-blast was clear, and fired the rocket.

Just as I fired it, I flinched, (This was my first time firing one in combat) and I aimed just a bit low. Lucky for me, just as I fired the rocket, I saw this rifle pop over that low wall I mentioned earlier, followed by a head and torso. It was a Jihadist popping over the wall to shoot at us. Just as he popped halfway over the wall, the rocket went straight through his chest cavity, and exploded on the wall about 4 feet behind him. The blast must have set off an ammo dump in the room behind the wall, and it literally blew him into tiny pieces that flew all the way down the road toward us. Little flecks of blood, clothing, and flesh rained down on us and I got a bit of him in my mouth. It was disgusting. I started dipping chewing tobacco after that. Grizzly wintergreen.

-   Anonymous US Marine. 3/5, Second Battle of Fallujah. 2004

"I killed two men with one round"
US Marine

For those who were there and those who know about it, Ramadi was a tough fucking fight and there was plenty of killing going around. I don't think a single guy in my squad hadn't gotten a kill. I was a designated marksman. So like a sniper, but not. Basically you get handed a 'high performance' rifle and a few weeks training on marksmanship. Still cool.

One day we are patrolling when it seemed like every Jihadist in the city opened up on us. An RPG came from a rooftop about 150 meters away and exploded right in the middle of my squad. Miraculously no one was hurt. I took cover behind a car on the street and started scanning for targets. I saw rapid muzzle flashes coming from the same rooftop the RPG had been fired from. A machine gun.

I did a quick range estimation, aimed my rifle, and aimed a few inches above the muzzle flash. They say time slows down when you kill, but not for me, I just squeezed the trigger and felt the recoil of my rifle. Immediately the muzzle flashes stopped, and we gained fire superiority. Afterwards, we moved forward to clear the buildings we had just taken fire from. Out of curiosity I checked the room I had seen the muzzle flashes from. Inside were two dead Jihadists. One holding an RPG, and another laying on top of him (the one who had been shooting the machine gun.)

When I inspected them, they both had been shot in the in the head or neck. I knew for sure I shot the machine gunner, but I don't know who killed the RPG gunner. The gunner had an entrance wound on his forehead and an exit wound on the back of his head. The RPG dude had a neck entrance wound but no exit. "I'll be damned," my buddy said. "You got them both with one shot." I have to admit. I was pretty proud of this unintentional accomplishment. After checking both their corpses I found two nice Seiko watches. My oldest son is now a Marine, and asked why I have two watches in my man-cave. I just smile and say "Two for one sale, boot."

-   Anonymous US Marine. 3/7, Ramadi, 2006

"Musheen gunz"
US Marine

Everyone knows machine gunners are meat heads. We make fun of them for being dumb but we love them. I remember in Iraq I was manning a VCP with my buddy (redacted). A vehicle approached from the south of our blockade and didn't stop. It ignored our warning sings, pen flares and my hand signals. The

Squad Leader came over comms and told us to open up on the car. My buddy, being a 0331 machine gunner, had waited for this moment his entire enlistment. He fired his 240 at the vehicle and damn near turned it into swiss cheese.

The other guys at the VCP went to check the car once it had stopped and when they came back they said the driver looked like hamburger meat. One of them said, "Damn, (redacted), did you really have to shoot that many rounds?" My buddy just smiled, spit out a mouth full of dip and said in a deep devil like voice, "I need kill. Need kill for machine gun god." And then lifted the gun onto his shoulder and kissed the buttstock with the world's biggest grin.

Some guys are just made to kill, I guess.

- Anonymous US Marine. 2005, Iraq War

"A dead man ripped ass in front of me"
US Marine

I was point man entering the house. As soon as I turned the corner in a hallway I saw a head poke out of a doorway, followed by an AK. My rifle was already raised and I fired two shots at him. The first round missed him entirely but the second one grazed his head. He retreated back into the room, and myself and two Marines took advantage of his injury and immediately followed him in.

He tried to raise his rifle again and I fired two more shots directly into his face. The top of his head came apart, leaving only his nose and below intact. It looked like a canoe. After we had cleared the house, I held a strongpoint in the room with the dead insurgent until our second squad came in and we could take a breather. Two Marines and I sat down and lit cigarettes. I leaned against the wall and we all just listened to the sound of battle a few blocks away.

For a moment it was dead quiet and we heard a, 'BrrrAAAAAAP. Braaaaap' come from the corpse on the floor. We all just looked at each other and my buddy said, 'Dude that dead guy just ripped ass.' And we all had a good laugh. "Excuse you." I said. "No one in this city has any manners."

- Anonymous US Marine. The Battle of Fallujah, November 11th, 2004

"I paid for this sword. I'm going to use it."
US Marine

I think every true warrior dreams of getting a kill with a sword, but no one actually takes steps to do it. It was 2005 in Iraq. My battalion was taking some rest after the fighting in central Iraq. We got mail call and my buddy (redacted) got a long package and seemed super eager to open it. A small group gathered around him, curious as to what was inside. He cut the tape on the box, and pulled out a sharpening stone and then turned away from us. He pulled something out of the box, and turned back toward us holding a mother fucking ceremonial NCO sword.

"What the fuck are you going to do with that?"

64

"Brother, I paid $300 for this sword. You bet your ass I'm gonna get a kill with it."

Our squad leader grabbed the sword and said, "(redacted), what's going to happen when we are on patrol and start taking effective machine gun fire? What are you going to do, you dumbass?"

(Redacted) took the sword back into his hands, pulled the sword out of the scabbard and said, "Sergeant, I'm gonna deflect the bullets with this bad boy, run up to them and stab them." During the following weeks, he came to be known as 'King Arthur. King of the Boots.'

- Anonymous US Marine. 1st Marine Division. Iraq, 2005

"GAS GAS GAS"
US Soldier

One day while I was playing with a camel spider in a palm grove. Really we were waiting on the buffalo to check out an IED, we heard 3 thump noises a good distance away. Then the whistle of mortars. We were in a shallow irrigation ditch already so we just tried to get small in the ditch. A mortar came whistling in and thudded into the ground about 25 - 40 meters away. It didn't explode. At first I thought we were incredibly lucky, then it started hissing and dust started coming out of it. My team leader leapt up and started dragging us toward the trucks shouting "GAS GAS GAS"

Literally ran up the back of the buffalo while it was checking out a suspected and started pulling all of the shit out from behind the A/C unit to get to our masks. My squad leader was screaming at me for approaching the truck with a suspected bomb in front of it. I looked at him and screamed "GAS" he practically shoved me out of the truck to start getting everyone's masks out

After the all clear, we went and checked out the mortars, apparently they were gas mortars but did not have any agent in them. Hajj would apparently get mortars and having no training in identification he would just lob them at us regardless of what they were.

- Anonymous US Soldier. Iraq.

"We waited to die in the blast"
US Army

Our squad was patrolling the main highway south of Kirkuk with a group of Iraqi police, October 2005. We had orders to set up a hasty checkpoint which we did next to a big field. Our Humvees were lined on each side of the southbound lane pointed north. It was at night so we used flashlights and headlights to signal people to stop and then they were directed to park in the field. There, the IP would go through each car or truck looking for weapons or bomb making materials. In that part of the country the Kurds and Arabs were constantly

65

battling each other with us caught in the middle. I was about ten meters from the checkpoint providing over watch on the vehicles.

It was all going pretty well. No problems. About twenty minutes into it a car was approaching and all of a sudden he stepped on the gas. He was coming at us like a rocket. Well, everybody knew that we were going to get the shit blown out of us so we all opened up on this car as it got closer and closer. Rifle fire, .50 cal., my 203. Everything. And still he came. Finally I just kind of closed my eyes waiting for the "click-boom" and the searing heat of the explosion. Something I was familiar with having just had my Humvee hit by an IED the month before. But the only noise was the screeching of brakes as the guy finally came to a stop at the checkpoint. Everyone ran over to his car thinking that this dude was going to be ground meat.

Not a fucking scratch! The IP pulled him out of the car. Through our interpreter he said that he was drunk, freaked out when he saw our lights and mixed up the brake and gas pedal. The IP changed his flat tire and sent him on his way. We, in turn, got the fuck out of there and RTB. We were fixing to rotate back to the states the next month so that was out last hasty checkpoint. And our patrols for that last month devolved into just driving around trying to stay out of harm's way.

-Sgt. Fred Hansen, 1st Infantry Division. Iraq 2005.

"Strange Breed"
US Marine

The first time I saw a dead body, I was 19 on my first deployment in Iraq 2005. It was like a dark scene out of a movie. A woman was holding a dead child with brains all over her garments. Her husband lay dead on the ground with half his brains scattered on the asphalt, half on his passenger window. We had to bag the bodies and toss them in the 7-ton like roadkill. After I stacked the second body on top of the first, my buddy 'Carl' handed me his digital camera. "Governale, take a picture." he said. Considering both bodies were already in body bags, the request came across as nothing less than some serial killer shit. I declined, but Carl insisted. "Governale, take the fucking picture." I pushed back. "Dude, I really don't want to take a picture." "Stop being such a *pu*ssy! Hurry up, I've got security." I paused with a sigh. (Sound of body bag unzipping) "Carl. Hurry the fuck up."

The deceased man was missing an eye, yet his other eye was looking at me and he had his mouth open. I clenched my jaw and held the camera steady. As the camera made a beeping sound, the flash gleamed off his brains. Carl laughed. "Haha you're going to burn in hell." Out loud, I said "Ohhh." As morbid as it sounds, that was the most dark, yet comical moment of my life. I handed him the camera and we finished the mission.

66

Upon our return to base, Marines from my section were gathered in a circle. Carl pulled out the camera and said "Want to see what sick fuck Governale took a pic of?" I started laughing, but Carl kept his bearing. He didn't crack a smile, looked at me and nodded his head in disgust; as he passed the camera off to Marines. Members of my platoon were saying shit like, "Why the hell would you take a picture of a dead guy?" I responded with, "Oookay I'm the weirdo." but everyone ganged up on me. The infantry is a unique place, filled with dark humor; with individuals from all broken walks of life.

- Justin Governale. US Marines. Iraq 2005.

"Hunger and flesh"
US Marine

I can still remember how hungry I was when I woke up to take my shift on post. It was about midnight and this wonderful smell of BBQ came wafting in. I dressed and went to the CP to find the cooks and get something to eat. I walk into the CP and I look around and there was no food, about that time a buddy of mine was walking past and I stopped him and asked where the BBQ was. He kind of laughed and said there is no BBQ. I was still smelling this wonderful BBQ aroma while we were talking, I shot him a puzzled look. He went on to explain that a few hours prior a family in the city had their house bombed by the Mujh because a family member of theirs hadn't complied to their demands. It wasn't a repulsive instinct that came over me, in fact I felt nothing at all. I just chuckled and said "Well, now I am hungry for BBQ".

People will say that burning bodies stink, which they might, but that day they didn't and every time I pass a steak house I remember that same hunger I had that night.

- Anonymous US Marine. 2/6 Marines. Fallujah, Iraq. 2007

"Market"
RAF

Op Telic 2004. Some shithole market on the outskirts of Basrah city. Driving around with a WMIK and Snatch Land Rover looking for trouble. I'm top cover in the Snatch with my LSW. Place is heaving, memory is a bit foggy as its two decades ago now but I remember passing under a bridge with crowds on it. Safe to say not British friendlies.

Some knob head with zero regard to the market goers lobs a hand grenade at us. I vividly remember it bouncing off the bonnet right past my noggin and landing on the ground amongst the shopper's. The *fucker* didn't go off! We start to cordon off when a warrior comes rolling down the road oblivious to our signals clearly in a rush goes right over our grenade which promptly exploded underneath. Tank and crew seem to not notice or not care and continue onwards. Cordon off.

- Anonymous SAC Royal Air Force Op Telic. Basrah Iraq. 2004

"Family"
US Marine

I was on post in Iraq during the early years of the war (2004) the guy with me was always the quiet one in the platoon. It was late in the night and we got sick and tired of being sick and tired and decided to do something we weren't supposed to do at night. Smoke a cigarette. I handed one to my buddy on post and he took it and gave me a nod in thanks. We smoked for a few minutes in silence and said something odd.

He looked up, blew out a breath full of smoke and said, "You know man. I grew up in an orphanage. Before I joined the Marines, I never had a family or any friends. This might sound fucked up, but this is the happiest I've ever been in my life." Now, almost 17 years later, I still think about those words almost every day. It's hard to explain. Being around death and destruction is a terrible thing, don't get me wrong. But doing it with a group of friends like that? It's closer than friendship. I suppose they're the truest family you ever could have.

- Anonymous US Marine, Iraq, 2004

"We go where we want"
US Soldier

DTG Early November 2006. Northern Hawr Rajab.

As we began to take over the AO from the previous unit we went on ride a longs with the previous unit. They showed us the routes the usually traveled and the problem areas they always experienced. During every ride-a-long the departing unit avoided turning south at one of the key intersections in our AO. "What's down that way?" SPC Fuscaldo asked one of the NCO's from the departing unit gesturing down the road to the south. "That's Hawr Rajab, you can't go down there. That road belongs to the insurgents." The NCO replied. Fuscaldo laughed and pointed to the airborne tab above unit patch "We're airborne, we go where we want." That next week after the unit hand off was complete, we would launch one of the most intense operations to retake the suburb of Hawr Rajab. This would bring our unit into some of the heaviest combat with the insurgency in Iraq.

- Sgt. Scott Wright 425th BSTB, attached 1/40th Cavalry Regiment 4th Brigade 25th Infantry Division

"I don't want to go back"
US Soldier

DTG Sometime in early March, 2007. Camp Buehring Kuwait.

While I was returning from my mid tour leave, I was assigned to a temporary barracks in Kuwait awaiting transport back into the shit. The temporary billeting authority tried to assign us in billets with other members of our units. The barracks were nothing more than an insulated tent with about 8 sets of bunk beds and an air conditioner. Better than nothing in the Kuwaiti heat, I guess.

While awaiting transport we did the usual things soldiers do, play spades, smoke cigarettes, swap war stories etc. My unit had been deployed for 6 months at this point and had seen some significant action. A portion of the 3/509th infantry had gone to support operations south of Fallujah, where they had seen some of the worst fighting our unit had been exposed to. The men from this unit were visibly affected by it and loathing the idea of returning to combat.
One night before I was due to return to my unit I awoke to sobbing in the dark. One of the soldiers in a bunk near me was crying himself to sleep. I lied there contemplating if I should offer my comrade comfort, but honestly, I had no comfort to offer.

Tomorrow he, just as I would be returning to a world of death, destruction and chaos. How could you not be upset about that? "I don't want to go back. I don't want to go back" I could hear him whispering into his pillow. "I don't want to go back either." I thought to myself. There was really no rationalizing it at the time. Here we were, across the world fighting a war for people who mostly did not want us there. For what? Oil? Glory? Prestige? I just wanted to return home to my new wife and forget about this sand box.
-   Sgt. Scott Wright. 425th BSTB, attached 1/40th Cavalry Squadron 4th Brigade 25th Infantry Division

"Brains on the road"
US Soldier

Our FOB was right on a highway, in BFE middle of nowhere. We were a few clicks away from the Iranian border. Several days a week our Battalion Commander allowed some locals to set up some tables in front, along the road and sell some shit. Knock off watches, pirated DVDs, and "ficky fickies" which were porns of course. Well we had some concrete barriers up front along the road, and some ICDC fellas that used to check vehicles coming through.
One day I was up front and looking at some knock off watches as mine had broken.

While there, I saw the vendor's eyes get big, and he said "Mister, mister! Here, now!" At the same time I heard an engine rev up, and the ICDC guys shouting. Then a .50 from a CAT, which was along the perimeter opened up. I was quickly in the ditch with the vendor, and looked up when the shit stopped, as it wasn't far from me. Some farmer got pissed off at being inconvenienced in his own country, I guess and wanted to drive through.

Well, he was stone dead. His passenger was screaming his head off. My First Sergeant was at the gate right away and saw me, and told me to check it. Fuck! I approached it slowly, and the door was practically popped open. The driver's body was leaning on the door, and it opened, half of his brain slid out on

69

the road. I had never seen a brain before and had no idea that it was grey and shit. It lay there for about ten minutes as my First Sergeant and BC checked out the scene, and the medic took care of the passenger.

I saw a dirty yellow mutt run up and grab that brain and take off into the brush across the road. There was a pack of wild dogs running around, and you could hear them snarling at each other over the take. Honestly, it didn't really register with me at that moment, because I hadn't really gotten over the shooting. It startled the living shit out of me. It was tough sleeping that night, as it was the first time that I had seen anything like it.

- Anonymous US Soldier. 1/17 FA, 75th Brigade, 4th ID. Dyalia province, Iraq 2003.

"I live a nightmare"
US Marine

On Oct 27th, 2006, I volunteered to be a part of the Casvac crew for my unit HMM-364, The Purple Foxes, and assist the Combat Corpsmen however they needed me. My opportunity came at 0730; I heard the alarm go off, causing me to sprint about 100-yards to the aircraft. I was putting on gear and waiting for the signal to get on the CH-46. Just before I boarded, I was told by the crew chief to be ready. It was a Point of Injury (POI), meaning that we are picking up the wounded right where he was injured, and the fighting is still going on. Over the next few minutes, we were flying low off the ground at full speed. I waved to the locals working on a Red Semi Truck and women hanging laundry. As they waved back before, I could see the column of black smoke rising up in the air. Reminding me that I was in a warzone. For a split second, I questioned my choice. Once, I realized my only way off this helicopter was by jumping off the ramp. I turned towards the burning tank and faced it like a Purple Fox. Within minutes we had landed fifty feet from the tank that hit a roadside bomb. From my understanding, The Marine was coming out after the blast and was shot six times.

Once we landed on the ground, I could see but not hear the two Corpsmen yelling and pointing at the windows. Next, the crew chiefs pointed their .50 cals while yelling frantically. Finally, the pilots were talking and pointing in different directions. To my left, I looked out the porthole, and I saw a Marine jump out of the tank half-exposed, waving us off, only to notice that my headset was unhooked. Once I had connected again, I heard, "PULL-UP PULL-UP, THEY ARE SHOOTING!!!!" The next thing I knew, we were in the air circling overhead, waiting for a new smoke signal to land once again. We came in low and fast this time. We passed a pink house with Marines taking cover on the Balcony. Until we landed near a grey house.

Right then, I saw a woman with a small toddler in her left hand and a young boy holding her right hand as they ran out of the house. My first reaction was drawing my pistol and watching the window right before me, about 25 yards away. At the same time, the Aerial Observer (AO) pointed his .50 cal at the very window. I felt a tap on my left arm and a Corpsman signaling me to the stretcher. Once I was off the ramp of the CH-46, I was in complete silence, black and white, and everything was in slow motion around me while I was able to move at average speed. The two Helicopter engines were perfectly silent even though I was close enough to touch them above my head. I watched each individual rotor blade moving in slow motion while they spun around. Marines in the distance were running in full combat gear and floating in the air as if they were stuck there in time like an artist drew them with a pencil. Pieces of mud were popping up around me, and one-piece, in particular, made me want to reach out and grab it during all of this chaos. Because it fascinated me that it was so close and just floating in the air perfectly still. A severely wounded man was placed at my feet carried on a blanket, which caused me to stand there and stare at him. I wondered why they put an Iraqi enemy wearing a Marine uniform at my feet. Once another Marine standing next to me screamed into my ear to get him the fuck on the plane. At this moment, everything zipppppped back to sound and color. My muscle memory kicked in, and I got him on the stretcher and helped carry him in.

I stood at his head and watched the Corpsmen work franticly to save him. I froze again as he was spitting up bile from one of the six gunshot wounds that hit his stomach, which was covering his hand that he was reaching at me with as if he wanted me to hold it. Once I made eye contact and watched him spitting up brown blood bile, I couldn't move for a few moments as we stared into each other's eyes. Until we hit some turbulence, and I had to help them again. When the wounded Marine's left arm began to dangle as it slipped off the stretcher, looking like Freddy Kruger sliced his bicep, fat, and bone. The two Corpsmen and I jumped back in shock, causing me to shout out, "IS THAT SUPPOSED TO HAPPEN?" The Corpsman quickly grabbed the arm and taped it to the wounded Marine's chest. We hit more turbulence when the foot of the stretcher popped out of the hook. Somehow I moved from his head to his feet with superhero speed and caught the stretcher in the air before it fell and dropped the patient.

Once back to the surgical unit, he was unloaded and taken away when I looked at my hands. They were the mechanic gloves I used to fix Machine guns every day, now they were soaked in blood. One Corpsman walked up to me and started to pour water at my feet because I was standing in a pool of blood and bone fragments. I watched the stream of water and blood run down the floorboards and off on the concrete. We made it back to the flight line, and I was told by the pilot that I was lucky because I was getting shot at when I came off the ramp explaining why the mud was flying up around me. We debriefed, and I was heading back to my shop when my legs gave out, and I fell to the ground. That was the moment that it set in what I had just witnessed. I used the small barriers to pull myself up because my legs were utterly paralyzed. Once I could stand, I made it back to my shop, where I talked to my SSgt about the mission. A few hours later, one of the Corpsmen I was helping told me that Marine passed away fifteen minutes after the transfer. So I had to wait a few months for the Marines Corps Times to get to Iraq. I looked up the names on the casualties list and saw his name was Sgt Luke Zimmerman. Over the next three months, I could not sleep due to the nightmares. During the day, on three different occasions on base, I would see him standing there perfectly clean unhurt, and just staring at me very, very angry.

- Anonymous US Marine. HMM-364, The Purple Foxes. Iraq 2006.

"I was shot by a sniper"
US Soldier

When I first arrived on scene, I glassed the area out, because no one had confirmed the sniper killed or gone. After a few, I made the mistake of assuming dude had fled because we had been on the ground 6 months and they weren't likely to stick around for a stand up fight unless we trapped them. I opened my TC door and stood behind it, I told my guys, if you're ever just standing around, open your door and stand behind it, it's not much, but it might save your life. After a few seconds I felt an impact like I had never felt before and it knocked me to the ground. I remember thinking "what the fuck was that?!!" As I laid on the ground. Never heard the shot or saw anything. My left arm was numb and I felt a pain in my chest and curled up into a fetal position. A voice in my head said, get up! Get up!

I shook my left hand like it was waking up sleep, pins and needles. Rolled into the prone and got my gun up. I remember seeing the red dot from my CCO and putting it on a lone tree about 200 meters out and thinking that's where he had to be, but I didn't see anything. The medic next to me, "Doc Archie" crawled onto my back where he saw the bullet exit through my body armor, he said, "its ok, I think it just knocked you!" After what seemed like forever, I told him, "Doc we're sitting ducks, we need to get behind the Humvee." I could see the other guys on the other positions scrambling. I knew they heard the shot and saw me go down. I keyed up on my icom and told them I had been shot, but was ok. I was still in a lot of pain and my left arm was still numb, but for some reason I told them I could still use it.

Doc crawled under the Humvee, through a puddle of his own piss he just left. I kind of 3 point football crawled to the front and sat down for some reason. I could still see the other guys scrambling around and I keyed up and told them that I think I'm ok. Just then I feel myself being lifted by my drag handle, doc picking me up. He sat me down leaning up against the rear wheel on the driver's side. By then he could see the blood pouring out under the collar piece and down the front of my IBA. The look in his eyes told me everything was probably not ok.

He opened the front of my vest and he looked shocked. Later he told me there was a big fucking hole in my trach. With big eyes, he told me everything was going to be okay. Just then, the LT pulled up a few feet away and asked what

72

the situation was, Doc turned around and yelled "We gotta get him to the fucking hospital right fucking now!" We got my IBA off and he started plugging curlex into my neck, I helped him hold it into place. Then they helped me into the back seat behind the driver. That's when that photo was taken, our photographer was riding with the LT that day. Heading northbound on Route Irish, an Iraqi car tried to merge next to us, my driver was screaming at the gunner to light them up, but the gunner was hesitant. The driver kept swerving the truck as he looked back and I thought, 'Great, I'll probably survive the gunshot but die in roll over.'

I looked past Doc through the window and could see it was just a few Iraqis not paying attention, that's probably why the gunner didn't fire. In any event, if it was a car bomb it would have detonated by now so I told everyone to calm down. (Yes, the guy with the bullet hole in his neck told everyone else to calm down) The People in the car quickly realized they were way to close to American vehicles and promptly pulled over but my driver was still very agitated. The driver was, and still is a good friend, so sharing the same humor, I tried to bring him some calm by telling him a joke (a quote from the movie top shots) I said, 'Mike! A horse walks into a bar and the bartender says, why the long face.' Except I passed out before I got the long face part out. That didn't work out.

At some point I remember hearing Doc scream, 'Stay with me! Stay with me!' And I could feel him pulling my eyelid open, but all I could see was light. I thought, 'Well, this must be it.' That bullet must have spun around inside of me and I'm bleeding out. My first child had been born right as I got mob'd up and was about 8 months old at that point and I started thinking of her. Shortly after I felt a sensation that I think was a second adrenaline dump and I opened my eyes.

Soon we were at the emergency gates of the 86th CSH and the Corporal in charge of the gate said everyone needed to get out and clear their weapons first. Doc was literally holding my throat and was like, "Are you fucking serious?" The Corporal was oblivious and insisted. That's when my driver pulled out and racked his M9 pistol and threatened to blow the guy's head off if he didn't open the gate. Fortunately, the LT walked up and threw the gate open before anyone got shot. I truly think he would have done it.

I walked into the ER and saw another one of our guys on a gurney and thought, "How many guys did this dude shoot?!", but it turns out he went into heat exhaustion dragging the other guy 6 stories off the roof. I went into surgery and that pretty much concluded the day's events.
-    SSG Christian Carpenter, Weapon Squad Leader, C co 1/184 INF, 4th BDE, 3ID. 22 June 2005

"Saved from haunting guilt"
US Marine

I deployed to Fallujah in 2007. A few years after phantom fury, it was no longer house to house fighting, in fact it was fairly calm at that point especially

73

since our unit shut the place down. 8pm curfew, very few ways in or out of the city and Iraqi police checkpoints at almost every intersection. We made it tougher for the insurgents to move around, but at the end of the day they still had home field advantage. We still dealt with IEDs, suicide dump truck VBIEDs, mortar and sniper attacks. For all the security, fortification and patrolling they still managed to get their licks in.

We eventually figured out that they were purposely spacing out their attacks long enough where just when we felt the threat was gone and let our guard down...BOOM someone gets sniped on post, or mortars start falling around the OP or a dump truck explodes.

We were on a foot patrol one night, staying in the shadows, bounding across streets, bumping each other from corner to corner and being quiet as possible. At one point we came to a halt right as I was at a street corner. I crouched down against the wall with my rifle pointed down the avenue of approach. As usual scanning, sweeping my aim from window to window, doorway to rooftop, when I saw the guy coming from out of nowhere.

A block away, on the same side of the street as I was, some guy was casually walking in my direction. Firstly, it was late night so no one was supposed to be outside with the curfew. Secondly, civilians in the city knew to stay away from our patrols as we regularly waved them off and occasionally fired shots to stop cars from getting close. This guy was coming straight at me. The problem was he carried a big brown grocery type bag in front of him, blocking his view. I yelled for him to stop, started flashing my surefire light in his direction and even waved my non firing arm. I guess he couldn't see me because he just kept coming.

At this point my finger is on the trigger, I'm watching him close the distance, I flip off my safety, and I'm panicking. I'm realizing I've already given every warning I'm supposed to, I'm supposed to shoot next. I'm breathing hard, yell out to the rest of the patrol, "Hey I got a guy! He's coming and won't stop!" Yelling "Aguff, Aguff!" (Arabic for 'stop'). I remember I told myself okay, I'll give him two more steps before I shoot, he would walk the two steps, Okay, two more, now he's getting close. If that bag is a bomb and he blows it I'm close enough where I'm gonna feel it now. I'm standing up, yelling, flashing, heart beating faster, I put a little more pressure on the trigger....then I hear the sound of someone in boots in a full sprint.

My squad leader had heard the commotion, and came running over full speed. He runs past me, in the direction of the man walking...and just like an NHL hockey player BODY CHECKS the guy with his rifle and bodyweight full force. The guy flew backwards, bag flying with food and things everywhere, almost doing a complete backflip. My squad leader lands on the guy screaming "Are you dumb? Are you trying to get killed?!" The guys face was pure terror. We figured out the guy was deaf, didn't hear my warning and didn't see anything.

I was seconds away from pulling that trigger. I don't know what my squad leader's reason for doing that was, instead of having me shoot or whatever. But he saved the man's life, and saved me from a lifetime of guilt. I fired my weapon on that deployment, in the general direction of the enemy, but that would have been an up close and personal kill.

I've seen what it does to someone when they kill a civilian accidently, scary to know it almost happened to me.

- Anonymous US Marine. 2/6 Echo Co. Fallujah Iraq, 2007.

"Stay Low"
US Army

On 16JUN2009, my platoon was tasked with patrolling the western side of Karrada Peninsula in the Babil neighborhood of Baghdad just outside the Western entrance to the Green Zone. An IED had been placed and detonated under a large diesel tank on "Saints" Street, just south of a large traffic circle. I was dismounted along with our brand new FO, our brand new 1LT, and my Platoon Sergeant, SFC Yakop. We were doing post-blast analysis, and immediately I knew this didn't feel right. The Iraqi National Police checkpoint had been moved several hundred meters north of where it should've been and the IED was just pieces of cast iron that had been duct taped to some HME. It didn't detonate the diesel tank, just blew a large hole in it. It seemed set up so Coalition responders would come to the scene.

We were on the ground about 10 minutes, and medevac status had gone red due to dust storms before we rolled out. Now, normally my Platoon Sergeant trusted those of us with prior deployments if we said something didn't feel right, and it really looked like a set up. I told him we needed to leave the AO, time now. Complacency must've set in because I was told "Those mother suckers ain't gonna do shit!"

Shortly after, the wind died down and I looked towards the LT just in time to see red spray from the side of his head and he immediately dropped. I had time to register what happened, and heard the "Snap" of the round. I grabbed the FO, who was next to me and threw him behind one of the Iraqi Police trucks that had been abandoned near the IED site. When all was said and done, he was treated at the Green Zone CSH, and was evacuated out of the country. He survived, and retired as a CSM/SGM.

- SGT Daniel R. Ames. Blue Platoon, A 1-319th AFAR, 3BCT, 82nd Airborne Division.

"They deserved better"
US Marine

I was deployed to Ramadi Iraq from September 2005 to April 2006 with a Marine infantry unit. We rotated through a reinforced observation post next to an intersection called 295 just down the road from a larger intersection dubbed "firecracker," by previous units. It was during one of these rotations we heard mortars firing at Camp Ramadi from a hospital to our west and my platoon set up an ambush if they fled our direction. When they stopped firing three cars left the hospital compound with one going west, north and east. The car traveling east drove right into our kill zone and an entire platoon of Marines opened up on this car. In the midst of shooting at this car a civilian vehicle came from nowhere and drove into our machine guns shooting at this other car.

We killed them. All of them. It was an accident and we just stared at this car full of Iraqi civilians from our positions understanding we just ended someone who was likely just going home. I felt nothing about the situation back then. As I have grown older I feel sad about those people. They didn't deserve that.

- Anonymous US Marine. 3/7 India Co. Ramadi Iraq, 2006.

"Find someone you can help"
US Marine

I was again in a rotation through OPVA with my platoon when I was coming off post. Usually to satisfy my curiosity and to see if I could spot any changes I walked around the entire second floor of the building and looked through windows people did not occupy. As I was doing it I saw two white puffs of smoke and what sounded like explosions to the west near the glass factory.

They were recruiting for the Iraqi Army over there and I feared something had happened. I checked in with the COC and they hadn't heard any radio chatter about an incident so I went to my cot. Literally five minutes later QRF was called and we responded to the glass factory. As we approached army strikers, tanks, and 5 tons were parked haphazardly blocking the MSR and we became frustrated trying to park.

When I opened my door and stepped into the scene the first thing I heard was the moaning and crying of 200 people lying dead, broken, and wounded on the ground. Army soldiers were stacking dead bodies in five tons and they were so high their hands and arms were hanging out the side. We were told "find someone you can help." So we did. We walked among the dead, torsos, and frozen faces. Piles of people near the blast zones seemed to be fused together. I couldn't tell where someone began and when they ended. Those piles were at least chest high.

We found a person barely alive laying in the dirt and we loaded him in a high back and took him to Camp Ramadi hospital. When we got there so many people were maimed they didn't have room and put them on cots outside. When I sat the guy down I stood over him, held his hand, and cried. I told him everything was going to be ok even though I knew he couldn't understand me. He just wanted a job. I don't know what happened to that man, but I'll remember him for the rest of my life.

- Anonymous US Marine. 3/7 I Co. Ramadi, Iraq. 2006.

"The true cost of war"
US Marine

I was a naive young man. People join the service for all sorts of things but I joined to kill people and not go to jail. What I didn't know then is what I would trade to achieve this twisted purpose.

My platoon was to ambush a car full of combatants firing mortars from a hospital at Camp Ramadi. When they finished three cars left the compound and spread west, north, and east. My platoon ambushed the car traveling east. As it approached the reinforced OP my platoon opened fire but the car continued to drive. I fired at the drivers face first, shooting without hesitation, remorse, or consideration to his humanity. I kept firing until the car came to a stop in the road in front of our OP. I fired at least 25 times at the drivers head and I had no idea if I had connected any shots. Two of the three men were killed and a third got out and started to run away but a fellow Marine shot him with a tracer round in the torso. He struggled but continued to flee. My squad gave chase.

I was tasked to test the hands of the dead for gunpowder residue with a kit I was not trained to use but I did it anyway. When I approached the car the driver and the man in the back driver side seat was clearly dead. I looked at the driver, the man I shot at and his face was unrecognizable as a human. The head rest was obliterated and he was caught on his seatbelt leaning forward, his face just a few inches from the steering wheel. Brain matter, blood and other bodily fluid was everywhere and the smell of death was overwhelming.

When I opened the back door to test the passengers hand his arm flopped out. When I grabbed his left index finger his muscle and skin slid on his finger bone and stretched. I vomited. It was in this intimate moment with men I fired shot at I understood how wrong I was and just how disgusting my perception was of war.

I have not killed anything I didn't have to since this moment. I heard once "when you kill, you kill yourself." On that day part of me died and it took years of helping innocent people to revive humanity in myself. This is the true cost of war. A person's sense of humanity.

- Anonymous US Marine. 3/7 I Co. Ramadi, Iraq. 2006.

"Hardest trigger I ever had to pull"
US Marine

I was in Iraq with a MTT team back in 08'. For those that don't know what that is; it's a Military Transition Team. It was our job to train the IA and start putting an Iraqi army face on the counter insurgency effort. Our MTT team was composed of eight SNCO's and officers. As well as six E-5 and below. One Captain, three Lieutenants, three Staff Sergeants, One Petty officer second class Corpsman, two Sergeants and four E-3 and below. Now that you understand the hierarchy you can imagine where shit would wind up when it rolled down hill. Being that I was among the E-3's and below it would fall on my lap as much as the others in the MTT. About 4 months in our captain decided the stray dogs on our patrol base had become a health hazard.

"We could pet them, forget to wash our hands and then eat."

Or

"Unknowingly step in their feces and track it in common areas around the patrol base."

So what us E-3's and below were tasked out to do was round up all the stray dogs we'd been feeding and grown attached to for the last 4 months and execute them. We zip tied their arms and legs and shot them execution style while they whimpered, yelped and screamed. Some of the cries almost sounded human. No matter how much time passes there are some things that can never be unheard. I participated in the executions.

This was an unlawful order I should have told my captain to shove so far up his ass that it would come back out of his mouth. But I didn't. I did it because the others were doing it and I wanted to lighten the load for them. Our corpsman carried out the majority of the executions.

In the end we executed around 30 dogs about 5 of them were puppies. It was the hardest trigger I ever had to pull. This made being around dogs difficult for a long time. And while I might benefit from a service dog, I haven't been able to bring myself to get one.

- Anonymous US Marine. 2nd MEF 2nd MHG Military Transition Team. Al Kharma, Iraq. 2008

"Warfighters"
US Marine/Army

In 2005/6 during OIF, myself and several other Army Infantry NCOs from 2nd Brigade, 1st Armored DIV, when it was still garrisoned in Baumholder GE, we're seconded to a Military Transition Team (MiTT) that was made out of hide from different Marine units on Camp Lejeune, NC, but mostly 3/8 Marines. The officers and Senior NCOs made up the staff that guided the Iraqi Army unit we were supporting and the Team Leaders for the actual three to four man elements that were embedded with individual Iraqi Infantry Companies. We and a few Combat Medics made up the Junior NCO Leadership and obviously medical support. All was warehoused on FOB Blue Diamond, right on the Euphrates River, next to the Damn/Bridge, NSW had Shark Base directly across from us, then CAG and SF both had COPs next to them daisy chained along the bank of the river. Blue Diamond was occupied by 3/8 Marines proper and 1/6 IN of 1AD. All right next to the large bridge on the MSR headed to huge FOB Ramadi.

Ok, so we did a lot of night raids, our Iraqis were sort of above par so we did some shit. It was legit, I had been in the Marines previously as a POG, then came in the Army as a Paratrooper then landed in 1AD after a reenlistment with option for orders to Europe. At this point in my career I was feeling pretty salty, Korea on the DMZ, MFO rotation to Egypt and now in the big show. Honestly I had no training for the type of stuff we were doing but I got along well with the Marines and I had decided, "Fuck it! When in Rome." So I went all in, when in charge be in charge and my new LT and I got along like peas and carrots. He had been to Haiti for some peacekeeping shit himself and was in one of the Fallujah dust ups. That and we were the exception and had a Navy Corpsman versus an Army Medic, true barrel chested freedom fighter, had been with Force Recon and done some shit. Good Doc. Best team.

So anyways we got the call to perform a night mission to hit a suspected HVT's location but the trick was we would be inserted up north by Marines who were running a Riverine Detachment. This was before the Navy redirected the program and brought it back. I was stoked, it was like a surprise birthday gift. I thought we were god damned commandos, this was some Vietnam MAC-V-SOG shit to me. Like going out LRRP style on PBRs in the Mekong Delta or something. (That's what was going on in my head, I was but naive at this stage still). However, as excited as I am, I am still a professional and I certainly didn't want to fuck it up. So I asked for rehearsals because I was sure none of my Iraqis hadn't embarked on boats before and dismounted then, potentially under fire, in the dark, in unknown territory. And the MAJ (great fucking guy to have as a skipper) agreed and we memorized the OPORD, rehearsed and Rock-Drilled until the LT and I were happy that this would work. And the Marine Boat Handlers were great to work with and accommodating.

So now it is "H-Hour" and we power up the Euphrates River in black-out, stealthily disembark the boats in some tall reeds, and made our movement to the Objective, the executed the raid. Now our HVT was not at home but it wasn't a total dry hole we recovered some IED components, some HME material and rat-fucked Soviet explosives that these guys had laid their hands on. So essentially the Intel was good, just not timely. The Iraqis did great and as we were getting guys back on the boats the LT whispers to me that was a good op. He might have been premature in offering his complements.

If you don't known this, when boats are putting folks on shore and picking them up, they operate in pairs or in teams of pairs. One boat will put in and one boat will loiter out in the open water to scan for threats and provide direct fire support with 7.62 mm Mini Guns, those Aviation .50 Cals that have such high rates of fire and twin 240Bs. Bow to Stern is armed to the teeth. Well we were the first extracted, then it's our turn to hang out and provide floating security to the next boat getting their dismounts. I am sitting on an ammo box making sure my headcount is right for the umpteenth time, when one of my Iraqis takes a flash photo of two of his battle buddies who were posing in front of the coxswain's station on the boat, throwing signs and grinning with their AKs pointed skyward. I immediately slapped the camera out of his hand, and the Marine LT who was the Coxswain, was giving me this stare like he was mentally throwing K-Bars at me with his eyes! Through his NVDs, But out of nowhere the Gunny who was the bow gunner on one of those Caliber .50 M3Ms had walked back to where we were midship and grabbed the offending photographer and swung him over the side of the gunwales and menacingly threatened to toss him into the drink. After a good shaking and more than a few pejoratives, the Gunny dropped the guy on the deck and went back to his gun, but not before he cut me a look that would cut through tungsten and advised me to keep my jundies under control, then flipped his NODs down. I replied, "Roger That.".

It was a long quiet ride back, only the sound of the diesel powered water jets propelling us along. The debrief afterwards was sort of cool as well. But afterwards the Gunny and Coxswain LT cornered me and said they understood it wasn't really my fault. I explained that's why I insisted on the rehearsals so nothing would go awry. But the MSG who was the MiTT NCOIC and my LT thought it was pretty damned funny and quipped something about the unpredictability of Iraqi Soldiers. But thank god there wasn't an irate, "I hate America", AQI asshole on the river bank with a PKC in 7.62 x 54 who saw the camera flash and decided to fire us up. Because that could have been bad.

All in all the point being, the best laid plans of mice and men. Anyways, that was a great deployment. Did some shit, and it was what propelled me to go on and do SOF stuff. There was some loss and bad shit. And I will keep that to myself for now.

-   Anonymous 2/6 Infantry SSG, Supporting 1st MEF in Ramadi, OIF 2005/6.

"Mass grave excavation…"
US Marine

In Iraq, 2004 in the Al Anbar Province. Our platoon was tasked with providing security for a group of Kuwaiti forensic scientists who were recovering the remains of Kuwaitis. The remains were from 1991 during the Gulf War. Saddam Hussein used captured Kuwaitis as human shields on his bases so U.S. and coalition forces would not bomb them. After the war instead of allowing them to go back to Kuwait, he has them taken out to different areas in the Iraqi desert. From there, a big trench was dug and they were shot in the head execution style and buried. Some were still alive when buried because their arms and hands (skeletal remains) were covering their faces as dirt was being thrown on them. I stood and watched as the Kuwaiti forensic scientists pulled the remains out of the ground. The skulls were men, women and children and they all head bullet holes in them. The Iraqi that led us to one of the sites was the same man who drove the bus in 1991 that took them to their death. Seeing this had me thinking that we were there for a reason and it was worth it.

-     Anonymous U.S. Marine. 1st Marine Division, Iraq, 2004.

"Shitty situation"
US Soldier

I advised an Iraqi Army unit in 04-05. We were on patrol one night, when the Iraqi 1SG started waving me to the front of the formation. As I moved up the sidewalk, something hit my leg with a soft popping noise. Grenade. I dove to my left and just as I was about to shout "Grenade!" I discovered there was no ground there. Nothing. Down an embankment I went, ass over elbows, winding up in a shit ditch that promptly soaked me. After a couple of seconds with no blast, I looked up the bank to see a row of helmets looking down and one of the American NCOs asked, "The fuck is wrong with him?"

I crawled up to discover I'd brushed up against a live wire that was sticking out of the pavement just enough to be dangerous. That, I think, was the pop. Now I'm covered in filth and its freezing. We get back to the vehicles and my driver just looks at me. I climb in the back, and we head home. It's very cold. When we get back to the FOB, my driver's evident amusement is getting old, so I make him hold the hose while I strip down and try to get the worst of it off. Man, its cold.

I decided to just walk the 10 or so meters from my room to the shower without bothering to put something on, despite the low temperature.
About halfway there, a female doctor and two female medics come around the corner. Double take, hard stare, followed by immediate diagnosis of acute, severe shrinkage. I determined that when they collapsed in gales of laughter.
For weeks after that, every time doc saw me, she giggled.

-     Anonymous US Soldier. US Army, Iraq 2004.

"Fuck you right back"
US Marine

I deployed to Iraq in 2006 with 2nd LAR. Being an LAR unit, we're far more mobile than most battalions so we got tasked out for missions throughout all of al Anbar. One of our missions was to protect the only bridge to cross the Euphrates between the Haditha Dam and the Syrian border. We had TCPs on either side of the bridge, as well as two TCPs in a town called Rawah and one that regulated traffic on MSR Bronze. My platoon got the shaft and got to go to Hesco hell on MSR Bronze at TCP 5. It was miserably hot and shitty living conditions but we made the most of it. Much of our mission was over watching the IA search vehicles and do route over watch on Bronze.

Well we would try to switch up how we got to different over watch positions but due to the terrain there were only so many ways to get to the high ground. During one of these missions the insurgents decided to lay an IED at a

known choke point. Luckily my VC was experienced. He spotted it long before we rolled over it in our LAV25. EOD was called and they blew it in place.
As a final "Fuck you." to whatever terrorist was watching, my LT shit in the IED hole.

- CPL Mike Tabor 2nd Light Armored Recon Bn A. Co. Iraq, 2006.

"Being pinned sucks"
US Marine

I was pinned by a machine gun in Ramadi. We were out and about doing Marine stuff, and we got caught in an ambush and I ended up next to a low wall barely 2 and a half feet tall. I was laying on my back face up.
It felt like an eternity. Rounds were flying right over me. Some hitting the very top of the wall sending chips of rock and dust in my face. It was fucking terrifying. I remember I just closed my eyes and screamed. I thought about my mom and dad and how I was probably never gonna see them again.

I thought about the Corps and how I must have made a mistake by joining it. Everyone else I knew was off in college and here I was about to be murdered behind this tiny wall on a street. I tried so hard to pretend I was somewhere else while this machine gun tried so hard to kill me. Suddenly the firing stopped and I realized he must be reloading. My team leader yelled for me to get up and move now if I didn't want to die. Man, I sprinted. I've never ran so fast. Once we were safe, my buddy pointed out I had pissed my trousers.
Being pinned is a helpless feeling.

- Anonymous US Marine. 3rd Battalion 8th Marines. Iraq, 2006

"Pieces of them were on the ceiling"
US Marine

I fired a SMAW rocket into a house and it had basically liquefied a room full insurgents. Stayed put in the room as my squad cleared the rest of the building. There was gore, body parts, and pieces of clothing and weapons all over the room. Guts were literally hanging from the ceiling. I approached a piece of a torso with a shirt attached to it and rummaged through the pockets. I don't know why I felt the urge to see what was in his pockets, I just wanted to. Inside a pocket was a picture of a man and who I presumed to be his family, and a Gameboy Pokémon game. I sat down on a chair and looked around the room, wondering which bits of flesh and blood belonged to the man in the picture. "What paths brought you here? What small decisions in our lives lead both of us to being in this spot, on this day? What lead us into this life and death struggle?" I didn't hate the piles of guts on the floor. I felt pride for doing my job, but an uneasy sense of dread for the family of whoever was in that picture.

He would never see his home again. Would I ever see mine? We're we both destined to die here? It sounds strange, but at the time, I didn't care. Whether

a grenade came through the window of the room, or I was shot in the street. I
didn't care. I was too tired and mentally drained. Death at the moment seemed like
a permanent rest. I just…didn't care.
- Anonymous US Marine. 3rd Battalion 5th Marines. Second Battle of
Fallujah, Iraq 2004.

"We missed every shot"
US Marine
So it's probably mid-July 2004 near FOB Kalsu in Iraq. Blue Platoon was
making our rounds outside the wire when we took up an over watch position on an
overpass for an approaching convoy on route Tampa. Not long after punching out
scouts and setting over watch we began taking indirect fire. My pig (LAV25) was
JUST missed by two mortars that landed within feet of it and blew out all but one
of our 8 tires. Me and two other Marines ended up under the overpass with some
motivators from bravo 2/1 or maybe 2/5 while the rest of my crew gave chase to a
suspected pick up leaving us at the bridge. We saw a white man dress flailing in
the breeze and all (maybe) 8 of us opened up on it. Some Staff Sgt ordered a cease
fire after about a mag and sent a fire team to get BDA. (Battle Damage
Assessment) When they returned an hour later, the man dress was well over 700
yards away and was actually a scarecrow...
Me and my other two Marines caught a ride home with Gunny who was
helping to recover my pig after playing LAPD and getting stuck in a ditch with all
8 tires now flat.
There wasn't a bullet hole one, in the man dress either.
- Lance Corporal Chris Kirkpatrick, Alpha Co, 1st LAR. Iraq 2004

"Medal Chasers"
US Marine
I was in 2/1 Marines in Fallujah from March 04 to Oct 04. I was an NCO
running a squad at that time. Myself and my peers had been in the invasion of Iraq
in 2003. We had a new platoon Sgt who was a recruiter in 2003. This Fallujah
deployment would be his first combat experience. This guy had a huge chip on his
shoulder from not having combat experience. His goal was to win medals. He was
constantly putting us in danger to try and win medals.
One day he is with my squad on patrol in the city of Fallujah. We turn a
corner we are looking at a crowd of 60 or more military age males. It was a
funeral for someone killed that morning (probably by Marines).
We were immediately seen and have this mass of angry military age
Iraqi's staring at my 10 Marine squad. The hate was palpable. I tell my squad we
are going to detour one street down to avoid a possible problem. This platoon Sgt
denied my orders and tells us to patrol straight through the angry crowd. He said
'Sometimes you need to take the bull by the horns'.

So my 10 Marine patrol walk through this angry mob of Iraqi's. I took point. I had my grenade in my hand with the pin pulled. I was showing the grenade to everyone as a warning to leave us alone. The crowd parted like the red sea seeing the grenade. As soon as we made it through, the crowd started chanting and carrying the dead guy off. On the roofs I could see locals with AKs holding over watch.

That was one of many times that platoon Sgt almost got me and/or my Marines killed to win medals.

- Sgt. Brad Simmons, 2nd Battalion 1st Marines. Fallujah, Iraq.

"Gotcha Good"
US Marine

In Fallujah I cut a man in half with my 240. We were holding a street on the edge of the battle area. Like the literal edge. Everything behind us had been cleared and everything in front of us was occupied by jihadists. I was laying on a rooftop overlooking a street with my 240. Things were relatively quiet at that moment. Quiet in the terms of gunfire not in our immediate vicinity.

At all times of the day in Fallujah you could hear the sounds of battle. Anyway, so I'm lying on this rooftop and I see a guy come out of the front door of this building with an AK in his hands. Immediately my first instinct is to pull the trigger and let him eat half a belt, but for some reason I hesitated. He didn't seem to know we were there. He walked out the front door as casually as a suburban dad checking his mail box. He slung his rifle and pulled out his dick and started to piss on the door step. I have no idea why he decided to do this, but he seemed completely unaware we were there.

I don't know how he was alerted to our presence on the rooftop, but he suddenly seemed to be aware of us, and without pulling his pants up, he swung the AK off his shoulder and started to raise it to the top of our roof. I just let him have it. In the Marines you're basically brainwashed to do short controlled bursts but for some reason I just held the trigger. I literally cut him in half at the belly button and his top half sort of folded over his legs onto the doorstep. I guess we really caught him with his pants down and he folded under the pressure. Machine guns are fun.

- Anonymous US Marine. 3rd Battalion 1st Marines. November 9th 2004. Second Battle of Fallujah

"Bombs in the sand"
US Soldier

September of 2005 and my platoon was temporarily assigned to FOB Speicher outside of Tikrit for convoy security up and down Route Tampa. We had made it down to Camp Arifjan in Kuwait with not much trouble traveling with 20 or 25 Army trucks driven mostly by females which we had never seen before so we thought that was pretty interesting. The convoy commander was a staff Sargent who had her shit together. On the way back up we pulled security for around thirty civilian trucks. Due to my total lack of directional ability the Humvee that I drove was in the middle. Which, of course, everyone knows is the primary target of any roadside bombing of a convoy.

Again, we didn't have much trouble on the drive up. Even driving around Baghdad. My TC had somehow figured out how to hook his IPod up to the comms so we could listen to music and it would break whenever someone would talk, incoming and outgoing. So that helped because this was about four in the morning.

We rounded a bend in the highway, slowly because of all the bomb craters and we pulled up next to an Abrams who had the over watch on the route we were heading to. Next to the tank was a semi that was just blown to shit. Apparently he had been hauling soda pop as the ground was littered with pop cans. The tank TC asked if we were thirsty and gave us a couple of cans of Fanta. After we passed the three of us had a philosophical discussion on why the tank was there. Did it mean that the area was secure or did it mean that the area was not secure so they brought in a tank?

About fifteen minutes later we had our answer. The three of us had just opened a fresh can of Red Bull and I was driving with my left hand and holding the can in my right as my TC was blathering on about stupid shit which you talk about at four fifteen in the morning. Out of the corner of my eye I saw the brightest flash of light I had ever seen. And the deafening boom. And then total darkness. It was explained to me afterwards that the explosion causes the inside of the compartment to become a low pressure area.

So all of the dirt, dust and debris from the explosion got sucked in through the gunners hatch and everything went black. Eventually it started to clear and both me and the TC were screaming to each other, "drive thru, drive thru", in near hysterics. This alluded to our training were if your convoy is hit you have to drive thru the "kill zone" or else those dudes waiting in the bushes take you out. Eventually we calmed down and he called back to our squad leader who was in the Humvee in the rear that we just got hit. His reply was something along the lines of "no shit-we saw the fire ball". The three of us were okay even though our gunner took the brunt of all that debris sucking through his hatch. Our windshield was completely shattered but we kept up with the convoy and didn't lose any power. Our thoughts at that point were of the Humvee that we had lost a couple of weeks before outside Speicher. The projectile entered through their passenger side door, missed the TC sitting there, hit and killed his driver and the resultant explosion seriously fucked up the TC and the medic sitting in the back seat. In the back of my mind I thought to myself that whoever set our bomb did a pretty shitty job. Thankfully.

Pretty soon both the TC and I (we are still great friends fifteen years later) just started laughing uncontrollably. Like with tears running down. Don't know if it was relief from cheating death or what but we just laughed and laughed. Then, at the same time we both looked down and we were still holding our cans of Red Bull. So we did all that with one hand. We clinked cans together to toast our adventure, chugged the RB and motored on to FOB Speicher. Uneventfully.

- Sgt. Fred Hansen. First Infantry Division. Iraq 2005.

AFGHAN WAR 2001-2021

"Watching a unicorn"
US Marine

Every combat deployment there reaches a point that you just don't give a fuck anymore. You don't care about anything anymore except those in the shit next you. Morale is generally low, and everyone is in a constant state of hate and discontent, we were no different.

One of these miserable days, while I was COG I was making my rounds to the posts, providing Marines with water, and relieving them if they needed to take a piss or whatever. Our compound had 4 perimeter posts and 1 VCP. The VCP was outside the compound on this shit dirt road and the only way to reach it was from the post's rear. While walking out there, the Marine on post was casually smoking a cigarette, helmet unstrapped, a few days passed a 5 o'clock shadow and a mismatched collection of clothes under his gear. He was every 1st Sgt's worst nightmare. He wasn't complacent but he just didn't give a fuck nor did any of us.

As I approached, I was about to call his name as to not sneak up on him. Gun shot was heard and his only source of cover, a 4 foot sandbag wall was struck. Clearly aiming at him. This Marine didn't grab his rifle, didn't dive for cover, instead without putting out his cigarette, he grabbed a LAW (rocket) we kept on the post and proceeded to "Return fire." Once the rocket was gone he just leaned against the wall and continued to smoke, completely unaware I was there. It was the most majestic thing I have ever seen.

It was like watching a Unicorn. I was in Awe. I just remember walking up to him and saying "Dude did you just return fire with a fucking LAW?" And he just shrugged in the most carefree manner. I was amazed. My Platoon Sgt and LT asked questions though but we got it sorted. The enlisted way.

-    Anonymous US Marine.

"He played our game for too long"
British Soldier

We had an enemy sniper who couldn't hit anything. It was quite annoying so we dubbed him 'Blind Boy Terry'. He would take shots at us from seemingly nowhere, and he was always concealed well. His aim was just very poor. One day we decided to have a good fun game with him. We outfitted a scarecrow with our gear and held the scarecrow just above a wall one day when Blind Boy Terry was active.

Every time he would take a shot at the scarecrow we would pretend like he hit him. We'd let go of the poll and our stuffed friend would fall to the ground. A few minutes later we'd pick him back up and have him bobbing from left to right across the wall.

It was good fun. Blind Boy Terry must have wasted 30 rounds on that scarecrow. Probably very pissed. I could only imagine his frustration before one of our own snipers got him for exposing himself for so long.

- Anonymous Soldier. 5 Rifles. British Army. Afghanistan.

"Shit happens"
US Marine

Everyone knows that if you need to take a dump, you do it before a patrol; not during. Well, sometimes those MRE poopies hit you at the worst time, and if you've ever lived off of those ya know that when you gotta go, it's time to go. We were patrolling in Sangin Afghanistan and everything was normal. We weren't in the part of the AO (Area of operations) where we normally got ambushed, so I figured it was okay to ask for a security halt so I could take a dump in a wadi. I put my machine gun down on the bipod facing toward a tree line, and asked my assistant gunner to hold my hands while I did an air squat in full gear to push that chocolate log out.

No sooner had it been halfway out when we took contact. 'Snap snap snap snap' over my head. I thought, "Fuck I'm gonna die with my pants down, dick out, and covered in my own poop." Without thinking, I pinched it off, stood back up, gained my balance, and then immediately hopped on the gun, which conveniently was facing the direction of the enemy fire and provided decent cover. So there I was, manning my machine gun, pants around my ankles, dick in the dirt, and my assistant gunner at my side. I could only imagine the laughs Terry would have had if they'd killed me and came across my body.
Oh, I also shit myself.

- Anonymous US Marine, 2nd Marine Division. Afghanistan 2011.

"I disassembled my light machine gun under fire"
US Marine

On July 4 2009 during operation Khanjari, which was the largest helo born assault since Vietnam, my squad and myself had finally gotten a short respite after being in almost constant contact with the enemy since the insert 48 hours before. No sooner than we could drop our gear and take our boots of in a little grain shed I heard our squad leader get summoned. We had been given an op to secure a cross road and push back the Taliban that were firing at the company from across a large field beside the village bazaar. In almost in instant we were in ranger file running to a canal that borders the field. As we were running I took a nasty fall due to me tripping and it caused the barrel of my SAW to go flying off. I get up and keep running trying to stay caught up with my squad. We get to the canal and part of the squad is slinging rounds at the talibs across a 100 yard field.

My squad leader directs me and another Marine to set up my saw in a poppy stack further advanced toward the Taliban position while the squad lays down covering fire. We finally get into position and I lined up my sights to squeeze of my first burst and realize that something is wrong. Right about that time the Taliban notice our position and start ripping off their own burst.

I start remedial action and it's not working. Still under direct accurate fire I start disassembling and then reassembling the saw in hopes that will fix the issue. Finally my guns is up. We lay down some rounds, break contact and fall back to the canal and watch Marine air deliver hell fire missiles and a 500 pound JDAM (bomb).

What a way to celebrate America's birthday.
- Anonymous US Marine. 2/8 Echo Co. Afghanistan 2009

"To the extremes"
US Marine

Early July 2nd 2009 we punched the time clock for operation khanjar with over 100lbs of gear on our back walking 26 clicks into uncharted Taliban land and they knew we were coming. At that point we already saw what they could do. We'd all done the same training and most of us were in the same firefights earlier in the deployment so we had an idea what to expect.

This was our D-Day. This was our Omaha beach, fighting head on into dug in enemy territory right in their gunsights moment. It was the biggest offensive any military did since Fallujah in 04'. And when it started, although it never got anywhere near the same level D-Day at Omaha beach was. It confirmed that they knew we were coming before the first shot was even fired.

They showed that to us with the amount of IED's they set and the complexity of how they initiated firefights with us. They could see us coming a mile away. It took us almost 3 days to move 26 clicks. They told us we would be living out the rest of the deployment were we wound up so we had nearly our entire packing list inside the packs on our back in full cammies with flack and Kevlar and it was over 120 degrees. That's how we fought the whole way.

Anyone that was there, that was on foot on that terrain the whole way would be lying if they told you it wasn't the hardest thing they've ever done. During that deployment our company took 7 of the 14 KIA's in the battalion. All 7 happened in one month.
- Anonymous US Marine. 2nd Battalion 8th Marines Golf Company. Helmand Province, Afghanistan 2009

"Brothers in Arms, and in Death"
US Marine

I woke up to the news Osama Bin Laden had been killed. That same, May 2nd 2011, I was combat meritoriously promoted to Sergeant. The company commander and company 1st Sergeant came to the ceremony and decided to patrol with my squad.

Immediately upon leaving Patrol Base Usman, radio chatter indicated there was a suicide bomber in the area and the target was a patrol base near a bridge. That Intel was passed every other day, so I didn't pay too much attention to it. The patrol for the most part was quite, a few key leader engagement here and there, and mostly consisted of showing the CO our area of operation.

We were about 500 meters from the patrol base and my squad was operating in two elements. My lead element was being led by LCpl Patton, and it had the CO, the Platoon Commander & some Afghan National Police guys, the second element was providing over watch. I was bouncing back and forth between the two. When I went to check on my second element, I stopped and started talking to some of the kids in the compound we were using for over watch and got this eerie feeling when the kids were apprehensive on conversing with me.

No more than 5 minutes into the conversation, I heard a motorcycle coming from the alleyway adjacent to the compound and then a large explosion. I ran out of the building and noticed all the members of my first team were on the ground. My first though was I lost half of my squad and platoon and company leadership. The first person I saw conscious was our Machine Gun section leader Cpl. Lindley and he seemed badly wounded. I ran towards him & dragged him by his flak jacket to the over watch compound to be triaged. I ran back out and the rest of the guys were getting up.

I initially thought someone triggered an IED but noticed all my Marines were intact. Then I noticed a pair of legs, and a messed up motorcycle. Most of the Marines within the lead element were concussed, peppered with ball bearings, but overall intact. The losses on the American side could've been much worse if it wasn't for Abdul. He stopped the suicide bomber and absorbed the majority of the blast. Our corpsman tried his best to keep him alive doing just about every procedure he could. Seeing him, I knew it was impossible. His left eye was blown out due to the pressurization, his testicles were scattered through his lower legs and his abdomen was completely exposed.

To this day I remember his labored breathing and the confusion on his face. Safe to say Abdul saved my squad and for that I will be forever grateful.

- Anonymous US Marine. 1/5, Afghanistan. 2011.

"Three straight days of combat"
British Soldier

Our platoon was ordered to move four kilometers directly south from our patrol base leaving at first light. About half way into the patrol we spotted a Taliban dicker watching our movements. We were just arriving at the compound we were going to occupy and the Taliban ambushed us from the west. I had a lot of close calls but that was the closest a bullet ever came to hitting me was that initial burst of machine gun fire. The Taliban were firing at us from the west and east, there was a lot of confusion with all the bullets whizzing past in both

90

directions with us stuck in the middle fighting back from the compound rooftops. The fighting went on and off all day and got pretty intense but the two snipers attached to our platoon were racking up some good kills.

After that first day I was exhausted and dehydrated and so was everyone else, the heat was unbearable. During the night our reconnaissance platoon managed to sneak to our location in the compound and re-enforce our position, it was great to see them, I had a close friend in the reconnaissance platoon.

The next day we were ordered to pull out but the Taliban were waiting for us. They ambushed the three Jackel vehicles that had moved out first to give us dismounted troops protection, detonating an IED under the middle vehicle in the convoy. We were all under attack from three sides, it was absolute chaos. The lads that got hit were in bad shape and four hundred meters away from us and still being attacked. The medic and some others from the reconnaissance platoon had to sprint over the open ground to get to them while being shot at, I have no idea how none of them got shot.

We eventually fought the Taliban off and chinooks came in and picked up our casualties. The next 24 hours we waited for recovery and support vehicles to arrive before the rest of us marched further south to a designated landing zone for extraction.

I will never forget the feeling seeing those chinooks arrive.

I was glad to be getting out of there.

I will never forget those three days in Koshkawah."

- Corporal Ross Smith. 1 Platoon, Alpha Co. The Highlanders. 4th Battalion, Royal Regiment of Scotland. Op Herrick 14 Helmand Afghanistan.

"I cried for his mother"
US Marine

As a rifleman you're trained to kill. From your first moments at boot camp you eat sleep and breathe 'kill kill kill'. You're almost brain washed in such a way that you just feel more than a desire, but a need to kill the enemies of the United States. I got my opportunity in Afghanistan when I was 19. I remember it clear as day. We were patrolling when we got caught in an ambush. My squad leader directed my fire team to maneuver on a compound with enemy Talibs inside of it.

I could hear our machine guns suppressing the walls and any crevice that a rifle could poke out of. We came to a gap in the wall and there he was. I was about 30 meters from the gap when he appeared. I saw his rifle, then I saw his face. Immediately I raised my rifle and fired into him.

The Marine to my left fired as well, and when our enemy fell, it wasn't like the movies. He gave out a little yelp and sort of just…collapsed into himself

91

and hit the ground. I ran past his body as we entered the compound and saw his eyes were still open, staring up at me.

After we had cleared the compound of Talibs I and another Marine went back to the body of the man we had shot. I looked into the dead boys eyes again and something in me just broke. I said I had to go take a piss and I went behind a wall and wept. I wept for that guy's mother. I wept for me. And I wept for the both of us being forced into that position.

War is a racket and the worst thing we have ever invented.

- Anonymous US Marine. 1st Battalion 6th Marines. Marjah Afghanistan, 2010.

"I ran faster than an explosion"
Afghan National

We got out of the FOB, to do a patrol in Sangin. Long story short, I wanted to get a cigarette light up. That day I was running out, I asked someone for one and he gave me a broken cigarette and it wasn't my brand. I lifted my head up to light my cigarette and suddenly I saw a big black thing rotating up into the air which was thrown from the other side of a wall we were walking next to.

In that short time from when I lit my cigarette till I saw that explosive device took me 2 minutes, so I was in the middle of line (patrolling formation) because after me the end of line was the beginning of the ANCOP. In that short circumstance I saw it (the IED) and started running with the fullest energy I ever had! Just imagine, that run had to be like a marathon runner to get off the arena. And I did it! Disappeared like an invisible man who never actually been at the line! I had run a couple of steps and the IED hit the ground and it sounded like a bottle of metal glass hitting the ground and then it exploded and I felt like a car hit my gloves covered hands, and I was still running.

A deep massive mixture of dirt surrounded the area and I don't know how long I was running till I stopped and sat down the ground. Then I heard voice of my team mate (W) "Hey Nick! Fucking Nick!" I came to the conclusion to stand up and shout out, "Hey W I'm alright!'"

- "Nick" (Redacted) Local National Linguist. Attached to 3/7 Lima Company. Sangin,   Helmand, Afghanistan.

"We blew his arm off"
US Marine

I saw one of the strangest things in my when I was attached to snipers. I was laying on a low rooftop during a firefight in Sangin Afghanistan when we saw some enemy fighters who had been giving our maneuver element some trouble. Naturally, when a sniper is in this roll, (over watch) we attempted to do our best to eliminate the enemy and lessen the danger to the Marines who were moving that direction.

92

My buddy (redacted) was using the M-107 .50 cal. If you know anything about these rifles; they are basically cannons better suited to shooting out engine blocks of vehicles than engaging human beings. It's just overkill. Literally. I saw a man running left to right across my field our fire. He (the sniper) led him a little bit so he would run into the round, and fired. I said, 'Dude you just blew his fucking arm off.'

I saw the man continue to run, but he had a stump where his arm should have been. He ran behind a building, and I lay there still observing the area. I saw a head poke around the corner, look around, and then run to the spot where the arm lay on the ground. The man picked up the arm, under fire, and then ran back behind the wall. "Did you see that guy? That arm must be made of gold or something." It's not a terribly exciting story, I just couldn't understand why someone would risk their life for a severed arm.

- Anonymous US Marine. 1st Marine Division Afghanistan

"Best Job I ever had"
British Soldier

I was a gunner on a 'combat vehicle reconnaissance tracked' (CVRt) Scimitar vehicle during Herrick 6 Helmand province. Up to this point in my career I hadn't been in a live contact, so being in Helmand I knew my time would come. It came. During an operation called Op Silicon my half of the platoon had been held in reserve during a battle group clearance of an area of the green zone north of Gereshk. This was 2007 so Terrys SOP was still small arms fire and RPG's.

We was called forward to over watch a patch of open ground in the green zone between areas of dense vegetation. One of our rifle company's was advancing with heavy fighting and pushing the enemy towards this open area... our 4 cars where set in over watch. We was there for approx. 40 mins before they started appearing.... In ones and twos at first. Little figures running right to left in the open. We could not miss. The Rarden 30mm cannon we operated was lethal, with an x20 zoom and HE loaded 30mm rounds. It was a case of put the mark on the Muj, targets will fall when hit. In 20 mins I went from no confirmed kills to 8 in x20 magnification, 30mm high definition goodness.
Best job I ever had.

- Anonymous LCpl. British Army. 1st Battalion. The Royal Anglian Regiment. 'The Vikings'

"I was just glad to be alive"
British Soldier

We were down in the Lashkar Gar area building a small check point. We were putting the HESCO in Bastion together when we started hearing the cracks of rounds coming down. We jumped off the HESCO barriers. One bloke broke his leg. We got our rifles shouldered and started shooting at the bushes about 200 meters away. We couldn't see the enemy but we could hear that's where they we shooting from. We all popped off rounds until an apache turned up. It turned the bushes into salad. We screamed and cheered as they fired into the enemy. Now look back and raise I didn't hate the Taliban. I'm just so glad they didn't kill me.

- Anonymous Royal Engineer. British Army. Helmand Afghanistan, 2012.

"Outnumbered 3 to 1"
US Marine

Towards the end our deployment, I'm talking right around the 30 day mark if I'm not wrong, I was standing post on an old British outpost called ANP Hill. It overlooked the ANP part of our main FOB on the backside, and on the front was a village that was, let's just say, sympathetic to the Taliban. Off to the right was this mountain that the Brits had nicknamed Lucy Pinder…the two peaks of the mountain looked like a set of DD's and if you've ever seen a picture of her well…enough said.

The mountain itself provided a great view of the valley and the Taliban had used it numerous times to shoot at us, as well as an overlook for a suspected supply line, so it was only a matter of time until we went up there and did something about it. That's what they were banking on. When the first Marines went up to set up our outposts up there, it was so mined it took a week to clear.

A couple of weeks later I was on our final OP rotation. I was getting ready to relieve my buddy (we'll call him JH) from his post on ANP Hill, and it happened to be the one looking at the village with good ole Lucy Ponder off to the right (keep in mind there's probably about 2000 meters between this village and the base of this mountain). Anyway, I ask him if there was anything I needed to know and he told me that our snipers had gone up the mountain to help reinforce the OPs because the Taliban were massing an attack of some two hundred fighters. There were roughly thirty marines and a handful of ANA….

After I relieved him JH put his shit down and came and sat outside my post while the night went on, just talking and making sure each other was okay and then it started. It was like watching real life star wars, only you're listening to your friends on this mountain call in contact. I remember yelling over to the other posts to my left and right making sure they were aware and had their gear on. Through my night vision all I could were tracers going both ways and all I heard were the sounds of AKs and the glorious sound of 240s ripping away. When you hear it from a not so distant, distant outpost, talking guns truly is the infantry version of Mozart.

With the guns ripping away I could hear the radio chatter. Our sniper platoon closest too us was what caught my squads attention. I forget their call sign (let's call them war party for fun) but when they reported their first contact it was during the first of the 240 fire. The initial firefight ensued, you could hear the other outpost on the other end of Lucy Pinder calling in their contact. All the

94

while my outpost had our GBoss (a surveillance camera with IR and night vision that can see for miles) pointed at the mountain. In the middle of the gun fight I remember watching a Taliban fighter get separated. As that was happening and he was trying to circle around we were trying to use a laser from the GBoss to mark this guy. We kept it on him and were radioing it up.

Then all of a sudden, everything goes quiet. The shooting just stopped. That's when my buddy from our sniper platoon came over the net and said "Cherokee main, Cherokee main, this is war party. there are nine enemy KIA, I say again have nine enemy KIA", stopped mid transmission and all you heard was the 240 let a burst loose into the guy we had laser designated and my buddy come back over the radio and say "break break, ten enemy KIA over."

The two outposts had apparently gotten into a gunfight with something like 90 fighters, the rest of them apparently hauled ass back to another village they were using as a staging point because they thought they were outnumbered. That was one of the last operations we had our first tour....March 2011
-   Kevin Reilly. 1st Battalion 8th Marines. Charlie Co. Now Zad, Helmand Province Afghanistan 2011

"The loneliest I have ever been"
US Marine

It was my last night of pre-deployment leave. I was 23 years old and had just finished saying goodbye to some of my childhood friends at the bar in town. I was sober and I came home at about 1 in the morning. I walked up the stairs and looked into my mother's room. She was asleep in bed with our family dog passed out on the floor.

I walked in and sat beside her and thought about all the times I was a kid when I got scared of the dark or had a nightmare and came into her room to be comforted. Now here I was, a grown ass man, being a combat veteran of two deployment last already, seeking my mother's comfort once again.

I laid beside her on top of the covers and whispered to my mom that I loved her. I fell asleep beside her like that until 4am when my father arrived and it was time to head to the airport to go back to Camp Lejeune in North Carolina. I'll never forget my mother's face as I buckled my seatbelt and waved goodbye to her to go to war one last time. It was the loneliest I had ever felt in my entire life.
-   Anonymous US Marine. 2nd Marine Division. Afghanistan 2012

"Doing my part"
US Marine

I enlisted the very day I turned 17. I dragged my mom down to the recruiting office in the fall of my junior year to sign papers to allow me to join the Marine Corps. When I was in 2nd grade, I watched 9/11 happen on live TV in my classroom. I watched thousands of people die and I knew then. I knew I would grow up with a desire to kill the men responsible for this, and men like them.

So 6 days after I graduated I left for boot camp and was on my way to being a Marine Rifleman and to kill the enemy. From day one you are indoctrinated and given a desire to take your enemies lives. "Kill" is a word used as a cheer. "Give him one" and we would all chant "kill" It never once, even once occurred to me that the war would end. I grew up with this war. Every day there was news about it. A roadside bomb exploding, a village being cleared, more coffins with flags coming home on them. I never in a million years thought that my chance to prove myself, as a Marine Rifleman, would never come.

I got to my first unit in February of 2013, and for the vast majority of Marines at that time, the combat was over. We just weren't going to see it. Our seniors, many of whom were veterans of the battles in Marjah and Sangin, told us "hey boot, be thankful. You don't have to experience what we did." And we would all nod and say "yes Corporal" or "yes sergeant" but it never erased that feeling of disappointment.

I cannot express to you what it feels like to train for war for 4 years, and never go. I've tried to explain it to my friends and family but they don't understand. I say "Pretend you're on a football team, you train day in and out for years, and occasionally you scrimmage with a friendly team, but you never get to play a real game." I suppose in hindsight, I am thankful I never experienced combat. But a small - no, fuck that. A large part of me; will always wish I had. Maybe then I wouldn't feel so ashamed for those free drinks at the bar.

-   Anonymous US Marine Rifleman. 2nd Marine Division.

"Friendly casualties"
US Marine

When the information about who was a casualty passed over the radio, a feeling of morbid relief always came over me when I found out it wasn't one of my close friends. Don't get me wrong, my heart broke for everyone who was killed or wounded, but a little part of me was always relieved when it wasn't one of my boys, you know? Better so and so than so and so. I don't expect you to understand. In the infantry we are all brothers, but some of us are closer than others.

I would have traded places with any single one of them in a heartbeat, but I was always relieved to hear that one of my best buddies wasn't the one who got hit. It's fucked up, but I guess that's just the way it is. I myself was a casualty once, and my proudest moment was playing a part in killing the man who shot me.

-   Anonymous US Marine, Battle of Marjah, 2010.

"My job is the worst day of your life"
US Airman

Combat flying, particularly launching off alert, can be addictive. When you're in the TOC and you hear, "troops in contact," over SATCOM with gunfire in the background, your senses become heightened. When the radio or loudspeaker starts crackling with, "attention on the net," there is an immediate adrenaline rush. For me, it was tremendously exciting not knowing exactly what I was headed into, and having to put it all together on the way to the LZ.

Naturally, all of the excitement was tempered by the fact that someone was having a very bad day, the worst day of their life, or sometimes…the last day, or hours, or minutes. It's such a paradox. You want to be busy, but you don't.

I'll always remember my first couple of missions in Helmand. In training, we were always taught to try and avoid compounds or built-up areas. For a traditional Combat Search and Rescue mission, this makes sense and can be feasible. You plan to fly over non-populated areas and avoid lines of communication or built-up areas, to avoid being spotted. When you're doing CASEVAC in an area like the Helmand River valley…far less so. On my first mission, I remember glancing down through the plexiglass chin bubble as we raced to the LZ at low altitude over dozens of compounds, and seeing people scattering about. The thought entered my mind that it could just take one round at the right time in the right spot to badly wound or completely end me. I had a moment of panic, and thought, "wow, this is for real. Why are you doing this?!" It wasn't long prior to that deployment that another pilot had just that happen and had been very seriously wounded. The feeling left just as quickly; almost like part of my brain told me to shut that other part out.

There were other times I felt that way. One time when we were scrambled at night to a Brit FOB in the valley, the missile warning system screamed, self-protection flares launched, which bloomed out the goggles, and I saw something bright arcing up from the ground. We had seen footage from Marine Cobras showing a confirmed MANPADs launch earlier in the day, from that area. Well, turns out this was an infrared illumination round launched by the Brits, to help us out. Still scared the crap out of me for a second. Then there was the time when I arrived to put my gear on the aircraft, relieving the previous shift, and the maintainers and PJs were still scrubbing the blood off the cabin floor from a mortally wounded Marine who had laid there not more than 10 minutes earlier.

But to be honest, for me, those moments were few and far in between. I found combat flying to be exhilarating, and the adjustment to coming back home after that was quite difficult, following my first deployment. I still feel guilty to finding some excitement over events which were obviously quite traumatic for those we picked up, and I fully recognize that they were – but I guess that's part of the absurdity of war.

- Anonymous USAF HH-60G pilot, Afghanistan, 2012

"I was a casualty"
US Marine

Cardy and Josh looked into the horizon over the compound wall, and I heard the whir of helicopter blades battering wind, then saw three dots in the sky closing in fast.

"There's your freedom bird, Burgess," Cardy said, smiling.

Doc and three Marines got me onto a litter and carried me out of the compound. As the helicopters lowered, their engines blasted away any other sounds, flattened grass, and sent dirt flying in all directions. One bird touched down while the two larger gunships hovered high above, circling our position.

The escorts, AH64 Apaches, looked like coiled bundles of metal muscle, rockets and cannons cocked on either side. Smoke wafted over me, and on the other side I finally saw the inside of the evac bird. They jostled me onto the litter in the helicopter, and I couldn't hear anything but the high whine of the engine. My ears rang, and my lower back tensed with sharp, needle-like pain.

There were two airmen inside, it seemed, along with an Army pilot. The one closest to me held up a needle and syringe, raised his eyebrows, and pointed at my hip. He injected me with the contents of the syringe, and I went up, high in the air, leaving the 'Stan below me, at least for a while. We sailed on, and I drifted home high, light and heavy all at once.

- Jonathan Burgess, Apache Co 1st Bn 5th Marines, Nawa 2009

"A dog's gotta eat"
US Soldier

February 2008, I was an Army Civil Affairs Team Sergeant in FOB Ghazni, Afghanistan. There was snow and ice everywhere. Simply put, it was cold as balls! It was a far cry from my time in Iraq as a Marine Rifleman. Anyway I was in my team B-Hut when there was a huge boom that shook the shit out of the entire place.

Next thing you know the radio went off saying that there'd been a VBIED (Vehicle Borne IED) attack against an ANA convoy about 400 meters outside the Entry Control Point and to roll the Quick Reaction Force. I was in the TC seat as we rolled out with the PSYOPS Team Sergeant SSG Rob on the gun. (SSG Rob was one of the most laid back and good dudes I'd ever met)

As we're driving up, you could see and actually smell the absolute mess that the VBIED had left. An ANA Ford Ranger looked like a giant hand had slapped the entire front end off of it and the remains of the VBIED were scattered for several hundred meters. There were parts of both cars and the dead suicide bomber everywhere.

As we set perimeter security, I dismounted in order to hold security for the Navy EOD techs as they exploited the scene for evidence and bomb residue. When I was done, I went back to my truck and as I was getting back in, I noticed a human arm laying out in the snow about 20 feet away. Thinking nothing of it, I got back in and called up to the QRF leader to let him know my truck was good.

As I was doing so, I saw a stray dog (damn things are everywhere over there) run up, grab the arm and haul ass with it. (The dog's movement made it look as if the hand was waving goodbye.) I said "Holy shit! Did ya'll see that dog snatch that dead guys arm?!?" About that time, then SSG Rob came over the intercom and said, "Yeah well homeboy shouldn't have gone all 'Allah Akbar' then if he wanted to keep his arm. Besides, a dog has gotta eat too."

The way he said it was so funny that even the Terp laughed. That's the kind of dark humor that got us all through what turned out to be a truly rough deployment.

-   SSG Jacob Bullion A Co. 451st CABN. Afghanistan 2008.

"It stays with you"
US Soldier

We were pushing down an ASR one day into a highly contested area. We were caught in an L shape ambush and unfortunately lost one of ours in an IED explosion. Fighting our way out after CASEVACing the dead and wounded was what seemed like days even though it was only hours.

Combat was fun and games up to that day. Washing the remains of a brother out of a makeshift casevac vehicle the next morning will stay with you.

-   Anonymous. JTF 101, RC East near Pakistan Border.

"We killed almost 150 enemy"
US Soldier

We performed several false landings under the cover of moonlight. I wasn't a cherry, had been in a few firefights... Hit a few IEDs, took plenty of mortars...but the fear of running into the unknown off the back of a chinook in the middle of the night was terrifying. The fear soon turned into exhaustion as the flat ground turned into steep hills, as the night turned into day, as the platoon stopped to rest after every hill rather than every hour.

A 48 hour mission turned into a week-long operation. We ran out of food and water shortly after the 2nd day and resorted to sucking the liquid from baby wipes, saving pee bottles (just in case) and contemplating the possibility of finding a local animal to eat and cook (the commander strictly forbid fires). Our first airdrop resupply was commandeered by a local Taliban patrol due to being dropped too far from our location. The second made it and the Gatorade never tasted better... the boys back in HQ added ACU pants, smokes, MREs and other quality of life things for us.

There was nothing quite like fighting at the apex of exhaustion, hunger, and raw emotion. We had already given 110% and each one of us had to dig extremely deep to find that extra determination and motivation to keep pressing on. It took us a long time to secure an exfil due to the insane slope of the mountain and sparse vegetation.

One of the choppers went down and they wanted to make sure we crossed our T's and dotted our I's before any other chinooks were sent to the area. As a 21 year old watching a JDAM get dropped on our fallen angel through night vision is something I'll never forget...

Our unit lost several good guys during that operation and a day rarely goes by where they don't weigh on my mind in some way.

- Anonymous US Soldier. 2-35 Infantry. Pech River Valley, Afghanistan. Operation Hammerdown, 2011

"World's worst road trip"
US Soldier

24 hour movement to cover 10 km from FOB Tombstone. In contact the whole way. We were trying to get a brand new caterpillar track hoe to the FOB instead of filling HESCOs with a shovel and we hit an IED that vaporized a truck load of ANA that we were training.

After we picked up what was left and put it in garbage bags we started moving again only to have the Afghan driver of the truck hauling the track hoe to get to close to the crater made by the huge IED and the track hoe rolled right off. The Engineer LTC wanted to try and save it but our Team Leader said burn it. After a heated argument during which we were in constant contact my TL told the engineer that he could stay with it but we were leaving. We whistled up some A-10s that were on station and blew it to shit. We finally made it to the FOB after 26 hours, black on ammo and exhausted. The only thing that saved us was those A-10s and some Apache drivers who took turns saving our asses.

After the 24 hour convoy from hell we went to sleep on FOB Robinson only to get woke up with a huge firefight. Trying to figure out what is going on and where the fuck you are after just arriving in the dark was awesome while you are getting shot at. Anyway we lost 2 of our guys, 1 KIA and 1 WIA along with 2 Canadians and a few ANA. Friendly fire is a motherfucker.
Always make sure the guys behind you on a 240 know what the fuck they are doing. SF tabs don't mean shit in that environment.

- Anonymous Embedded Tactical Trainer (ETT) 4.0. Musa Quala Afghanistan, 2006

"We killed them with science"
US Marine

About a month after getting into Afghanistan and specifically the Nad Ali district of Helmand, I ended up flying a Puma in a rotation with three other guys. It was an invaluable ISR tool because we could follow enemy combatants home after they took shots at our patrols. Aside from that we had good enough cameras that we were credited with something like 40 confirmed IED finds in the battle space and this is from 700 feet in the air or so.

That area had produced to date our only friendly casualty via IED and as of that day I caught a group of three men in the act of planting another on the very same road. I called to have my commander confirm what he was seeing before getting IDF assets on station, originally he wanted to use mortars but we didn't have the right munitions for an effective kill of all three. Higher denied HIMARs because the enemy were too close to buildings and in 2012 the Roses were pretty tight. We settled on Hellfire's from RAF pilots, because that was what was approved and God bless those pilots.

Once I was properly offset and still maintaining observation I was given the radio to talk the helicopter on, and he asked me about a fourth person across the street and about ten meters away. They appeared to be laying command wire for the IED back to a nearby compound or perhaps power source. Both were common TTPs for the area and time. I made the call to take them out and this is where the story gets interesting.

Later I was going through the footage frame by frame to see if I could find the exact moment when the missile made impact and I did. But what was funny was how the two men standing attempted to run away and the man on the ground who was actually building the bomb just looked up and to the left as if to say "Oh, fuck." Like in the movies. About this time a motorcycle with two men rode past and wobbled a little bit and it wasn't until the second missile that he was hit by either shrapnel or just concussion. The second missile was a direct hit on target and cut the young girl assisting in the attempted murder of my friends in half. All told, four enemy combatants killed, two unlucky guys injured but I believe they both survived after we got them adequate medical treatment and it was all from the only airstrike from my platoon the whole deployment.

- Anonymous US Marines. 2/7 Weapons Co. Nad Ali district, Helmand province. 2012-13

"Be gentle with the bodies"
British Soldier

In Afghanistan, on operation Herrick 17, we had been given the remit of training the Afghan National Police. They were pretty terrible at their job and were mostly populated by young boys who didn't have any idea what they were doing or older more corrupt men who had links to the Taliban or were in it for personal gain. We lived in a FOB with around 60 of them with the only British soldiers being Squadron HQ and our bolstered troop as the patrolling unit for the local city where we conducted training and routine patrols.

One day we heard that the AUP had killed some local Taliban who were driving in a car. About 6 police just stood in the road and unloaded AKs in to the vehicle as it drove at them with three guys in it.

I briefed our soldiers who had to go out to swab/ID the bodies to scratch them off the known list. Told them to be respectful due to the sensitivities around treatment of bodies in the Islamic community etc. and not to touch more than needed.

Went outside to find the AUP kicking the three bodies around the car park and spitting on the corpses. Told the boys not to worry about being careful and just get the swabs done. They had to break their fingers to get the finger prints they needed as rigor mortis had set in. One guy had taken rounds in the face and jaw and that's where we got the swab from for him and the others from their mouths.

A bad day to be Terry Taliban.

- Anonymous Officer, British Army, Afghanistan 2012.

"War takes from us"
US Marine

December was rough for us. We were operating out of Leatherneck, driving far from the base and dismounting for patrols in enemy controlled territory. After spending a few months doing helo ops this was a whole new ballgame, our movements were being tracked much more easily by the Taliban. EIDs became our new big threat. I was driving the second vehicle of four. We came down into a small hamlet surround by rocky hills. The fields in this area were never wet and we would often avoid the roads by driving across them. Today the fields were flooded and a muddy mess. Alarms started exploding in my head but the lead vehicle kept its speed down the road.

As we passed through the few buildings in this little "valley" I looked to my left and there was a guy standing 10 feet from me. We locked eyes for a moment, he twisted away from me, and the lead vehicle disappeared in a violent explosion. Time stopped for a moment and I was sure my friends were dead. I looked back to my left and the man was gone.

We dismounted and started to prepare for the ambush that always followed IEDs but one never came. Everyone in the vehicle was alive but the gunner was badly injured and the rest were dazed. Some of those guys never truly recovered from that day. One took his life, another lost his marriage and was medically retired because of a severe back injury from the blast. I'm positive to this day that I was making eye contact with the bastard that buried that explosives that hurt my brothers and it bothers me that I didn't kill him. War is disgusting and the only people that escape it are the dead.

- Anonymous US Marine. 1/9 Walking Dead. Afghanistan 2013

"Zombies!"
US Soldier

We were a month away from getting out of Afghanistan I was getting relived from guard duty and sitting there bullshitting when I saw the truck coming up from Pakistan. I always hated that road and where they put that damn outpost, it was an Afghan border patrol compound that sat beside a major road. With no damn hescos around it just a concrete wall and one strand of C-wire. After two tours in Iraq I knew a soft ass compound when I saw one. But the Afghans thought it was secure and our command wouldn't let us force the issue. We did after that damn day though, we made it secure like only combat engineers can.

When I saw the truck turn left everything in my mind snap tight cause I knew what was happing. I grabbed my MK-48, they made me leave my 240 on the truck because they thought the MK-48 was better cause it lighter? But always had issues with it, my buddy saw me throw it up on the wall and sight in and he froze for a second till I told him this is gonna fucking suck, cause the truck came to rest less than 75 feet from us. No one in the platoon had ever heard me say that, most of the time I just dealt with it. I will say that even though his eyes got big as saucers he didn't run. He stood beside me with his M-4, I was proud of him that day. He could have ran, a smart man would have. Never said I was smart but I refused to lose or back down just that redneck part of me I guess.

Right as I was sighting in to shoot, heard behind me an Afghan border patrol yell, 'Shoot, shoot!' All I could yell was 'No shit you dumb shit!' I emptied the 50 round nut-sack I had on the weapon, the one and only time the damn MK-48 worked for me; into the driver side window. I watched it shatter and the driver slump over. I stood up for a second and then I saw the vehicle explode.

Seems the asshats remote detonated it from the mountain side. I remember seeing and feeling the blast then waking up screaming cause my head hurt. My buddy looked and saw me unfurl myself he said I looked like a pretzel. I ended up with a massive concussion and shrapnel to the head. All I could think was my head hurt but I need to get up cause there was no way it didn't blow a hole into the wall.

We found out later from EOD that is was estimated 3000 pound VBIED, I pulled myself up and my buddy and there was a big ass hole in the concrete. Luckily that was all it was, which was bad enough. Four of us ended up getting our brains rattled, one lost a leg and another didn't make it. To this day I always think if I could have acted faster I could have got his ass before it went off. Maybe it would have changed the outcome.

I remember afterwards watching first platoon pull up, I was still in the tower and there was a car across the road that had tried passing the truck when it went off. I yelled at the guys that there were people still in there. He walked up to it and saw an arm raise up and heard the dismount yell 'Zombies!' and watched him run back to the truck. I remember having to hold on the wall to keep from falling over laughing. Black humor was all that kept me going that day and for many days after.

- Anonymous Soldier. U.S Army Machine Gunner OEF. Kwost Afghanistan. 2009 to 2010

"Modern Vikings"
Swedish Soldier

I deployed to Afghanistan in 2010 to Mazar-i-Sharif as a rifleman. Swedish troops were supposed to have it pretty easy in Afghanistan, and generally the news in Sweden quite seldom would report on us getting into contact with the Taliban.

So we were out rolling in our CV90s and we got pretty close to a village that was quite ambiguous towards us. The vehicle commander reported to our squad leader that they say women and children leaving the village, and we knew that shit was about to hit the fan. It sure did. We had two guys standing up in the fighting compartment, hatches open, and an RPG came spiraling towards us from behind a stone wall. The rocket landed about 10 meters away from our vehicle's broadside. Me and another guy leapt to our feet, stuck our heads up and we just unloaded on that guy. One of our machine gunners sprayed a full cassette, 200 rounds, before our squad leader told us to close the hatches. The vehicle pivoted and we heard the thick bass of the 40mm and several long bursts of machine gun fire from the co-ax.

Our squad leader listened into his com helmet. He turned to us and grinned, and said "They got his ass." We cheered, and we decided to return to base (RTB) shortly after. I was elated, but most of all maybe excited. Looking back, with everything that happened to Afghanistan, I can't help but feeling rather feeble, and that I in hindsight probably would have not done it again. Knowing that it was essentially all a waste.

- Anonymous Swedish Soldier. Afghanistan, west of Mazar-i-Sharif, 2010

"A shitty way to die"
US Marine

I was on my second deployment to Afghanistan and my company was conducting Heli borne raids throughout Helmand Province to disrupt the production and distribution of HME (homemade explosives) and opiates. It was a really cool deployment in the sense that we would go out on these ops, sometimes get in a fight, then come back and eat ice cream at midrats on Leatherneck.

I can't remember the exact name of the place we went to but I do remember hearing people refer to it as "The Spine". There was this village surrounded by large hills and mountains. I was a machine gunner so while the clearing element worked its way through the village I was with the over watch

104

element walking up and down these hills and mountains to keep one step ahead of them. It ended up being a 10-12 hour op and I believe it was a dry hold.

We waited until nightfall for exfil in this farmland nearby the village. We were doing night exfils because we got lit up the last time we did one in the daytime. When the birds were inbound we would break down our perimeter and bunch up so we could get on board as quickly as possible. I could see the CH-53's coming in and I remember thinking "That looks like it's going to land right on top of us." Sure enough it was.

Once everyone realized what was happening we scattered to get out of the way. I just picked a random direction and started to run until I tripped on something. I rolled over to my back and looked up to see the 53 still right above me. I'm not sure how high up it was but at that moment it felt like it was right on top of me. I guess I chose the wrong direction to run. All I could think about was how much it would hurt to be crushed. In what felt like the last possible second the 53 started to ascend again and the rotor wash was so intense I thought I saw Marines who were still standing up get knocked down.

The following moments were chaos as we tried to get accountability of people and gear. One of my fellow machine gunners somehow lost his 240 but it was found nearby. By some miracle no one was injured or missing any major pieces of gear.

I still get a good chuckle thinking about how absurd that night was. Of all the things that could kill you in Afghanistan, imagine getting crushed by your own helicopter in some muddy field. That would have been a shitty way to go.

- Anonymous US Marine. 2/9 E Company. Machine Gunner. Afghanistan 2013.

"Turtle"
US Marine

A few days after our glorious Corps' birthday we left our OP and went on an 18 click (11 miles) movement to contact at a village in a place called Kurgay. We left with full packs, fully expecting and knowing we'd be out there for at least a few days. We knew it was a village sympathetic to the Taliban and quite honestly we wanted to see how close we could get to the village before they shot at us....turns out it really wasn't that long.

We stepped off at 0400. I was walking point as I normally did. Everything went pretty smoothly (as much as it can in the mud on foot). We walked through this village a few hundred meters from the base of a mountain we and the Brits had called Lucy Pinder on the right and what we called the Hershey Kiss to our left. We had shaken hands and done the bullshit hearts and minds thing.

I remember shaking with this one dude though, I remember looking down and he was tatted, thought that was kinda funny but didn't say anything, a few of my guys behind me picked up on that too. Anyway as I walked south through the village and came to the backside heading toward Kurgay, I noticed we were walking towards a choke point. Following the one dirt road that lead between the Hershey Kiss, and this little hill a couple miles off of Lucy but on the same side of the road.

I can honestly remember looking at that and every alarm bell as a point man was going off....quite literally the last place you want to walk your patrol, but we had no other options. I turned around and told my team leader we should take a cigarette break, he laughed and told me to keep walking.

Not soon after I turned around we had about an eighty to one hundred round burst of PKM fire rip through our patrol not 3 inches from my side of the column. No shit this asshole walked that gun down our entire squads patrol. To this day, I don't know how I'm still alive. It was a textbook ambush. This dude and a few of his friends got us. I remember having a Sgt of mine shooting over my head at one point and then it felt like everyone and their mother decided to shoot at me.

What I had neglected to realize was that I was the only one still out in the middle of this dirt road, everyone else in my squad had made their way to this ditch next to the road and were taking cover. I distinctly remember asking myself if I was ready to know what it felt like to get shot. I was one hundred percent convinced it was happening, but then I had a not so amazing idea while everyone was yelling at me.

Instead of trying to inch and shoot and inch and shoot my way to this ditch…I was just gonna roll and go for it...except one problem....you guessed it...I was wearing the full pack. I wish I had remembered I had a full Elbe pack on, because if you've ever tried to roll with one on your back...I'll never forget the sounds of bullets whining and snapping past me, while I'm in the middle of this fucking dirt road, in bum fuck Helmand province Afghanistan, the dirt kicking up all around me as I'm looking at my friends who are in cover, holding out an ankle and my arm saying "Turtle outta water bros!"

...they still call me turtle. People wouldn't believe half the shit you hear in a gunfight in terms of comments and conversations.

- Anonymous US Marine. 1/8 Charlie Co. 2010-2011 Now Zad Afghanistan.

"A shot in the dark"
British Soldier

Afghanistan summer 2012 this was my 6th deployment 3rd in Afghanistan. I was 29 at this point. I was tasked to lead a Night patrol of 12 to an Afghan Local police station that was on the edge of the green zone. The police were being attacked most nights so the idea was to go and support them.

We'd been there a few hours and they started getting a bit anti and the interpreter suggested they we leave through some of the things they were saying I took this on board as the previous tour 3 from my unit had been killed in a police station along with 2 military police as well as many injured.

The ALP checkpoint was over watched by a small friendly CP so I was happy with the fire support I had should anything go wrong. I did the checks I needed to check for icom chatter etc. Got my guys together and head back to the main fob via the friendly CP. After leaving and only 100m from the police my point man saw movement close to where he was and the terp told me icom was going crazy this was the exact moment I knew we'd walked into an ambush. For a split second it felt calm the world stood still no noise just calm then they opened up from 3 locations as well as illuminating our position with a device causing fire (still to this day don't know what it was).The patrol turned into the fire and started to fight back. We'd trained for this and started to peel out of it. I changed magazine lifted up my rifle to fire and everything just stopped. I felt like someone had taken a 100m run up and hit me in the face with sledgehammer.

I wasn't seeing the normal green of my night vision and my the radio chatter in my ear from command was distorted, I was struggling to breath I put my hands on my face and knew that I'd been hit I found a hole that was deep in my face under my eye. The round had gone through my NVG and into my face and up.

The pain came quick but if I'd stayed here I was I would have been useless and didn't want my lads to have to carry me out, all the lads I had were young under 20 most were in their first gunfight so I needed to make sure they got out of it. I got up and carried in peeling with them unfortunately the ambush had a cut off which opened up luckily no damage was done by that and at this point we had good fire support to suppress them. We extracted to the main fob on route back I knew I was in a bad way I'd been injured twice before but RPG frag but this felt different I couldn't see or hear on my left side and I could feel the blood coming out quite fast. We got back, I counted my men in and was treated then casevaced back to bastion then to the U.K

The gunshot wound cost me the sight in my left eye. Made me dead in my left ear and did some damage to my brain which after 9 months in hospital and rehab was discharged from the military. I count myself lucky really could have been a lot worse for me and I'm also lucky none of my men were hit.
A lot of people will say they don't respect their enemy but I did that night they laid a good ambush and other than setting their guns too high executed it well. I'm also proud of how all the young guys performed that night.
-    Anonymous British soldier. Grenadier Guards, Lance Sergeant.
     Afghanistan Apr 23rd 2012 Helmand Provence, Rahim Kalay

"The kids don't stand a chance"
US Soldier

As a hot headed saw gunner in the infantry, I was trained in the art of violence. Mentally and physically ready for anything, my unit trained hard for one year to be ready to deploy to an IED and combat heavy COP Sabari in the Khost province of Afghanistan. Mentally I was ready for anything combat had to throw at me, or so I thought.

About a month or two into our deployment, we stopped for a KLE in a small village right outside our COP. It was a typical warm March morning and my platoon was setting up security around a qalat, my team leader does the usual rounds and places his firing team to pull security. My location however was particularly different than my other team members. I was placed next to a tree which is not unusual, however I noticed behind my location I had some company.

There in the open behind my location, I noticed there was a boy no older than four, sitting out on a high chair all alone. The boy most likely belonged to the qalat right next to my location, I looked down and noticed a chain about 30 feet long that connected his high chair to the tree I was using for cover. As I kneeled behind the tree for several minutes making sure no one snuck up behind my squad, I couldn't help but take quick glances back every few seconds at the child behind me. The glances quickly turned into me slowly inching my way back standing next to the boy still facing my sector and keeping an eye on the open field in front of me.

As I stood next to the boy I noticed he was a special needs child, he couldn't speak and couldn't close his mouth. I also noticed he didn't have full control of his hands or feet, and the flies were finding a home on his face and mouth because he couldn't swipe them away, as I swiped at the flies he made eye contact with me and a sudden rush of emotions swept through out my body. An overwhelming feeling of guilt and shame swept over me, I remember thinking to myself, "How could I ever complain about anything, when this kid is literally chained to a tree." As I kept swiping the flies from his face, I couldn't help but think how different his life would be if he was American, and how lucky I truly was to be in a position to care for myself and blessed to be in a country where this type of treatment of a special needs child was unacceptable. Standing alongside him, my role that day slowly changed from infantryman to unofficial guardian. I remember standing out in the open and feeling such a strong feeling of duty and commitment to the safety of this child. A child who I knew nothing about 20 minutes prior to our encounter, a child who I couldn't speak to or communicate with. I stood right next to him out in the open behind no cover, a literal sitting target for any Taliban. During that time I remember saying to him, "I got your back bud".

If the very real possibility of getting attacked would arise, my plan was to pick up the child and run him into the house as fast as I could, while somehow trying to simultaneously fire my saw with one hand from the hip like Rambo. Fortunately the moment never came and the only attack I was fending off was that of the relentless Afghan flies. My plan was to find this child every-time we returned, and spray him with some insect repellent to help keep the flies off.

I carried the repellent with me every day and every day I kept him in the back of my mind. Thinking next time I see him I'll help him out and give him some water, and leave the repellent on his chair and maybe his parents would use it. That day never came and I never saw the boy again, but I still think about him every time I start to think about my deployment. The feeling of overwhelming guilt always comes right after;
'What could I have done?'
'I didn't do enough!'
'Is he alive?'

I was a hardened soldier an expert of violence and death, and ready for any threat that came my way, but for a brief moment in time I was defeated by compassion and emotion, the very last thing I thought I was going to be confronted with in that country.

I believe subconsciously that moment changed me more than any combat situation I encountered. After the military I decided to start a career in education, my wife and I also foster two amazing children that we plan to adopt. It all began there for me, and in some way shape or form I believe small moment changed my life forever.

- SPC Danny Frescas. US Army. B. Co. 1-26. Khost Province. Afghanistan.

"Time for a laugh"
Australian Commando

My name is Gary Wilson and I was deployed with the 2nd Commando Regiment as part of the Australian Special Operations Task Group (C/S NZ) in the Shah Wali Kot, and was one of the diggers on the ground for the battle of Eastern Shah Wali Kot.

I was positioned near the crest of one of the hills as an over watch / cordon with my platoon commander, sergeant, medic, JTAC and one of our sniper teams. It was mid-June so it was getting really bloody hot sitting in the sun with no shade getting shot at.

We'd received word that the Taliban had located either us or our other platoon on the adjacent hill and were going to begin engaging us. Then, we all heard the pop, and a bit of dust was kicked up over my equipment from right near my feet.

I shit myself and made myself as small of a target as possible when after hearing the pop my platoon sergeant yells out "contact" and the rest of the lads dug in for cover as best they could.

Then nothing, no more shots, so everyone gradually sits back up and keeps their eyes peeled.

I get back into my radio to keep working then thought, "Shit, I need a smoke now" but couldn't find my lighter. Our JTACs thermometer had died a little earlier that day when the temperature read 48 degrees Celsius (118F)

And at my feet, remained little bits of shrapnel that used to be my lighter. The rest of our platoon who were resting in a small shaded area at the base of the hill we were on radioed up to us and asked "Are you guys still in contact?"

'Nah, the Zulus lighter blew up'

Amongst all the explosions, gunfire and Apaches racing overhead, were could all hear the other lads' laughing at us from down the hill. No matter how much shit is hitting the fan all around us, there's always time for a laugh.

- Gary Wilson. 2nd Commando Regiment. Australian Operations Task Group (C/S NZ). Shah Wali Kot, Afghanistan. 2010.

"Casper's calling your name"
Australian Commando

Following on from my last about always finding something to laugh at in combat. In the same battle I was talking about, The Battle for Eastern Shah Wali Kot. My platoon had a silly childish game where the "joke" was if you called out someone's first name, (normally it was their nickname, call sign or a variation of that) and they funny part was everyone would avert their eyes making the "victim" think they were hearing things.

Back to the battle, because we were so focused on the task at hand (not getting shot) I wasn't thinking about that stupid fucking game, I hear a voice calling 'GARY!'

I sit up, look around like a dick to see the rest of the platoon looking up and laughing from the trucks they were taking cover behind. Fuckers.

- Gary Wilson. 2nd Commando Regiment. Australian Operations Task Group (C/S NZ). Shah Wali Kot, Afghanistan. 2010.

"Children of the corn"
US Marine

I grew up in rural Indiana and was always surrounded by corn. Cornfields were always a sign of home until I went to Afghanistan. I was expecting a sandbox but to my surprise, Afghanistan had some large cornfields too. Looked a lot like the Midwest. Almost made it seem surreal. One of the first patrols we had in Sangin was on a 24-hour operation where we took this mud hut for our own. We were told there was some Taliban activity just across this cornfield from where we were.

Me and two other guys were sent into the middle of the cornfield to hold security. The corn was high and you couldn't really see us and we couldn't really see out. We heard on the radio that the Taliban were in sight. I looked at the two Marines next to me and said we should lay down.

Just a second after that we heard the machine guns firing and I watched the corn stalks getting chopped in half above my head. I yelled to the next Marine we need to communicate with the squad leader to get us out of there. The Marine was a boot, like me, and he tried to be formal in a conserved voice. I yelled at him that he needed to FUCKING YELL. It seemed to be we were getting shot at from the front and the rear. I hugged the dirt and put my ear to the ground trying to get as low as possible.

Come to find out there had been a miscommunication and the guys in support of us with machine guns thought WE were the Taliban. Getting shot at by the enemy is not fun. Getting shot at by your own guys is even less fun.
It's eerie that now, whenever I see corn, I get a warm feeling of home and a fear of the unknown at the same time.

- Anonymous US Marine. 1/6 A Co. 2nd Platoon. Sangin Afghanistan, 2011.

"Nobel Peace Prize"
US Marine

So, we were conducting a RIP with one of our sister platoons in Sangin. The guys from the other platoon were offloading and guys from our platoon were hopping on the birds. My squad was on LZ security. While this is happening some ANA guys roll up with an ambulance freaking the fuck out. We look up and see the ANA birds are circling overhead. We basically told these guys they had to wait and whatever. So our dudes get done and bounce, the ANA birds land and the ambulance rolls up and they throw two bloody and lifeless bodies on the birds, all the while grilling the fuck out of us. So we're bullshitting and joking after and talking about how we really didn't care that the ANA guys died. Finally my buddy loudly proclaims 'Have some fucking humanity.'

So naturally we all laugh at him. The running joke the rest of the deployment was that we'd put him up for a Nobel peace prize for that comment.

- Anonymous US Marine. 1st Battalion 7th Marines. Afghanistan.

"Oopsies"
US Marine

I was with 1/5 from 2004-2010. C Co for my first 3 pumps and ended up with the PSD/Jump for my last deployment in 2009, Nawa AFG. There wasn't a single day that we didn't leave the wire. Whether it was escorting higher ups, EOD, React, Mail Call, whatever was needed we would be there. We had just put in this badass engineer bridge not only for us but for the locals. We have had issues with the culverts in that area. We are on a mission and hear a faint explosion in the distance, we all listen to Geronimo Main to see what the hell happened.....silence. We go about our business and we get tasked with heading to Jaker to do something or another.

We stumbled upon a complete S-Show like 10 locals scrounging up body parts, there was already a pile going with 3 different pairs of shoes. One still had a foot in it. We look at the bridge we just put in and there were pieces blown to hell, it was trashed. We are there for a good 10 mins when we hear yelling in the corn field, they are unsung a dishdalla cover, and they drag this nub of a corpse out of the corn. No arms, no legs, no face, only a torso and back of this guy's head. Turns out 3-4 dudes were of them emplacing an IED and when they went to set down the part of the ramp they moved they detonated the damn thing. With a bunch or young Marines around wide eyed and never seeing a dead body before, I asked them "Am I the only one craving a steak right now?" They didn't appreciate my humor.

Fast forward to us getting back to Geronimo, I run into our OPS O (operations Officer) and he asks what we found out. Unexplained the above with the multiple pairs of shoes and body parts and torso. He looks up like he's doing a math problem and looks at me, and goes "1.5 million dollar bridge...3 dead bad dudes...eh I'll take it, we've spent more on killing people." And walked off.

- Anonymous US Marine. 1/5 Afghanistan

"Living with the impossible"
US Marines

It's been over 10 years since my point man was killed and I still feel the weight of guilt over his death. I can think about him, though, and not cry or breakdown. To this day, I feel most guilty about the fact that when I think about him, I only cry when I consider how close my best friend and APL was to being killed that day too. He's alive, but the thought of how close he came to dying because of a tactical decision that I made hurts me more than the actual death of my point man.

It's a shitty revolving door or guilty feelings. I feel guilty that my point man died, and guilty for being glad that it was him instead of my APL because if my best friend had died...I don't know if I could have survived that. Just the thought of it makes me break down.

- Anonymous US Marine. Marjah Afghanistan, 2011.

"Enemy radio chatter"
British Soldier

We moved into Babaji during the night to secure the area to allow the ATO (bomb disposal) to come in and destroy some IED's. The insertion was a success, we wasn't spotted or compromised and we set up a ring of steel. Later as the sun started to rise and warm out cold bodies the boys started to get a brew on in the village. As the sun grew warmer the ICOM chatter (enemy radio) started and there was a panic in their voices. I ask the 'Terp' what they were saying. He said a local fighter was describing the situation to his commander. He said there's hundreds of us! When asked what were we doing the local told him that we were having a picnic. The enemy commander said "Why don't they fuck off back to their own country to have a picnic?!" We just laughed at what they were saying and the whole situation as ATO wouldn't come in unless it was secure and not hot.

Later on the enemy Commander told him not to worry he was going to send the sniper and the chatter died away. We just had to sit tight and wait! We waited for over an hour and still nothing, we were still waiting for the ATO to come forward but they were after reassurance that it wasn't comprised and we were on the net telling them all was quite.

Then the ICOM started again angrily, the Terp translated that the local had asked what are you waiting for? The reply came as "Shhhhh the sniper was about to shoot the guy with the cigarette." At that point my whole patrol and I spat out our cigarettes. We looked at each other and we all started to nervously laugh.

Luckily for us he was the worse sniper I have ever experienced. Had tripped up holding his rifle he would struggled to hit the floor. That being said ATO wouldn't come out there was firing from him and us returning the compliment so they deemed it too hot. So I guess he achieved his aim!

- Anonymous British Soldier. British Army, Household Cavalry Regiment. Afghanistan Operation HERRICK 11

"Moving forward"
US Soldier

Back in the day, when we deployed (Army) we'd get 15 days of R&R leave midway through deployment or whenever it was workable for your unit. I got mine in early May 2008, about 5 months into my deployment to Afghanistan. It hadn't been too bad up to that point aside from the extreme cold and the occasional rocket or IED. Nothing really to write home about. It was a cake walk.

Getting home and being there for those 2 weeks was awesome. I spent time with my wife, kids, friends, and family. It was great. Then it came time to go back. The day I left, I woke up with this crushing sense of foreboding that I just couldn't explain. Kissing my wife and holding my kids at the airport in Houston became something that just put an enormous weight on my very soul. At the time my little girl was 2 and was just barely talking but she knew enough to grab my face in her tiny hands, give me a kiss, and hug my head. It was as wonderful as it was gutting. It took every ounce of discipline I had not to cry in front of them because I knew it'd only make it worse for everyone.

I got on the plane and 45 min later I was at the DFW airport. The weight on my heart hadn't lessened as I made my way to the USO. When I got there, they had this program where they'd film you reading a book to your kids and then they'd send the DVD and the book home to your family. I chose the book "The Little Red Hen" because I remember it was a story my mom read to us when I was kid and I figured my daughter would like it. It took me a couple of tries while trying to maintain my composure but I was finally able to get through reading the book. I filled out the paperwork and left shortly thereafter back to Afghanistan.

I stepped off the Chinook back on to the helo pad at Ghazni the day of my 30th birthday. Let's just say the Taliban had a "celebration" waiting for me and everyone else in RC East. The entire area of operations went absolutely nuts and for the next 5 months it was constant. We logged countless patrols and were involved in numerous TICs, got IED'd multiple times and saw some things that it took me years to talk about. When I got home, everything was the same but I was different. I was a shell of my former self. I was lost and I didn't know how to find my way back. I almost lost my marriage, my family, everything, all because of me. I'd be lying if I said I never considered taking my own life. I thought about it and worked it out in my head numerous times. That was not who I was and thank God I didn't have the courage to go through with it.

Then one day about a year after my return, my little girl brought me The Little Red Hen book and DVD that I'd made for her at the USO at DFW. She asked me to watch it with her and to read her the book again. So I did and it made her so happy! I wept when I saw the man I was in that video and I wept again at the happiness that I gave my little girl. After that, I began to heal. 13 years later and still going strong.

- Anonymous US Army Soldier. 101st Airborne. Afghanistan 2008

"What no one tells you"
US Soldier

After sustaining several gunshot wounds I was made out to be some sort of hero for continuing to fight and save lives. Medals were pinned on my chest, and command spoke highly of me. What they don't tell you or talk about is how your life instantly turned upside down. I could no longer do simple things for myself. They don't tell you that once you are wounded your real fight has just begun, the fight to return to some resemblance of normal life.

They don't tell you that your family now has to take care of you. They don't tell you that your small children won't understand why dad left for deployment a Superman and returned, crippled and disfigured. I have never fought harder to do anything in life as I did to be a functioning father/ husband. Three years, numerous surgeries, countless hours of therapy, fighting through the pain and suffering all in an effort to simply walk through my own front door.

- Anonymous US Soldier. Gahazni, Afghanistan/ recovered at Walter Reed. 10th Mountain Division (LI)

114

"Doc"
Navy Corpsman

     I deployed as a corpsman with an infantry battalion in 2012. The training up to that point was phenomenal. Within my first 2 weeks, I saw a man exposed to an IED. He had no legs from the knees down and part of his left hand was missing. I looked directly at him and thought it wasn't real. The most significant thing I remember about him was his balls were the size of softballs which left his dick not viewable. This became a normal experience for me as I tried to make trauma a normal thing. I worked mainly on Afghans that were either Tali or civilians that were in the wrong place at the wrong time.

     Plus the Marines were really good at killing mother fuckers so less people for me to treat.

     I would say my biggest struggle and still over 10 years later is knowing the dudes I helped save are probably dead. Especially that little boy with no legs. It haunts me knowing that he is probably out there in a country ran by some of the worst humans I have ever experienced.

-    Anonymous Navy Corpsman. 2/5 Marines Afghanistan 2012

"Fucked up game"
US Marines

     I was a designated marksman in the Marines. It's kinda like a sniper but not really. You get a pretty nice rifle with an optic and it basically gives your squad or platoon the ability to reach out and touch the enemy a bit further than your average rifleman. We had this kind of fucked up game going with our machine gunners to see who could touch the enemy the furthest distance out. So far our machine gunners had gotten the furthest kill at about 450 yards. I was laying on a rooftop and had ranged a few buildings at 650-700.

     One morning one of our patrols pushed out and myself and a few machine gunners were on the rooftops just giving them over watch for as long as we can. The patrol starts taking shots, and I see movement in that group of buildings I mentioned earlier. Bro, when I say the competitive part of me got giddy when I saw a rifle in a dudes hand, I mean I got giddy.

     I looked through the optic, adjusted for the range, and fired. My target fell to the ground and rolled over onto his back. His rifle was still in his hands. I was trying to control my excited breathing to take another shot when I saw little puffs of dirt start flying up around him.

     It was those fucking machine gunners trying to poach my kill. Before I could get another shot off, I could see their impacts and bits of the enemy fighter get blown onto the road. I looked to my right (where the machine gunners were located) and they were flipping me the bird. I still count it as mine. Just like Han Solo, I shot first.

- Anonymous US Marine. 2nd Marine Division. Helmand Afghanistan 2011.

"Absolutely zero fucks"
US Marine

Dog handlers are special dudes. Not only do they have to worry about themselves on patrol, but their dogs as well. Marines love their dogs. I don't trust anyone who doesn't like dogs. We were patrolling in Helmand Afghanistan, and on this patrol we had a dog and it's handler with us. Both of them had been on previous deployments and were pretty salty and knew what to expect. The handler and the dog both didn't give a fuck. Literally. Not. A. Single. Fuck.

I watched, with my own two eyes, our entire squad take contract on a patrol…round snapping overhead. Clumps of dirt flying into the air. Everyone immediately dives for cover and starts trying to figure out where it's coming from so they can return fire…but not this dog and its handler. The handler took a knee, put a dip of grizzly wintergreen in his lip, stood up, raised both his arms above his head while rounds are COMING AT HIM and yelled to the Taliban,
"Y'all fucking SUCK!"
It was the craziest shit I ever saw in my whole damn life. Even his dog didn't give a shit.

- Anonymous US Marine. 1st Marine Division. Helmand Afghanistan, 2010.

"The other side"
Taliban Fighter

I would like our experiences to be represented. My father and uncles fought the Soviets. We fought the Americans. Many of my brothers and cousins were killed in our war. Face to face fights with Americans were not favorable. We are not superior soldiers. Once we were in these face to face fight. Americans were trapped in an ambush, and we managed to shoot their vehicle with a rocket. Unaware if we gave them casualties. We ran because a plane was coming and for that no defenses we had were good enough.

I am proud we fought so long. Many, many Taliban died. I would not like to repeat this experience we endured. My father spoke of victory against the Soviet when I was small. I did not know this would come at such a cost.

- Anonymous Taliban Fighter. Participant since 2012-2020

"We all bleed red"
US Soldier

During the BDA (Battle Damage Assessment) of a gun run from the air, I was with several soldiers on a hillside in Northern Afghanistan going from corpse to corpse of dead enemy fighters in case any needed medical aid. As we came to a

116

slope in the hill I heard a groan below us and immediately the soldier to my left raised his rifle. We had always joked about offing a wounded enemy if we ever came across one, and for a split second I thought this guy might do it, but instead the soldier approached him, checked the wounded guy for weapons, and then motioned to me. 'Doc, he needs help.'

I came over with my med bag while some of the other guys got a bird in the air for our wounded EPW. He was a younger guy. Maybe 20-22. I knelt beside him to treat him. He had deep cuts in his abdomen from splinters of rock blown around by the explosions. As I treated him, I observed the look in his eyes. It wasn't hate or animosity. It was a mix of fear and gratitude.

I think he expected us to walk up on him and shoot him instead of helping him. After we got him in the air, I looked at my gloves and saw his blood was red. The same color as ours.

-   Anonymous US Medic. 10th Mountain Division. 1st Battalion, 32nd Infantry. Kunar Province, Afghanistan. 2009.

"Adrenaline"
US SOF

After you experience combat, like, real combat; nothing is ever the same. When you come home, water tastes fresher, food tastes better, and sex feels euphoric. You survived the litmus test of the varsity team of the human experience. But after a while, once the death and explosions get further and further in your rear view, all those things lose their luster and shine. You find yourself missing it in a weird sort of way.

To be surrounded by alpha males in an environment of kill or be killed. It's terrifying, but exhilarating. You'll never feel more alive and life will never seem simpler than those months you spend behind a gun. War is terrible. It's disgusting and unnatural. But it can be the most addicting drug you'll ever take. Your friends become your brothers, and your brothers become your tribe. Once you're separated from that high and your tribe, the pistol in your drawer seems friendlier and friendlier after a few drinks.

-   Anonymous Green Beret. US Army. 2010, Afghanistan.

"Society lies about what war is"
British Soldier

You're a mad cunt if you think you're the only one in combat who pretends he isn't scared. You can watch footage today of lads in fights, none of them look scared, but I promise you they're all just a minute or two away from pissing themselves. Modern culture has skewed our perception of war. That it's some fun game the lads get together and play. 'Slay bodies! Moons out Goons out!' These TikTok hype videos and games that just distort what it is.

117

No one tells you about your mates who get their jaw's shot off. Their legs blown off. No one tells you what it sounds like when your best mate gets one in the stomach and he screams bloody murder all the way into the helicopter ride out. I was scared shitless every step I took in the Stan. Every time a round came round I heard those screams of the wounded in my head. Don't get me wrong, mate. Courage is real. But no one but psychopaths enjoy killing. I'd clench my teeth, close my eyes, and pretend I was somewhere else to calm down. Then get the job done because that's what men in uniform do. Just don't be misled. There's nothing good about war other than the bond you build with your mates. That's a lesson society won't tell you.

- Anonymous British Soldier. 2 PARA. British Armed Forces. Afghanistan, 2008.

"Forbidden love"
US Marine

I fell in love with an Army Nurse. It was my second deployment in Afghanistan. We were on Camp Leatherneck and would take turns rotating to one of the smaller FOBs a few miles to the south. I somehow ended up always being one of the Marines who was tasked with escorting enemy wounded to the hospital. I'd sit next to their bed in the hospital and just watch them. An Army nurse and I would often talk while she would treat these guys. She was a Captain and I was a Corporal. So fraternization was a big no no, but we immediately bonded. I fell in love with her voice and the gentleness of her touch on the patients.

One day, I came back to the hospital after one of my buddies was badly wounded with an enemy prisoner who was also wounded. I was covered in both of their blood. She held me in the hallway as I cried. It's been years since I've seen her, and I never told her that I loved her. We never even kissed. Still to this day I've never dated someone who has been as gentle, kind, or beautiful. To me she will always be the one good memory of my time in war. She will always be on my mind.

- Anonymous US Marine. 1st Marine Division. Helmand Afghanistan.

"Dead bodies sit up by themselves sometimes"
US Marine

Our squad was on our rest cycle from patrol or post when we got the call that first platoon had a MASCAS. (Lots of casualties) They pull up in the MRAPs with 5-7 wounded and we get them in the med tent. I help get one of the AUP (Afghan Uniformed Police) with a gun-shot wound to the head on a stretcher inside and stay with him. Doc checks him out and says, 'He's gone.' and moves on. So we're about to move him and this motherfuckers eyes roll to the back to his head and FUCKNG sits up shaking!

118

It lasts a whole maybe 3-4 seconds and I almost shit myself. Start yelling for doc again but by the time he gets there he's down again and said that shit happens and that he's dead. It's weird thinking back now because a man died and that's terrible but we couldn't help but laugh at it after.

-   Anonymous US Marine. 1/7 Baker Co, Sangin Afghanistan, 2012

"Human fragments"
British Soldier

It was mid-March. The heat was beginning to really crank up. We had a patrol out (5 platoon) and they were patrolling just up the road when the pictured Taliban member opened up on them by firing his weapon at our platoon. Thankfully, the Taliban aren't very good at aiming as he didn't get any of us.

Our OC, Maj Wearmouth and our FAC (Forward Air Controller) W01 Hunter were quick to react and called in an exacter (guided artillery shell that is designed to land in front of you, throwing all the shrapnel up and towards you). The devastation caused by this was immense. As QRF my job as section 2nd in command was to make sure we were ready to deploy as back up, from our mastiff vehicles. We were about eight strong. As soon as we got the call, our Sgt Major (with some very aggressive enthusiasm) told us to load up and get moving. We did. We went to the area where the exacter struck and there was the Taliban member lying there limp, bloody and full of holes. He was moaning and asking for help. This is the same guy that just fired over 30 7.62mm rounds at our mates. Asking for help.

Our Sgt Major, (Redacted) asked the medic that was patching up the holes if 'he was finished patching him up' to which he was, at that point (Redacted) marched over, grabbed the limp enemy, picked him up and began marching him towards the back of the Mastiff. To say he wasn't able to before (Redacted) moved him would have been an understatement. (Redacted) literally made him walk/dragged him in to the back of that wagon. Blood pouring out of him.

We took him back to the FOB were I TQ'd (tactically questioned) him. We had recorded the Taliban's movement from before he opened up on our patrol. We recorded the movement of the weapon he used as it was grabbed by a local and hid in a hut. Later on in the week, someone tried to retrieve that weapon and the OC ordered for that hut to be destroyed with the person going to collect that weapon inside the hut. When we went to the hut, there was fragments of the person all over the inside of the hut and a hole on the roof where the artillery round came through.

I still remember how young he was. His full life ahead of him. I saw him as a kid looking for a little adventure. Playing a game. Clueless to the life he was throwing away.

- Lance Corporal Quinn, British Army. FOB Wishtan, Sangin Afghanistan. 2010

"My consequences and guilt"
US Marine

As a Combat Engineer I found it solely my responsibility to protect the Marines around me and the local populace safe from IEDs. We were supporting an infantry platoon and ran daily patrols disrupting enemy movement and searching compounds for IED materials and weapons caches. This scavenger hunt became an obsession for me. There is nothing more satisfying then unearthing a pressure plate or yellow jug of explosives, to this day I haven't found a similar thrill.

During one patrol, we halted outside of an abandoned compound to take a break from the heat and do wellness checks. During the break I began sweeping with my CMD (combat metal detector) around the compound to make sure the area was clear incase if one of the Marines started to wander off some. After about 10 minutes, I came to a side entrance to the compound and swept the head of the detector across the doorway. The CMD instantly began to sing, at that same moment the patrol leader was rounding everyone up…to push on with the mission. I wasn't sure if what I found was an IED but it had all the signs of it, the placement was ideal and the metal signature was there. I struggled to make a decision whether to halt the patrol and investigate or leave it and let the platoon commander know about it in the post op brief. The patrol we were on was time sensitive so we were not trying to waste time, I remember telling myself "mission comes first" so I left it.

The patrol was RTB (returning to base) about an hour or so after the break when we saw an explosion in the direction we heading, maybe ½ click out. We re-routed and went straight for the blast site, as we got with-in 200 meters we realized it was the compound we had taken our break at. A man was walking toward us with a wheel-barrow with a white sheet over it, the man was weeping. Under the sheet was a young boy maybe 8 years old missing a foot and had half of his body torn up. Our Corpsman went to work and called in the 9-line.

As this was going on myself and a fire team pushed up to the blast site. As I turned the corner to see where it was my heart stopped beating and the world started to spin. The boy had stepped on the IED that I had found but decided to ignore. The children were always curious and would follow behind us to see if we dropped anything, this was something that I didn't consider. There isn't a morning or night that I don't live in regret and shame because I failed to keep everyone safe. I have nightmares of that man with wheel-barrow and when he pulls the sheet back, the boy laying in his own blood with the torn up body is my own son.

- Anonymous US Marine Combat Engineer. Trek Nawa, Afghanistan, 2011

"We serve"
US Soldier

Our Company had just been assigned to assist security efforts of Brigade engineer assets constructing a TI between two towns in our AO. At the time it was merely an approx. 70m x 70m square of hescos with an approx. 6m moat around with run ups in 3 corners and an ECP. Not much but it became home frequently. We worked in three shifts, one manning towers and ECP, one assisting just outside with the engineers, and one cleaning/resting.
It was my first shift, still early on in the (my first) deployment, and I was still wide-eyed excited about each and every "mission".

About an hour into my shift it became fairly obvious to us a large crowd of MAMs were approaching from the western town hoisting a platform of some kind. We watched with anticipation as the gaggle approached to within 25m of the ECP. Our WSL, my TL and a few of us with our terp approached asking what they wanted.

From within the crowd the men carrying the platform, which was now evidently a bed, emerged and threw the bed down. Sprawled out on the bed was half of a child who was no more than 5 or 6. His torso was halved, as if someone had taken a hacksaw from his left shoulder down to his groin. What stood out the most was what was left of his heart hanging out onto the bed. This was the first corpse I have ever seen.

What became of the matter was known to those above my paygrade. All I recall was the group was attempting to claim ISAF mortars has fallen upon the boy and our side claiming he stepped on one of their IEDs. That matters not as, despite what this lad may have grown into, he could grow no longer. It's been nearly 10 years and like many others, the imagery remains just as vivid now as it did through the eyes of a 19-year-old.

-   Anonymous US Soldier. C CO 1-23 INF, 3-2 SBCT. FOB Zangabad, Horn of Panjwai, Kandahar Province OEF '12.

"Fighting Ghosts"
US Marine

The now ill-fated war in Afghanistan is a great example of irregular warfare. The enemy was everywhere and nowhere at the same time. Look out for military age male with a man dress? That describes the entire population of Helmand province who ventured outside their compound walls. Females never went anywhere alone and most kids didn't venture out too far away.

I showed up to Helmand province in June 2010 as a 20 year old Lance Corporal. One of my best friends had just been KIA the prior month in the unit we were slated to replace. He was just 19. I was angry and sad, I wanted to shoot somebody soon. I was assigned as a gunner for a gun truck and attached to a line company. We took turns when it came to dismounted operations. Keep the roads clear of IEDs, provide heavy guns and be the quick reaction force every day. Easier said than done.

Life was very expeditionary and austere at the patrol bases. You could hear gunfire and explosions in the distance every day, a lot of patrols would take contact that summer, anything ranging from a random potshot to a complex ambush. The multiple army or air force Blackhawk's buzzing overhead daily meant somebody got hurt somewhere in Indian country. Motorized units like ours with the big MRAPs and guns were good at scaring the Taliban away.

However, we were bound to the few roads available. Any movement implied guys walking in front of the trucks with a metal detector, it was a slow methodical process every day. We quickly became friends with the EOD techs, ever seen a man dig a bomb out of the ground with a knife? They do crazy stuff. The cat and mouse IED game was daily, the Taliban was always watching but they were nowhere to be seen. The Afghan Police abandoned a checkpoint which we held for several days, we left once to provide QRF and upon our return the checkpoint was demolished. We secured a chunk of road for a week then we left for another QRF; upon our return a few hours later an IED was buried where a vehicle had been parked all week. One day they got ballsy enough to walk up to another vehicle and a Taliban fighter tried to toss a couple grenades in it, he missed and was shot dead by that crew. We finally saw the enemy.

A different day we stumbled on another IED, a young guy walked out of field with his hands up. It took a moment for us to realize this was the trigger man and we were a few steps away from walking into his kill zone. We detained him and played by the rules of war. It was very rare to come face to face with a living Taliban... I wished he had not surrendered so we could have shot him.

The enemy initiated all the fights and the Marines ended them. It's very frustrating as the Taliban always chose the time and place for the fight, then melted away once Marines achieved fire superiority. Back at the patrol based I overheard a Marine from a different platoon say that fighting the Taliban was like fighting ghosts, the same thing the Soviets said before us. That Marine would later earn multiple purple hearts and a Silver Star for his actions on deployment.

Manning a turret gun I always felt a sense of responsibility towards the guys walking around with rifles. They counted on us to save the day when things got bad, and they certainly showed their appreciation when our guns came into action. Whenever it was my turn to dismount I would share all of their frustrations, physical exhaustion sometimes followed by rounds cracking overhead. During a small ambush I saw a suspicious man nearby, I asked the nearest NCO if I should shoot the man, he said it was my call. I made up my mind but the man didn't step out again. After we closed in I came face to face with him. Why would he stand outside of a house when bullets are flying and Marines are in the neighborhood? Was he Taliban? If he had lingered there any longer I would have shot him. Taliban spotters were a concern, once I even saw them with binoculars peeking from a window.

A different day I saw a man kneeling on the side of a road during an early morning, my crew was asleep in the truck. Burying an IED was good enough reason to shoot somebody and these roads were littered with them. I put my sights on him, took the safety off then waited and hesitated. I decided not to do anything, moments later an old man stands up and picks up his rug. He was just praying... Holy fuck I thought to myself. I was shaken up.

The routine of war continued over the months. I considered myself extremely lucky, by the last month of deployment most of our platoon had triggered IEDs and been blown up at one point or another. Some multiple times, some even were on their first few days there... but not me or my vehicle, I was one of the lucky few. The line company we mainly supported had suffered a lot more, many faces from the summer weren't there by the winter. Some guys would get sent to the rear when wounded and then found their way back to their platoon's weeks later. They could have chosen to go home but would not leave their brothers behind. A flow of combat replacements did trickle in over the months, new faces.

The battalion insisted on launching more clearing operations in the final weeks of the deployment, not sure why since our replacements would be doing that exact same thing. As a token of the futility, a Marine in a different company became an amputee days before the extraction birds showed up.
 Mere days before our relief arrived we all were back out looking for bad guys, this time in the freezing cold rather than the blazing summer. That day our snipers in over watch were engaged first, then trucks joined in with the machineguns while the rifle squads maneuvered up. We could finally see groups of military age men lingering in the distance, my team leader said "Let them have it" as we drove up and engaged with the M-240B. Enemy fire picked up dramatically and we kept trading lead for the next 45 minutes, it ended up being the biggest firefight of my deployment. At one point a white sedan comes out of nowhere and drives up a hill, everyone shifted their focus and fire to it although gunfire still poured from multiple directions. Nonetheless we all engaged, Taliban must have been trying to egress and we caught them red handed, or at least we thought so. Air support showed up and did gun runs on the car. To our dismay once the riflemen charged up the
hill moments later they found wounded children...the car had been occupied by a family fleeing the engagement. A horrific scene in the fog of war.

A few days later our extraction was delayed and we spent Christmas at the patrol base, we would finally fly home after the New Year. We would refit, replace, retrain, and redeploy again 10 months later. That second deployment was less kinetic but had one of my closest calls with the death. Once I came home I decided I had enough. I felt exhausted so I left the Marine a few months later. The older I get the more I dwell on that incident from December I don't think it's something I will ever clear from my mind, the guilt sticks with me to this day.

- Anonymous US Marine. 2nd Battalion, 6th Marines. Marjah, Afghanistan 2010

KABUL AIRPORT EVACUATIONS 2021

"I remember…"
US Marine

Before we got to Kabul, we had seen the videos of the Afghans falling off the C-17 and the airfield being stormed. I remember sitting on the C-130 into Kuwait watching those videos on my phone and realizing that we were headed into some wild stuff. Our CO briefed us that we would see and do things that would bother us but that we had a job to do and we needed to be prepared for anything. He wasn't kidding.

I think about the things I saw and did there every single day. We were forced to escort people out who didn't have the proper documents. Some of them had no business being there and made fake documents to try and sneak through so it was no problem tossing them out. But some of these people were people who had been supporting our military since the very beginning of the war.

I remember there was a man who had brought his very old grandparents with him and him screaming at me that I couldn't throw them out because they would be killed. I realized that nothing I said would justify the fact that this man had been risking his life for our military since I was 2 and now my scrawny 22 year old ass was the one sending him to die.

There was another time where there was a kid, about twelve years old, who had his brother with him. His brother was probably about 8. I was on the outside perimeter by the canal where we would pull the people out of. My job was to send people with the right documents through and escort those who didn't out. This kid and his brother were on their own and they had been sent back out for me to remove. I can still remember every feature of him.

I remember his bloodshot eyes with tears streaming down his face and him grabbing at my sleeves saying "Please, my family, my family, please!" He was resisting me and I had to shove him along to the barrier that separated us from the people. His brother was behind him, I don't think he understood what was happening. I'm sure this kid saw me as horrible person but I don't think he understood that I saw myself as a horrible person as I was sending him and his brother to die.

When I got home, there were signs in Horno that said 'Heroes' and similar things and my family was telling me that I should be proud of the people I did save. But I never think about those people. I think about the people I didn't save, or the people that are dead because of me.

- Anonymous US Marine. 2/1 Golf Co. Kabul Afghanistan, 2021.

"Real GWOT Marines"
US Marine

Ever since I joined the Marine Corps I wanted to deploy to Afghanistan. I wanted to become a "Real GWOT Marine". Needless to say I was ecstatic to go into Afghanistan and help with the evacuation. I would soon learn how foolish that thought was. Our priority during the evacuation was to control the "comfort area" and escort people to the airport. At one point we had over 5,000 refugees with only 100 Marines and some Soldiers to control them. Riots and fights broke out daily. Grown ass men stampeding and hitting babies, little kids, and even kicking a pregnant woman in the stomach, resulting in a miscarriage and vaginal bleeding immediately. All of this just to get some food, water, or the cardboard from the MRE box to sit on.

After a few days we finally had the go ahead to get these people on buses and get them the hell out. Little did we know that they still had to get vetted. We were under the impression that they wouldn't make it this far without knowing 100% that they were good to leave. The consulate came and vetted people, resulting in over half having to be sent back to the north gate, after having lived in that hell for days. I didn't care about the single guys because they were all assholes anyways. But having to shove women and little kids out, that I had fist bumped and reassured hours earlier, is what makes me hate myself. A fist bump will never be the same…

I'm mad at the organization and the administration for making me do this. I'm mad that I didn't have answers for them. I'm mad that I had to shove women and children towards the Taliban, knowing full well what their fate would be. I'm mad…. and I'm sorry.

- Anonymous US Marine. 1/8 E Btry. Kabul Airport, Afghanistan 2021.

"It just makes me sick"
US Marine

So many emotions come to mind when I think about Kabul. I feel guilty, not for the military aged men but for the innocent women and children who just wanted a better life. I'm proud to say we did our job and I think we fucking kicked ass given the situation we were put in and in some moments with all the adrenaline it was a blast.

The emotion that I feel the most though is anger. I would have much rather stood, fought, and died than to work with or support the Taliban. Hearing about how the Taliban do things like throw acid in women's faces is more than enough for me to know these dudes need to be put down.

But when the countless innocent women beg and pleaded with me to kill them over being killed by the Taliban it made me sick knowing we were "working" with them. It just makes me sick. First time I had the most solid PID anyone could get we were told not to fire. I don't blame my leadership though. I know they were just following orders like I was.

It's the ones in DC that'll never truly know what went on that make me angry. Overall though the whole experience gave me a new perspective on life and words will never describe how grateful I am to have been born in the US. We are still a beacon of hope for a lot of people around the world and I just hope we learn from our mistakes.

- Anonymous US Marine. 1/8. Kabul Airport, Afghanistan 2021.

"Lord of war"
US Airman

It's been a little over a month since we finally left Afghanistan. And every day it's been on my mind, never ending like when a telemarketer calls you every hour of the day and night. I have been trying to put things into perspective for me to cope with this and I don't even know where to fucking start to tell my story as to why I feel guilty... Working Air Transportation in the Air Force on a deployment is one thing but I lucked out and received a J.E.T. tasking deployment where I got to be an arms dealer, a "Lord of War" as the organization liked to nickname itself or officially as C.S.T.C.A. that's my guilt... A DOD weapons dealer, the only ones in country who did it "legally" we were told.

Now fast forward to present day after seeing & speaking with friends, seeing the comments on social media, the news, and the entire world upset about how MUCH we left behind. It gets to you after a while, this was the highlight of my military career. This was by far the wildest military tasking I ever got to do and nothing will ever top it. But now reflecting on it, seeing how everything has played out I'm not enthusiastic about it. Feeling uneasy about what the future holds for Afghanistan, how many civilians will die from the ammo/weapons, what our adversaries will learn from all the equipment we left behind.

We had flights coming in on US gray tails, US cargo commercial and especially on Antonov's. I remember all the different types of ordnance that we flew in and which countries they came from, 7.62, 5.56/.223, 40MM HE, 40MM training blue, RPG 7VR, RPG 7V, 55MM Rockets, M4's, M16, M60, 240 - 249 SAWS, AKs, thermal scopes, most definitely NVGs GEN 3, 105 Howitzers, GShG 7.62mm mini guns, land mines, claymore, boots, socks, uniforms, jackets, body armor, hand grenades, flash & smoke grenades, generators, medical supplies and of course thousands & thousands of vehicles. And that's just the stuff we gave them for "free". I hate to imagine what we really left behind.

- Anonymous US Airman. Kabul Airport, Afghanistan 2021.

We were in Afghanistan before the evacuation. We had a different mission. We were at the embassy first when it all went down. We were amongst the last to leave. We left at night to HKIA barely slept, barely ate. We were up all day and night the day before doing our best to destroy any sensitive items/ equipment. When we first got to the airport the situation was under control but the marines needed help controlling the situation because they were in the same boat as us. No sleep and hungry. I had no idea how bad that day was going to be.

We were told we needed to stop anyone from getting on the tarmac, no ROE no guidance whatsoever. At first the crowds weren't rioting, they tried to talk to us and show us their papers but I had no idea what to do. I remember all their faces vividly. I see their faces and desperation every night. I turned away so many people who had proper documentation but I had no clue what to do. I had a few water bottles in my pocket and there was families begging for water. I had 3 bottles I gave it away to the woman and children first. I didn't get water until hours later...the first day at the terminal the crowd hadn't gone crazy yet.

They were trying to reason with us. Trying to show us their papers. We couldn't do anything until the situation was under control. Suddenly we heard shots popping off from outside the gate. Ak47s. I didn't know what to expect in that moment, I was expecting a fight but this wasn't something I ever trained for. Thousands of civilians in the way of the enemy. This man comes in shoots his AK in the sky, I try to get a good shot of him but at that point the crowd was running towards us and people kept getting in my line of sight. I decided not to shoot. I couldn't live with myself if I had killed an innocent person. He pointed his gun towards us and the crowd and started firing. Eventually he went to the top of the steps of this white shack and immediately he was gunned down. People will say "Oh I was the one who shot him, no I was" you couldn't really tell. Point is he got lit up and fell like a sack of potatoes. I for sure thought that was just the beginning. I was right to an extent.

Chaos ensued afterwards. Once word got out that the Taliban were setting up a perimeter outside of the airport and flights were canceled for the time being the civilians tried to do everything in their power to get by us. Trampling each other. Kids. Women. Everyone. It was like world war Z. Thousands of people. I had no choice but to put my hands on them to defend myself. One point a man with his child who was about 15 years old came up to us begging us to render medical aid to his son... A giant hole in his arm, surely from the AK earlier. The kid was leaking blood and was passing out in his arms. We couldn't help him. He's dead now most likely.

The crowd started to run towards our military planes and so we retrograded as well and set up a line of basically MRAPS, soldiers and marines. Side by side. We could not let anyone pass. At one point we were surrounded by thousands of people I was gassed just by shoving everyone out of the way to create a path. The plane that took off with people attached to it saved my life. While it was still taxing is when I was surrounded by thousands. I felt the heat of the jet engine and surely thought I was gonna die right there. Then suddenly the engine roars and blasts me about 5-10 feet away. It created enough room for me to regroup with my platoon.

Eventually the civilians knew it was fruitless. There was no more planes left so they started to leave one by one. However throughout the whole day more and more would come in waves. One point there was this man and his family. He was carrying his limp child and begging us. I couldn't understand what he was saying but we just stared at him. We couldn't do anything. There was mother's holding babies who weren't crying anymore. Mothers holding their limp children begging us. One point the crowd died down but there was this mom, with a younger woman and they were holding a young girl. She was limp. And they were both sobbing. One of us walked up to them and handed a water bottle but didn't say anything. What could we say? What could we do? Later in the evening we got word that the Taliban were gonna help with crowd control and not to shoot them. Eventually they came with bull whips, rifles anything. Just beating the fuck out of these people. This one old lady ran up to us and was just crying and begging us. While this guy was just beating the fuck out of her with a whip. I have never wanted to kill someone that bad. I didn't think it was possible to witness that much evil. All we could do was watch. I felt helpless...

- Anonymous US Soldier. 2-30 IN, 3/10 Mtn. Kabul Airport, Afghanistan 2021.

"Welcome to the Infantry"
US Marine

Music makes stuff a bit better. When I get out I wanna make music. Because one song helped me get through the daily shit show that was Kabul. "Welcome to the Infantry" by Fitzy Mess. He's a Marine Corps vet.

There's a line in it that says, "To be completely honest, yo. It makes me quite uncomfortable to think of all the things you'll suffer through before you're 22; but the thing that's fuckin' cool is your boys all gotta suffer too."

And that line is so true. Whenever I was like, "This sucks. I can't keep doing this. We have barely slept or ate since we got here." I remember that all my boys are here with me you know? I'm not alone in this shit.
"This will suck a lot worse if you expect it to be nice." God, the truest shit I've ever fuckin' heard. It's definitely the little things that get you through the day on a deployment. I'm just grateful for some good music and some good dudes to help me out.

- Anonymous US Marine. 2/1 Kabul Airport, Afghanistan 2021.

"It's all so vivid"
US Marine

The days were getting monotonous. It was nearly six months of doing the daily grind in Kuwait. Training, classes, more training, chow, more classes, some gym time. My platoon was getting restless. The thoughts of how much of a disappointment this deployment has been was all I could think of. What looked like what our deployment in the Middle East has been will always be. Until we got the green light for Afghan.

Spirits went up, nerves were racing, and some Marines were suspicious not to believe we actually got the mission until we touched down in Kabul since we have gotten our hopes crushed so many times before with false promises of a mission.

We arrived in Kabul a few days after the chaos that took place on the landing strip occurred. That being said, it was calm and quiet when we exited the aircraft. Some pop shots came flying at the tarmac we were on but nothing noteworthy occurred, that day. The storm seemed to have passed, but I guess it was just the calm before the storm.

As for the rest of the mission, it was chaos, confusing, tiresome, and a whole host of verbs and feelings that can't be put into words. Most importantly it was never boring. I felt purpose. I am sure I can speak for many other Marines they felt the same way.

Many Marines who have been giving testimonies of their experiences regarding the evacuation have expressed views mentioning "I didn't sign up for this" or "What was the point" these are views and phrases I just cannot wrap my head around.

Speaking for myself, I loved every second I was up. Working, holding security, searching civilians, the whole deal, I loved it all. Then, on that fateful day the bomb went off. Everything from that point forward moved in slow motion. Every second can be recalled in the back of my head and picked apart like a Claymation movie. Every dead and dying body that rushed by, every sector of fire I held, every single "suspicious" individual I called out to my gun team leader who then relayed it to snipers. Everything is still so vivid.

Of course without needing to say, it was tragic. I lost a close friend and fellow Marines. Others lost many close friends that day... They will never be in our lives or their families' lives ever again. That is a hard truth to swallow. Though, in the end I finally felt like I did something. I felt fulfilled. Not because I necessarily did my job of being a machine gunner, but the simple fact that I got to fulfill somewhat of a duty to the country I chose to serve. Maybe it's my naiveté speaking, but I have no regrets about being sent to Afghan and I would do it all over again. In my eyes, no sacrifice that was made over there was in vain.

- Anonymous US Marine. 2/1. Kabul Airport, Afghanistan 2021.

"Suffering is international"
Australian Soldier

An Aussie perspective on the entire situation that happened in Kabul. We sat and had many smokes and fed your lads some of our highly sought after ration packs after they had been on the gates. I sat and comforted some of the younger blokes that were pretty fucked up and literally fucked from fatigue. The biggest thing they needed was a reassuring ear to listen and some support in any way we could offer it. Your lads worked nonstop and it was a privilege to see the work ethic and resolve of the Marines and the Airborne blokes that we worked with on the South Gate. I sincerely hope that these guys are being looked after returning and if any of them want to reconnect and say g'day my door is always open and would be happy to have a yarn with them.

-   Anonymous Australian Soldier. 1st Battalion Royal Australian Regiment. Kabul, Afghanistan. 2021.

"What we saw"
US Marine

Our first shift was the day we arrived. We went out to the ECC as a group and begun receiving the brief of our daily operation. 30 seconds into standing there talking to our Gunny, a car came flying across the flight line and onto the back road to the ECC. A foreign military contractor stopped the vehicle and called over to us asking for help. We all turned around and set up a perimeter immediately. I went around behind all the Marines spacing them out, racking one in the chamber, and telling them to get the fuck down on a knee. 2 men stepped out of the vehicle dressed in Cammie bottoms, t-shirts and head wraps.

The situation reeked of a VBIED. I got on a knee 10 yards away in front of the vehicle. I was scanning everything for wires, vehicle sagging, vests, switches and weapons. Gunny yelled at the 2 men to get on their faces and interlock their fingers on the back of their heads. My weapon was trained at the drivers head, and my adrenaline was coursing. I was thinking to myself "I'm gunna kill these motherfuckers" the whole time I was in front of that vehicle. More military personnel came running out and yelling at us to stand down but I didn't hear them until they were right behind me. They cleared the men and turned them around to where they were supposed to be. They were allowed to be here, they just got lost. That was the first time I really thought that I was going to kill another person.

The next day I worked on the NTS kits registering people. There were so many locals that thanked us for saving them. One man showed us a recent surgical scar from the removal of a bullet. He said the Taliban shot him in his stomach. Another man was in tears because he lost his wife amidst the chaos outside the gates and she couldn't get in. Many situations were hard to listen to. We were asked to help retrieve somebody's father because the Taliban captured him, but there was nothing we could do. Our operation was strictly inside the walls. Almost everybody thanked us for registering them and getting them on flights.

Whether their language was English or their native tongue, it felt great to get them out all the same. What hurt the most was turning people away and sending them back to the gate. They had already come all this way. The women, children and men alike were all beaten and bloodied. Not all, but a really big number of them. I will forever be haunted by that. Not knowing what they are doing or if they even survived.

- Anonymous US Marine. CLB 24. Kabul Afghanistan, 2021.

"I was thrilled...at first"
US Marine

My story is the same as every other grunts: join the Marine Corps to deploy and kill people who needed to be killed. Needless to say when we were in Kuwait and we got the word that we were going into Afghanistan to help conduct the evacuation I, just like everyone else, was thrilled. Finally I'd be a real Marine and not just a UDP or MEU baby. I wish I realized how naive I was. When we touched down it was a mess. Our first day in country I was standing post on the one of the gates and within the first hour of being on over watch I watched the ANA shoot a six year old kid in the stomach with a 12 gauge rubber round. I was horrified, and I'll never be able to get the sound that poor kid made out of my head.

The next day my platoon was conducting detailed searches of the refugees and this one kid who must've been 15 or 16 said his brother had his ID but he was at the front of the gate. I took him down there to look, and immediately I saw a father holding his little girl over the gate trying to get us to take her, and the ANA hit her in the stomach repeatedly to get her off the gate. I was sickened.

I recall after the Abbey Gate incident that everyone was paranoid and tense, and rightly so. About 12ish hours after it happened, I was on post and we were given a handful of BOLOs. The one that concerned us the most was a white Toyota corolla followed by an oil tanker. Intel had reported the oil tanker was a 2,000 IED. After being on that post for about 2-3 hours, a tanker ended up rolling up and stopping about 50 meters east of our gate, let a military aged male out of its passenger seat, then drove up and parked on the road directly in front of the gate.

After it had stopped, the driver just looked at us and had his hands somewhere near his lap. He sat there watching us, and we sat there watching him knowing that if that was our IED, we'd be dead before we could do anything due to our rules of engagement. We still don't know what he was doing, but he stepped off after about 3ish minutes. I'd never been more scared in my entire life and I still haven't forgot what it feels like.

It was all just terrible in every aspect. Men beating their wives and kids, women using their kids as human shields, escorting families back out the gate as they begged us to shoot them instead of turning them back to streets where the Taliban would eventually find them, dead/dying civilians being carried back and forth, the bodies of dead babies being discarded into the wadi that ran next to the gate. It was a mess. And what I hate the most is having left knowing that we could've saved more people. I'll never forgive myself for any of it. And worst of all, I feel bad for the families of the men and women who gave their lives trying to save others. They deserve better, and unfortunately, they'll probably never get it.

- Anonymous US Marine. Kabul Airport Evacuations. Afghanistan, 2021.

"Those Marines saved us"
Afghan Civilian

Like a nightmare, the Taliban were everywhere. They had blocked roads to the airport, and we had to walk in darkness for more than two hours. We were told to be in front of the black gate at 11 PM sharp, and a team will get us inside the airport. Looking at my old mother, who struggled to walk with us, made me feel the worst pain ever.

At 10 PM, we arrived at the gate and waited for two hours, and no one showed up. God, I wanted to cry so badly looking at my poor family, who had no choice but to wait. My brother, who lives in the US, told me that this was the only chance we got, and we should not leave the gate until getting inside. We waited till 8 AM in the morning, and still, no one showed up. Suddenly the gate was opened, and Marines came out. Hundreds if not thousands of people were rushing to get into the airport. Marines got control of the situation and pushed people back. They were only letting US citizens and Green Card holders inside.

I saw a Marine who was standing close to us. Along with my sister, we reached him and tried to speak to him and explain everything so that he could help us get inside. We showed the documents that we had, but it was not enough. I called my brother, and he said, 'Wait, I will talk to someone inside and see if he can help.' He shared a number and told me to call this number and pass the phone to the Marine. I did what he said, and the Marine was talking to the guy. He cut the phone and said, "Wait here."

Those moments were the most critical moments of our lives. Whether getting into the airport or being killed by the Taliban. The guy called me again, and I passed the phone to the Marine. He spoke with the guy for two minutes. The moment that the marine told me to bring my family inside was the happiest moment of my life.

I felt like he freed me out of the cage and gave me the wings to fly. He carried us to the airport and left us with a big smile on his face.

- Mostafa Anwari, Afghan Refugee. Kabul Airport, Afghanistan. 2021.

"I don't feel good"
US Marine

One of the biggest things that sticks with me from that place was how much unnecessary death there was. Men were trampling and hurting little kids, pushing women holding babies into c-wire obstacles set up to control the flow. We were authorized to have warning shots and the Afghan contractors accidentally shot several people on several occasions.

One time we were outside of the gate shoulder to shoulder with riot shields. We had to use non-lethal on them regularly because if we didn't then they would literally kill each other to get through to us but it was brutal. We threw flashbangs over their heads, shot them with rubber bullets, beat them with batons and I just told myself it was because we didn't want them to trample and kill each other.

OC spray and CS gas was also used and I just thought damn this shit fucks me up how are these kids dealing with this. I watched one woman get shot in the chest by an afghan contractor in front of her family and I just don't even understand why. Between that and kicking families out because I was forced to kick them out because they didn't have the right paperwork and after trying every way in the world to bring them in as the children pulled on my arm and begged me while the fathers would say to just shoot them because that's a better death than they would receive.

I just don't feel good about any of it. We let them down and we tried our best. I'm angry that this all could've been avoided if we had started evacuating before the city fell. The whole city was petrified of the Taliban who claimed they were helping despite the decapitated bodies they would bring to the gate to warn citizens that would be their fate if they didn't leave.

- Anonymous US Marine. 1/8. Kabul Airport, Afghanistan. 2021.

"Bombs away"
US Airman

My deployment was nothing major, a pretty cake deployment for all intents and purposes. For me, the war always ended at 4:30. About 2 months in, a couple of us got an invite to check out the MQ-9s for a little Disney Land type tour, complete with a feature presentation of HVT strike footage in HD. Before I go any further, I'm an AMMO troop by trade, so I've seen my fair share of what the Air Force's explosive arsenal can do to soft and hard targets alike. Hell, for some of them I can even tell you how they work inside and out. For some reason, this was different.

I remember they sat us down and told us that the footage we were about to watch was the feed for that dude that made the bomb at Abbey Gate. He was sleeping on a mat outside, with one of his family members sleeping on a cot next to him. After about 6 seconds it was over, they used two low collateral munitions on him. There's no explosives, it's just a weighted bomb body with 3-6 razor sharp blades attached to the end of it, so he got turned into human hibachi meat. Twice. They stopped it just as his homie within 10 feet of him woke up, ran over, and began to sort through his blood and guts. It was over in 20 seconds, a silent movie of big-brothers ultimate prowess, but all of a sudden I found myself wondering why they made it so quick. He probably didn't even feel a thing. Then I wondered how they even knew if it was the right guy, and if it was the right guy, why didn't they do this before he was able to kill 13 service members?

I wasn't bothered by the footage, really. After 5 years of being an AMMO troop, you learn that your job is to enable all of that stuff. That's your job. Killing people with pinpoint accuracy from 25,000 feet. Wouldn't happen without you, because you're the one that builds the bombs in the first place. Then moments like this happen, and you realize that that's the thing about being in the rear; they give you ice cream, beer all that shit. It's like they try to convince you that the war isn't happening. For some reason, that's the frustrating part.

- SrA Brian E. Carlson, USAF AMMO

"Honestly, I had fun."
US Marine

I enjoyed my time in Kabul. The smell was terrible and the place was disgusting but when we pushed out the gate the first time I was expecting decent people, half-assed lines, but that was not the case. It was chaotic people, shit, cwire, gunshots, trash and babies getting tossed around.

Then they tried breaking through the line and we had to beat the fuck out of these people. And it wasn't mostly women and kids it was 95% military aged men fleeing their country like cowards. By day two my hard-knuckle gloves where shattered from fighting them off. Now the kids maybe under 16 I felt bad for, and babies that got fucked up because of their shitty parents; not us. Splitting families didn't really bother me because I watched them make up bullshit families right outside the gate.

Soft-ass Marines trying to let everyone in didn't help either. And women, get fucked it's not like the Taliban took the country in a day they had time and waited until now. So I had no sympathy for these people. If they would have turned around and fought back they would have their country. And all the Marines that said this isn't what they signed up for. But yet they signed up to kill and possibly be killed and see their buddies die then that's fucked. I enjoyed the violence and thought the experience was fun.

- Anonymous US Marine. V1/8 Bravo Co. Kabul Airport, Afghanistan. 2021.

"I'm only 20"
US Marine

I know I signed up to suffer. But I straight up feel used and abused, dude. I can't even legally drink alcohol and they made me separate families and watch people beat children. Bro, joining the military was the worst decision I ever made. I didn't sign up for THIS. I love my platoon and my friends but this isn't it.

I wanted to serve my country and now I can't sleep or even be around little kids now. That shit at the airport was so unbelievably fucked up that I have to force myself not to cry like all day long. I can't even go to my chain of command or they will label me a sad Marine and kick me out. A bunch of Marines in the Corps right now are saying they're jealous of the dudes who "got to go" to Kabul and do their jobs. Bitch, don't be jealous of this shit. All we did was save a few people and send literally ten times more to their deaths. I'm gonna live with this shit for the rest of my life and I'm only 20 years old.

I should have gone to college but I got sucked in by a pair of dress blues and clever commercials….I hate that they made us do that…I'll never forgive them for fucking this up so bad. This isn't the war my big brothers got to fight. There's nothing for me to be proud of. Don't get me wrong, I'd never become one of the 22. I'm not saying that. I'm just so unbelievably pissed off about all this.

- Anonymous US Marine. 2/1. Kabul Airport, Afghanistan. 2021.

"His jaw was missing"
US Marine

It was an absolute shit show of a place. The parents of their children were abandoning them. The children were abandoning their parents. I had to split families and I had to push families out of the gate where I knew that they'd die due to the Taliban's presence. I fight to sleep some nights because I don't know which is worse! Pulling the trigger or sending innocent families to someone that'd do it anyways. People are upset about the harsh reality it was.

I was close to the IED when it went off and worked on Marines and Afghan Civilians after the blast and that was probably the hardest thing was having to let people know that their buddy was dead. Going completely internal for the first second because it never registered in my brain that it was an IED. In my mind I suppose I wished it was a flash bang and it wasn't. I came into realization of the fact it was an IED when the first guy walked out of the hole in the gate missing the bottom half of his jaw.

It was honestly the scariest part of being there. I assisted in the aid of many people there as I was at the blast site. We had intel that there was an IED but the marines there and corpsman were so dedicated to helping those who couldn't help themselves that they were willing to sacrifice themselves. No one that day died in vain which is what I need to tell myself because I personally put interventions into someone who didn't make it.

136

Nobody wants to hear it but after you get there and you put interventions in to save people and they still die it makes it feel like it was your fault.
-    Anonymous US Marine. 2/1, HKIA Kabul Afghanistan. 2021.

"Fuck *the Taliban"*
Afghan Civilian

By the time the withdrawal started we were in a military base. Everyone was leaving. Contractors and Military personals. They send all linguists home. I was the last local national in the base then I got a flight with ANA Helicopter. I went home to see my family, they closed the Bagram Base and things got serious!

We left our homes, we rented a house in Kabul near to the airport. It was so quick! People were talking about Talies that they are coming, people were freaked, politicians, President Ghani…they all left the country! Fuckin' Puss!

Everyone was trying to get ahold of their supervisors. I contact my friends in State. Friends in Marines and Army, they were calling me, texting me saying, 'Hey Sayed, don't worry we got you man! I went to the airport there was so many people and so many checkpoints from the TB. I received passcode and names from the 2/5 Marines. (Organizing his evacuation) The Marines from 2/1 were waiting for me, they knew that I'm coming I had a passcode with names. On 24th AUG Abby gate I got a chance to talk to those Marines.

There was a Marine from 2/1. I told him, "Pass the passcode and names to your LT." Then the LT comes over and told us to get in. We were in safe hands. We took some pics with 2/1 Marines then we got out. We were lucky. Rest of my friends were still stuck there some of them got out on 25th. On 26th that explosion happened. I was worried about everyone and there was 13 Marines and more than 100 Afghans! Rest in Peace! Jawad was one of them he was interpreter for the Green Berets and a good friend of mine.
-    Sayed Jan. Afghan National. Evacuated from HKIA, Kabul Afghanistan, 2021.

"Mothers in Arms"
US Marine

I didn't have an opportunity to deploy, but I've certainly dealt with the fallout of deployments and war. When I enlisted in the Marine Corps, my mother could not sit at home waiting for me, sending care packages to soothe her anxiety. She decided to get into the fight too as a DOD civilian contractor.
As an Afghan-American woman, she had the language skills to do a much needed and difficult job. She was ultimately medically evacuated while on her last deployment to Afghanistan. I don't want to go into too many details, but her last deployment was harsh, and I'm glad she is alive.

Last year, right before the pandemic, she was diagnosed with breast cancer. I was her primary caretaker. She is currently in remission. I wonder how much of what she was exposed to during her time fighting the war in Afghanistan contributed to her cancer. Now, after the fall of Kabul, I'm saddened for both my fellow Afghans and military family. The past few months have not been easy. This is not the outcome any of us fought so hard for.

I just want to assure you that you did make a difference. As bad as things are in Afghanistan right now, you still gave the people there a chance. You gave an entire generation opportunities and a better life. Please stay in the fight. As the years unfold, things come to light and make sense, you will find a purpose and another way to fight. Fighting is not just done on the battlefield. The world needs you more than ever.

- US Marine Arya Khoshal. Global War on Terror.

"I forgive you"
Afghan Civilian

I am in hiding. I seen other Afghans sent stories. I was at the airport to try to leave Afghanistan. I have no family and am wanted by the Taliban for serving in the Army. I want American soldiers to know I do not blame them. I could not escape. I was turned back at the gates day after day, but I do not hate them. (Americans) I know it is not your fault. I saw you give food and toys to children. Try to play with them and make them feel safe.

It is not your fault. I know that orders are the orders. I said I was in the Army so I know commands must be obeyed. Very few Afghans blame the soldier. Children are different. They are small and do not understand as well as us. They see what is in front of them, not the whole book of the story. I speak to the Marines who shared their story here. I see that you mourn Afghans. I beg of you dear, you are forgiven. If not by all Afghan people than by me. I will find another way out of here.

- Anonymous Former Afghan Army soldier. Kabul Airport, 2021.

"Two generations. One experience"
US Marine

My grandpa was one of the last ones to leave Saigon at the end of the Vietnam War. Now 46 years later, we were the last to leave Kabul. I won't speak much about my time there, but I'll tell you how I felt at home.
It's hard. It's hard knowing that so many people are alive or dead right now because they had the right or wrong piece of paper. I came home and talked to my grandpa. Like I said, he was in Saigon. He asked me how it was. I just shrugged and said, "That was the worst thing they could have ever asked us to do." My grandpa came over to me and gave me a hug. He held me so tight and I could feel a frog in my throat.
I started to cry.
"I know", he said. "I know, boy. I know."

The only good thing that's come out of this is my grandpa and I understand each other on a whole different level. I never imagined it would feel like this. But now I understand why he never talked about Saigon much.

- Anonymous US Marine. 2/1. Kabul Airport, Afghanistan. 2021.

GLOBAL WAR AGAINST TERROR (ext.)

"Fitzy Mess"
US Marine: Sana'a: Yemen

I was just thinking about a really profound moment during a deployment, when my unit got activated to re-enforce the US embassy in Yemen when their country broke out in a civil war in 2011.

I was trying my absolute best to suck every bit of nicotine I could out of a shitty, lite, off-brand Middle Eastern cigarette with another guy from my platoon. We were venting about how much we hated the celebrity-worship, social media obsessed, childlike tendencies of people in our age group. Here we are, 19 years old holding down a compound surrounded by constant firefights and heavily armed and organized groups of people who have less than positive opinions about the good ole US of A.

Meanwhile, people our age back home were partying, bitching about college, and going about their normal lives like a bunch of selfish pricks! This was a weird psychological phenomenon I had when I was that young, having that kind of experience, and I couldn't comprehend the fact that the rest of the world doesn't come to a screeching halt because I'm going through some miserable shit.

As silly and self-centered as our complaints were in hindsight, as long as I live I'll never forget this. My friend turns to me and says: "Sometimes, I feel like we have more in common with the enemy than the average American."

The realization that I had no refutations to make was sobering, to say the least. Fast forward to the present day, I'm on social media giggling at the most absurd low-effort memes, going on bullshit political rants, shitposting, feeling like I experienced personal loss when a rapper I like dies, keeping up with all the juiciest political and celebrity gossip, and taking selfie videos of me rapping in my car for a bunch of strangers on the internet to watch like some narcissistic sociopath. I've become what I once loathed.

- Corporal William "Fitzy Mess" Fitzpatrick. Charlie FAST, Yemen 2011.

"I realized I was not immortal"
US Marine: Iraq

Operation Inherent Resolve isn't as glamorous or cool as OIF or OEF but it's all I got to experience. Depending on where you were with OIR you got to experience some kind of real world events. Our unit was deployed to the TQ airbase in Iraq in 2016 and mainly stood post. Many long monotonous hours spent standing post looking at piles of trash left over from OIF and chain smoking. Every once in a while you would get lucky and help treat some causalities the Iraqis brought in. This was the first time I ever saw someone die.

The poor guy was an Iraqi soldier in his early 20s at most; my age. Sniper apparently got him in the head and he was barely hanging on. We had to turn him away because we didn't have the capability to help him at our base and told them to take the guy to Baghdad. Unfortunately for him, or maybe fortunately at that point, his labored autonomous breathing suddenly stopped. That day made me realize my own mortality and to be thankful for an otherwise boring deployment.

-    Anonymous, Marine Corps, 2/7 in 2016

"I thought my best friend was dead"
US Marine: Syria/Iraq

I deployed twice in support of OIR. Both times thinking I'd finally be able to do my job. Machine gunner. Once to Iraq in 2015, and once to Syria in 2017. Iraq was pretty much standing post for 7 months. Very easy to become complacent. But one day, while on post we saw an Iraqi tank pull up on the causeway not thinking anything of it. Later that day, right around midnight, we're getting ready to get relieved off of post and all of a sudden a SVBIED blows up 300-400m away from us killing 15 civilians and wounding 40+.

We took cover behind a tiny wall on the rooftop we were on, went condition 1, and then watched everything unfold before our eyes. People running around holding body parts. The shockwave and heat wave of that explosion that I felt. The chaos that ensued after it blew up. The helplessness that I felt, I will never forget.

Syria 2017. We were the first ground troops in Syria. We pushed down south near Raqqa and set up a little fob/firebase. We did a few patrols, stood some post, and watched our arty guys absolutely destroy ISIS positions. Isis would hammer us with mortars and rockets daily. Arty would take them out or air strikes would. One day I was on QRF right near the VCP but inside the wire and my best friend was on post at the VCP. We start hearing what sounds to be like explosions in the distance and I say to some of the guys "Do y'all hear that? Are we taking IDF?" Then finally after about 4 explosions, the air horns we had for IDF attacks started going off. We start hearing the mortars impact closer and closer. Hearing the whistle of the enemies mortars flying overhead of us, not knowing if one would hit and kill us.

One of the mortar rounds landed 10 feet in front of my best friend and we all thought he died. The fear right then struck me, thinking that my best friend was dead and I couldn't even kill the enemy. Our LT did a Medal of Honor run across the entire fob checking on everyone. Our Plt Sgt was taking cover in our fighting holes between mortar impacts just to check on his guys. After about 25 mortars/rockets hitting all around us, artillery finally took them out. And we could finally see that our friends were in fact not dead but shaken up from the attack. EOD then did post blast analysis and was talking to my buddy and said that if that

141

round was 1 foot closer to them that they would've died. I'm so grateful that my best friend is here today. I love you man.
- Anonymous US Marine- 3/7 & 1/4. Global War on Terror.

"Oh shit its happening"
US Soldier: Syria

We were in southern Syria since December 2020, and it was going on four months and absolutely nothing had happened. Yes we would see a few Russians here and there but we would look at them, and they would stare at us. One day we were on a 5 vic patrol and sand storm had picked up so we pushed our matvs to a file. All of a sudden over the net I hear contact right contact right from my 4th truck. Myself responding with "Haha ok bulllshiittt" simultaneously tracer rounds impact in front of my truck and thunk against the side armor. My gunner who was facing to the 9 (we were taking contact to the 3) screams over the headset "contact left" and starts sending rounds with the 50. I was trying to tell him no no contact is to the right, and noticed through the little matv window that sure enough I could see the distinct X muzzle flash of a DSKA that we were getting.

Shot at from the left as well. I put two and two together and was like of fuck were in a kill box. I screamed over the net push through push through and we began to zip out of there. The dudes engaging us began to follow and my platoon Sgts vic lit into the hilux and it immediately pulled of right as if the driver was killed. The sand storm then got a lot worse, and not knowing who else was there, we broke contact and proceeded back to the outpost.
- Anonymous Soldier. US Army. B CO 3-156 INF. Syria 2021.

"Inherent Resolve"
US Marine: Iraq

I was in the first batch of Marines back into Iraq when the ISIS thing kicked off. We were there when "there were no boots on the ground in Iraq." We took rockets every morning and every night for probably the first 2-3 months we were there. It was my first deployment so I didn't really know what to think of it. They sounded like trains flying through the air. You could hear them fire, usually 2-4 at a time, and then listen to the train come screaming over and explode somewhere on the base. Some landed pretty far off and a couple landed pretty close.

I was never really that scared, but I remember the first time I was caught completely in the open when it happened. Nowhere to go, nothing to jump behind. Just standing there in the open hoping it didn't land on you. Total helplessness. They went screaming over and hit a few hundred meters away and I was fine. That experience taught me that it didn't matter how good of a grunt you were;

sometimes you just get blown the fuck up for being in the wrong place at the wrong time.

You have absolutely no control over certain elements of living or dying in war. That's when I let go. Just completely stopped letting myself worry about what was going to happen to me. Never bothered me again. Had a few closer calls, but always found it easy to keep it together once I let go. Only thing is, it's hard to get that back after you let go of it.

- Anonymous US Marine, Al Anbar, Iraq 2016.

"Fighting ISIS"
British YPG Volunteer: Syria

Roughly six-year's ago now this was taken alongside Danny an ex US Marine. I and he were in the Kurdish YPG and both of us had roughly been in Syria for the past 7 months. Both of us had taken part in two operations previously before al hol, during the operation to liberate Al hol we had moved to the Iraqi side of the border in Sinjar to a staging location ready to push into ISIS territory.

When the day came we pushed from across the border into Syria; along the way we captured a village in which we witnessed roughly 7 or 12 ISIS members run towards us in the open as our Heavy Weapon Trucks gunned them down followed by a failed car bomb which the driver bogged in the mud from the previous days rain.

Eventually we would cross over and spend the night. At this point we were in an old Syrian border post near in the outskirts of the town of al khatuniyah observing some ISIS fighters and trying to spot where the mortar position was on the Sinjar that was harassing our position, it must of been roughly 9am at the time ISIS had started mortaring our position with the closest landing within our position compound.

Our unit commander came over to us as we took cover in a foxhole dug out overlooking the plains, he came to tell us if I wanted to come film the airstrike that was coming on one of the positions in front of us that we were waiting to push forward on, only problem was that he gave the Coalition the wrong coordinates for it and we ended up getting hit by an coalition jet which took out 4 of our technical's and killed 9 of our guys while wounding 5 more.

Had it not been for Danny and the fighting position we were standing in we most likely would have been killed or badly injured as he heard the missile coming in at the last moment and pulled us down the Toyota which was less than 15 meters behind us was hit and was now popping off with ammunition and the other missiles targeted our DSHK trucks just next to us on the other side of the berm they were shooting at the time.

The bombing seemed to last for ages but in reality it was less than 30 seconds while all this was going on I remember Danny's shouting a prayer Psalm 23:4 while our bodies and minds were vibrating from the shock waves. I'm not religious but I certainly was in that moment, my heart was racing my face filled with dirt as tried to bury myself into the dirt, the only thought rushing through my mind was "Please be quick. Please be quick."

Once it was over the screams of the injured and those shouting out for to check people, me and Danny were still stuck in our foxhole with the ammunition still cooking off from the Toyota behind us, we both decided to hop over the over side of the berm to try and assess the situation and make sure we didn't get left behind if they decided to retreat hastily, at first I thought it was artillery but Danny said it was the jet and once that set in I started to grow anxious hearing the jet in the sky again and thinking back to all those videos I had seen of them turning round to finish the survivors off.

Eventually help arrived I ended up going to the rear of the operation my mind wasn't right and I couldn't do my job without having a panic attack every time I heard a jet fly over, my biggest fear being the Americans would come round to finish us off, eventually I would end up leaving Syria because my anxiety and panic attacks were triggered every time a jet flew over which was 24/7 being a war zone.

It took me one year to get over my fear of jets and back to normality.

- Anonymous British Volunteer. YPG. War against ISIS in Syria.

"Mosul or Stalingrad?"
Iraqi Officer: Iraq

It was the largest force assembled of my countries soldiers (Iraq) since Saddam held power. Mosul was turned to powder in some places. Daesh had occupied Mosul for a long time, and my men and I were eager to take it away. Many died in the fighting. Several men I know were on the same street as Daesh and ended up in an argument during a lull.

"Give up! You will all die here!", 'We will show no mercy if you don't throw away your guns!' We tried to convince them to let themselves be taken prisoner but they wouldn't listen. One tried, but he was accidentally shot as he entered into the street. One of my men shot him and that put a stop to any thoughts of the others giving up.

We tried to coordinate with NATO artillery to fire into the buildings but we couldn't communicate well with them. We had to rip them out ourselves. Daesh resorted to using civilians as shields. Several were killed in the crossfire. My boys were not mad killers, but men who wanted their city and families back.

- Anonymous Iraqi Officer. Battle of Mosul 2016.

WARS IN THE 2000's – CURRENT

"I was ready"
French Soldier: Africa

It was my first real dep, and I'm like hanging in the sun with my flak and all relieving duty of my one of my fellow boots at the gate. And so as I come I'm like "Yo sup my man." to get éléments and he tells me 'Ah fuck this shit, this sucks ass big time.' Within hours an African dude came with his AK and a helmet on his head (they don't normally wear it if things ain't about to get sideways). And he pointed me.

Soon after exchanging a few word with this soldier probably on drugs I understand there's no way outta this, he's probably gassed outta his mind so I take my FAMAS and off I am *RACK* I load my gat. His nose trill are moving in anger, we are looking at each other in the eyes. And he put the selector of his AK all the way down and load it. By loading my gat I escalated the situation and there's no way outta this I'm thinking.

It's time to either way have balls or die on a stupid-ass watch at the gate. So I'm pointing at this dude my mind is racing, making plan of shooting him and jumping behind the wall to cover after the first shot. All that in a quarter of a sec but it felt like it took ages. I'm wondering if I'm gonna get my ass chewed for killing an 'ally soldier.'

And then I push with my index the selector of the FAMAS and come to press the trigger, slowly but surely as I reach this point where all my questions are answered and I'm just doing it. As I come mid-way to the shots fired point, he put his weapons down and laughed, then leaves. I'm contemplating shooting this motherfucker in the back, but I get back to the world I get behind the wall ASAP and I point at him as he's leaving....pressure is coming down and I'm somehow thankful I didn't shoot him but also regretting.

Turns out I found out why he acted that way: When the official convoy were passing in the avenue we had to lock the 2nd gate and put the tires on block thingies, but the asshole who I relieved on duty never told me and passed on the information. So I learnt that despite the aspect of our job being dumb, a lack of communication could result in real situations. The second thing I learned is: I was ready.

- Anonymous French Soldier. 21 RIMA – 4th Unit, Africa.

"Boring Deployment"
US Soldier: Horn of Africa

I grew up watching others join and deploy to Iraq or Afghanistan and enlisted myself fresh out of high school hoping to deploy. Instead my first contract was spent in garrison doing mundane Army day to day, motor pool Monday or partying. My second contract time for deployment finally came only to be told we were going to the Horn of Africa, not exactly the grunts dream deployment but we trained up hard anyway. Finally we arrived in Djibouti and went about our mission some guys got to go to other places throughout the Horn away from the flag pole right away much to envy of other grunts.

Then one day EARF and was called up to go to Kenya after an attack by Al-Shabaab that left 3 Americans dead. After arriving in Kenya we were quickly put to work in providing security and improving our fighting positions working with Air Force engineers building hescos, putting up c-wire around the perimeter, etc.

Going on actual patrols and securing our AO made us proud and we felt we actually earned the patch on our right shoulder. One thing that stuck out was seeing the wreckage and burnt out aircraft from the attack along with sweat aroma smell that most of us never knew before which was the combination of human remains as well as burnt metal, plastic and fuel. That was the moment I knew this shit was real and a seemingly "boring deployment" can change real fast like it did for the soldier and two contractors who gave their lives. Rest Easy to those Americans.

- Anonymous US Soldier HOA 2019-2020

"Cartel showdown"
Mexican Marine: Mexico

We were patrolling down Avenida International, it's the road that takes you from Zona Centro to coast of Tijuana. It was unusually busy due to a makeshift military checkpoint manned by the army but we took the shoulder on the left to bypass all the other vehicles. A military truck (a four door Silverado equipped with seats and guard bars to hold yourself up as you rode in the back along with six others) stopped, and before I had a chance to even put my FX at the ready the element in front of my squad opened fire on a green SUV in traffic.

The five men who were in my squad opened up as well. I stood there frozen. Fire ceased and we kept advancing along the road. As I passed the SUV we fired upon, I saw the carnage and what looked like three dead bodies and I was able to see a broken AK stock on the passenger side covered in blood.

To this day I don't know if it was because I really had no clue of what was about to happen is the reason why I froze or it was just that one first time you see someone lose their life so violently before your eyes; but I felt like my heart was going to explode and I leaned over the tail gate and puked as we drove away.

146

We had close calls after that but nothing ever felt like that day. We traveled that same road hundreds of times after that and I could see the US on the other side of the wall and I often wonder now if Americans really know what happens on the other side of that wall and really want a civil war like so many claim with so much political division we have today.

When you go fight in another country such as Afghanistan or Iraq you are made believe that those people are not human but in your own soil with people you have so much in common with its different. Also we are blessed in the United States because when we come home from other countries people here blindly thank you for your service. Countries such as Mexico and Afghanistan the military often holds a different place in peoples mind set.

American service men now feel betrayed by their government because after 20 years of fighting Afghanistan is back where it was in 2001. Mexico is back where it was in 2007 and we did terrible things to our own people here thinking we were on Gods side. Reality is that since the beginning of time men have killed their fellow men while being the same side, the poor manipulated side.

- Anonymous Mexican Marine. Amphibious Brigade. Mexico 2011.

"Sicario"
Mexican Soldier: Mexico

Cartel members are full of bad men and I don't mind terminating them one bit. They say it's a shame to kill your own countrymen but not when it comes to these guys. Bad men all around. A few years ago while I was in the Army, we were driving along a road in (redacted) when we got the green light from our commander to open up on a few cars with known cartel members inside of them. I was on top of the truck manning the machine gun and when they got close enough, I'd say 200 meters, I emptied the gun on them.

They tried returning fire by poking their arms with guns out of the windows, or shooting through the windshield, but it was no use. I had a clear line of sight and a 300 round belt for them. Both SUV's were riddled with holes. I'll admit, maybe they tried to give up after the first 100 rounds, but we all know how the Mexican justice system works. They'd be back out on the streets hurting people within a week. So I let them have the other 200 rounds just to make sure.

- Anonymous Former Mexican Soldier. Mexico, 2012.

"Litmus test of combat"
KNLA Burma

CRACK, CRACK, CRACK enemy bullets fly over us, leaves and twigs fall out of the bush above as the guerrilla next to me looks over, smiles and gives me a big thumbs up. We have found the enemy, they are in the gully below us and judging by the smell of cordite close.

They might be close but we still can't see them. We fire a few rounds back, each and fall back. There is 50-75 enemy in a resupply patrol, once a month they send these patrols out to supply their outposts along the border and they are easy pickings for ambushes. As they retreat back down the gully they hit a couple of mines that have been laid behind them as we engaged them from the front.

Our job done, we slip away, later one of the guys finds a bullet hole in his pack. The bullet had entered his pack and passed through, tearing a hole in his bible before exiting out the other side. This has been my first contact and now after years of training, for the first time, I feel like a Soldier.

-    Anonymous Western volunteer, Lieutenant, KNLA, Karen State, Burma.

"Honor Restored"
KNLA Burma

Sometime in late 2000 a 12 man Thai army patrol had bumped into a Burmese patrol of 50 troops, along the Thai/ Burma border. Rounds were exchanged and one of the Thai soldiers was killed. There was a lot of activity along the border with guerrillas operating there as well as criminals smuggling people, drugs, gemstones and lumber so it wasn't unusual for mistakes to happen.

It didn't help that there was no love lost between the two sides but with no war on officially there was nothing the Thais could do in response. So a faction of the Thai army approached the Battalion of KNLA I was with and asked them to attack the camp of the Burmese soldiers responsible.

What made this operation even more unusual was that we were to be driven through Thailand in trucks by members of the Thai army to an area opposite the enemy camp. We were then to cross the border back into Burma, carry out the attack then fall back to the trucks to be driven back to our camp.

There were several European volunteers there at the time but as they were quite tall and broad shouldered the Colonel decided they should stay behind. I was only a little taller than the average local. I have never been a big guy and after a steady diet of rice and hills could easily blend in with the group. When the time came to go I covered my face and hands in brown cam cream and further enhanced my disguise with gloves and a balaclava. I must have been convincing because one of the NCO's came up to ask me who I was and where I had come from. I am not going to lie I felt a little like a Selous Scout about to go on an external op.

About 60 of us boarded the trucks and off we went, the drive was only 30-40 minutes but would have taken days to walk if we had followed the border around. Once we got there we disembarked, crossed the river and got into a LUP to wait for dawn. The enemy position consisted of DKBA and SPDC camps next to a village. The soldiers had gotten lazy and were forcing the villagers to do guard duty.

About 30 minutes before dawn we attacked. With the first group going to the SPDC camp and the group I was with going to the DKBA camp. The DKBA weren't interested in a fight and took off as soon as the shooting started. We ransacked the camp, grabbed some Intel and set it on fire before going to link up with the other group.

As we were coming back we started taking heavy fire from the village. We were in the open and luckily there was a small mound we could take cover behind. About six of us got down behind the mound, the fire was murderous and too heavy to return. Bullets were cracking overhead and dirt was flying off all around the mound from bullet impacts.

The officer in charge was a short fellow with no weapon but two radios. He started talking into the radios at 90 MPH. After about 10 minutes the enemy fire lifted as they were forced to withdraw by the other group and we made our way to the village. The villagers had all taken refuge in the pits under their huts, they were probably more annoyed with us than pleased and I hope the Burmese would not take retribution out on them.

One of the NCOs had been wounded in the face, with blood dripping from his cheek, he was firing 40mm rounds back at the Burmese with a huge smile on his face. Sadly about six months later he lost a foot to a land mine.

We crossed the river and headed back to the trucks. One of the Thai officers was enthusiastically shaking everyone's hand as they boarded. It was now daylight and my disguise didn't work so well face to face. He gave me a surprised look as he shook my hand but didn't say anything. The mood in the trucks was happy but quiet and the trip back went by a lot quicker. On disembarking I slipped away before attracting any more attention and started cleaning my weapon and sorting my gear. The raid was considered a success with only a few light casualties on our side, three enemy killed and an unknown number wounded. Thai honour had been restored.

- Anonymous Western volunteer, Lieutenant, KNLA, Karen State, Burma.

"Everything is food"
KNLA Burma

In the jungle everything is food, including you. It's funny how once you leave the West, ideas on what food is expand. During a mis-spent youth I spent a bit of time in the jungle. I hadn't been there long and was sharing a hut with among other people one of the cooks. He often wore a heavy metal T shirt and had a chain around his neck, at first I thought it was a fashion accessory it wasn't until later I realised he was a prisoner serving a sentence for drug use, as one of the camp cooks. The chain was fastened with a piece of string and more symbolic than anything else, I never saw him or any of the other prisoners mistreated. There was nothing to stop him running off except that he had a decent life here, probably better than in the refugee camp where he had gotten himself in trouble previously.

149

The camp had a few cats and one in particular would catch rats then retreat under our hut to have its meal, why I don't know as the cook would always take the rat off it. My friend and I were discussing how this was odd. Surely it was better to encourage the cats to catch rats? We didn't figure it out until later, the cook was taking the rats away to cook and eat. Food in the camp was pretty simple, mostly rice with chillies and vegetables taken from the jungle, like banana plant (pretty much the whole plant is edible and the leaves can be used to cook with or serve up on).

Meat was a rarity in the camp and rats were a great way to supplement our diet. There's not a lot of meat on them and they taste quite gamey but on the positive side it's very lean. Bush rats are a lot smaller than sewer rats and importantly clean and safe to eat.

- Anonymous Western volunteer, Lieutenant, KNLA, Karen State, Burma.

"The day I realised my life's a holiday"
KNLA Burma

This villager was forced to work as a porter for the Burmese army. Overloaded with equipment and taken far from their village they would be beaten for any offence. As if that wasn't bad enough they were forced to walk at the front of the column as impromptu mine clearers. Burma has been at war pretty much continuously since the end of WW2 and now is one of the most heavily mined countries in the world.

After stepping on a mine the Burmese dismissed him and he was carried through the jungle for three days with no medication until they reached this band of KNLA guerrillas. KNLA medics were able to amputate his foot under local anesthetic. The procedure was carried out in a jungle clearing on a bamboo platform that had been built for the purpose that morning. The sound of the medic going to work with the bone saw is not one I will forget in a hurry.
The operation took just over an hour and watching it I realised I really had nothing to worry about, my life is a holiday compared to what could be. Since coming home I'm always amazed at the things we get upset about here in the west, while our countries aren't perfect they are a damn sight better than anywhere else I've been.

I have worked and travelled around Africa, Asia and the Middle East. My time overseas has taught me to be grateful for what we have, there's always someone worse off. Take responsibility for your own life and don't be so easily manipulated by those that would divide us.

- Anonymous Western volunteer, KNLA, Karen State, Burma.

"The Russians attacked"
Georgian Soldier: Georgia

I joined armed forces at the age of 18, it was way back in the beginning of 2007. My parents were strongly against it, moreover my father was veteran of war in Abkhazia in 1990s and was heavily against it. But being teenager with hot blood running through my veins I thought it was best thing I could do with my life, plus joining army and "patriotic cause" was heavily propagandized by Georgian government during that time. Good insurance and free collage afterwards seemed attractive as well. So I joined.

I signed the contract without hesitation and got assigned in 42nd battalion of 4th mech INF brigade. It was mostly made up of young boys like me who wanted to serve their country, we were lacking experienced officers. But God damn we were motivated to hell. We thought we could tear any enemy apart. No second thought.

In summer 2008 we were preparing for Iraq. We were scheduled to leave in September. On early evening of August 7, I was at home, tensions were building up between Russia and Georgia but no one thought we would have war. I got call from Ministry of Defense - "combat alert". We had those before, I thought it was part of regular exercise, maybe we were heading to Iraq. I said regular bye to my parents and brothers and sisters. No one was worried, except my father, like he felt something was wrong. I got to the base and what I saw made my heart pump race fast and scared me to hell. Everyone was packing bullets in magazines, tanks were being loaded with combat shells and prepared for March - it was war.

Still, no one thought we would have war with Russia. We received simple order - unknown military formations had crossed border from side of South Osettia and threatened ethnic Georgian population. "Destroy those units and protect civilians"

We got loaded in military Krazs and marched to South Osettia, in opening hours of August 8 we were at the staging area. I tasted war there - artillery firing, I was shocked, scared, excited and happy all at the same time. Picture of BM-21 Grads firing into night and lighting the skies is still one of most beautiful and horrifying things I have ever witnessed. We still had no idea we were at war with Russia. We were instructed to not to fire at Russian peacekeepers present in the area since they were not the target of our operation. So we went very motivated and sure in ourselves that we would crush rebels in no time and return to our homes in several days.

Around 12-1 pm August 8 out battalion was stationed in the woods near Tkshinvali (rebel capital). We had no idea Russian aircraft have been bombing Georgia for several hours already, communication between units was very bad. We were resting from night marches and skirmishes that took place at night. Everyone was relaxed and motivated, ready for action again. Suddenly I heard aircraft noise, we saw SU-25s passing over head, and we thought those were Georgian Air Force SU-25s bombing rebel positions. We waved and cheered as they passed.

After passing, they turned and went for second pass but that seemed weird. Thought they were returning at base? I felt pain and force over my whole body and got knocked over, everything went pitch black, I was alive but I was struggling to open my eyes. Ringing in ears, felt like my bones were turned into metal and I had no force to lift them. We were bombed.

When I opened my eyes, words won't describe what I saw, blood, human parts and knocked down branches of trees everywhere. I could not configure what happened or what to do. Chaos. I did not knew where my squad or officer was, I did not knew where my weapon was. I saw guy picking up his ripped of arm near me. My uniform was covered in blood and shrapnel. I was bleeding from everywhere.

I sat down and close my eyes, I did not wanted to be there anymore. I did not want war anymore. I did not want to be in the army anymore. SU-25s returned, firing unguided rockets and cannons, thankfully they targeted our trucks which were empty. After they left, we started retreating from the position, after the bombardment Russian tanks and infantry begin assaulting our position and there was no way we could hold. War went for several more days, Russians overwhelmed us. We were outnumbered and outgunned.

That day changed me forever, for several years I struggled with heavy PTSD which almost drove me to suicide. I was scared of airplanes passing overhead for several more years. My advice to anyone who is thinking of joining army - ask the veterans first what it's like. They won't lie to you, and even if they do with words, their eyes won't.

- Anonymous Georgian Soldier. Bravo Co, 1st Plt. 42nd infantry battalion, 4th Mechanaized Infantry Brigade, Georgian Armed Forces. 2008

"Absolute loss and destruction"
Georgian Soldier: Georgia

After the SU-25 bombed us in the forest, there was chaos everywhere, wounded screaming for help, those still on feet trying to evacuate wounded. I was standing and sitting down, now knowing what to do. Stunned. There was just so many bodies lying around. You could not tell who was wounded and who was alive. The image I won't be able to take it away from my head. Forest full of bodies and branches fallen from trees.

My officer grabbed me and got me in Hilux truck. The whole rear body of the pickup truck was filled with wounded. I was sitting next to driver. Behind me was young fella, probably 21-22. He was wounded in stomach. He died on the way to hospital. We had to drive several dozen kilometers to Gori military hospital (which was only military hospital in country).

When we arrived there. Absolute chaos, hospital was filled with wounded civilians. Russian aircraft raided Gori several hours before. They struck living flat block of civilians, killing and wounding many. Those who had hardest condition were treated first, so those who could still hold on had to wait, I remember seeing fear and confusion in the eyes of civilian hospital staff, but may lord help them, they saved thousands of lives in those days.

I remember sitting in the waiting area, still in body armour and vest filled with 5.45 magazines and grenades, even had RPG-22 on my back. I just could not notice them. Officer from military police approached me and I handed all my weapons and ammo to him. I did not knew where my AK-74 was, I lost it somewhere in process. I got treated some time later. I had shrapnel in my hand and a bit in leg, my ear drums were busted and I had difficulties hearing. But apart from those I had survived quite lightly. Also I am lucky I did not have my helmet strapped on, it would snap my neck.

I stayed there for 2 days, on the 10th I got out of hospital. Just like that just walked out. I approached some troops in the Gori to get basic information what situation was like. It was complete chaos, my battalion and brigade was simply put out of action and was retreating to Tbilisi. Remnants of 4th brigade arrived in Gori during late evening, I linked with what was left of my battalion, and my officer was killed in action day later after bombardment on 9th.

There was complete chaos. The army was not retreating, the army was escaping as fast is could. Russian aircraft circled over us and strikes anything target like. Everyone was on their own, just trying to save themselves. We just knew what we had to get near the Tbilisi (capital) and defend it at all costs.

Our large armoured convoys went during night, only time when Russian aircraft could not take us on. On 11th we were near Tbilisi. It was chaotic scene, tanks, artillery, civilian cars, buses all roaming on highway and Russian aircraft strike anything that moves. When we got to Tbilisi, situation got little better, other Georgian units had not taken such great casualties, communications and air defense got set up near the capital. We got in coordination with each other and we prepared for defense against Russians which had already taken Gori. But fight never came, war ended on 12th of August.

One thing, I never forget was - face of civilians when we retreated from Gori. You could read lost hope and feeling of betrayal. We left them to face Russians on their own, they were killed burned and raped by Russians and were not there to protect them. We, soldiers, who had sworn to protect them, just could not do so.

- Anonymous Georgian Soldier. Bravo Co, 1st Plt. 42nd infantry battalion, 4th Mechanaized Infantry Brigade, Georgian Armed Forces. 2008

"From Russia, With Love"
Russian Soldier: Second Chechen War
     We had this guy attached to us called Chuchella, it means scarecrow in Russian. He got attached to us about half way thru my deployment to Chechnya. We were VDV and he was a GRU operative but the dude was real scary. In Russia it's pretty common to wear a balaclava or scarf or face wrap because it's cold and it keeps the wind out of your face. But it's one thing to wear one, and it's another to never take it off. I mean I legitimately never saw this man take off his face wrap.

     He even slept with it, and he wore a Gorka suit so he almost always had his hood on. The guy was crazy, he never really said anything to anyone but whenever we would catch a survivor from a skirmish he would "interrogate" them by taking them up to the Domas (apartments). You could always hear the guys screaming so we'd move our camp a little bit further out.

     One time my platoon Sgt had enough and he made us pick up camp in the middle of the night and move like five clicks away. We didn't tell anyone over the radio or anything and we hid inside a building in the middle of this blown up city. We didn't even hide from the enemy, we hid from him.

     Well it didn't matter. We woke up to him staring at all of us in the entranceway to the building we were sleeping in. He had knocked out the two guys on door sentry and he just stood there, eyeing us all down like we were fucking meat to him. I've never been more sure that a single man could take on a room of soldiers and win.

     Needless to say, our platoon Sgt was relieved of duty when we got back to the base and that shook up the platoon, and also put me in a leadership position. One of the only things this guy ever said to me was 'Human flesh is a lot like pate, it's soft and malleable. I don't need special instruments to cut, I have my whet stone and my spoons.'

     And no shit this guy had a little mat with sharpened spoons that were almost razor sharp, along with a bunch of needle and thread. He explained to me that he liked slicing a finger a piece at a time, and then sewing the cut closed just so someone could feel the pain over and over again while losing very little blood. Fuck Chuchella

-    Anonymous Former Russian Soldier. Beta Company, 218th Battalion, 45th Independent Guard Brigade. VDV. Chechnya 2008.

"My worst day"
Russian Soldier: Second Chechen War
     One time, during a fight in a depression things got pretty hectic. We had started out on top of this bowl like depression, but we slowly worked our way down into the centre of it all. There was a thick patch of woods it was suspected that an enemy cache was present.

It was real early in the morning, there was a thick fog that rolled all around us and the air was heavy from the previous day's rain. This would be the worst day of my life as I knew it. We lost three people and almost every single one of us were injured in some way. I think that event singularly made me a different person.

As we reached the thickest part of the forest, we started receiving small arms fire from the trees. We expected this and didn't suspect anything strange about it. However, as we chased these two riflemen down, we started receiving more fire from different parts of the forest. Maybe 5-8 guys shooting at us from all around. A 12 man squad can handle that, but walking into an ambush that surrounded us had us worried.

Then the mortars started happening. Luckily, I don't think those guys had the location pre designated for fire. But they started walking rounds on us, and then it started pouring. I'm talking about thunder clapping above us, with thick heavy rain drenching every part of your body. As they walked rounds on us, we pushed outward and to the NW, as that was where there seemed to be the least amount of fire. We tried breaking contact but we realized too late that we had run up into a clearing in the woods. This was visible from the edge of the bowl and not even 300m away we had insurgents firing at us from the top. We took cover and me and my buddy laid down behind a felled tree. It was a fairly large tree but we were basically laying prone with our backs to the tree as bullets zipped past our heads.

He stood up to take a shot and all I remember seeing was him stumble back. He fell over on his ass and wheezed. I saw what had hit him, a VOG-25 (grenade launcher round) had hit him square in the chest and was stopped by his body Armour. He seemed fine but as I went over to him a burst cut through his body and one specifically had punctured his throat. I pulled his legs to drag his body back over to me and by the time I had pulled him back he was already dead.

I turned around to tell my squad leader but instead was met with a flash of light and a red spray.
Our RTO had taken a direct hit from an RPG-7, and had now become a red paste and bone fragments on the ground. I actually don't remember much after this. I don't remember fighting back and I'm pretty sure I just sat there behind that tree. But I'm here. No one talked about it. No one explained to me what happened. Honestly, I don't know if I want to know

- Anonymous Former Russian Soldier. Beta Company, 218th Battalion, 45th Independent Guard Brigade. VDV. Chechnya 2008.

"Russian and Chinese training"
Russian Soldier: Gobi Desert

The first time I worked with the Chinese, it was this massive cooperative training event that's the equivalent to JRTC. It's the one that you sometimes see on the news in America and causes everyone to freak out, even though it's just Russia and China training in the middle of the open plains, and it's scheduled like clockwork

It takes place in Northern China, close to the Gobi desert. The Chinese aren't very good hosts, and usually they just sit there for an hour boasting about their might while you sweat your balls off in full kit in the desert sun. Regardless, that training exercise was probably more dangerous than any of my three deployments. The Chinese military has zero regards for safety, which is saying something coming from a guy who signed up to get shot at and jump out of planes for two different countries. I watched Chinese privates dump a box of 60 year old grenades on the ground and just start throwing them in the open, with zero pit and zero cover

Like, I'm talking about a field as flat as table, and these guys are throwing grenades with fragmentation sleeve into the open, with no consultation or regard for anyone standing near them. During the night it would get freezing cold because of the wind blowing thru the plains. So we would find purpose built hills and shit that they would dig with excavators. Well little did me and my squad know that the Chinese army was using those as fucking ramps for their Jeeps! They were literally driving them up and off these massive dirt mounds mere centimeters from our heads.

I could actually see the tires treads at night, that's how close they were. The worst thing I think that happened was the Chinese Marines tried demonstrating one of their amphibious armored vehicles in this massive lake. Well it got about halfway through the lake but these massive bubbles started surrounding it as everybody looked on. Then it sank to the bottom like a rock, but the Chinese observers didn't even flinch! We went out there with a bunch of zodiac type boats and tried to rescue them. That was my first experience working with the Chinese. Underpaid, underperforming, and unprofessional to say the least.

- Anonymous Former Russian Soldier. Beta Company, 218th Battalion, 45th Independent Guard Brigade, VDV Gobi Desert, 2011.

"Strong wind"
Russian Soldier: Venezuela

This is the shit that SHOULD make America worried. So for as long as I can remember, Russia and China have been doing a military exchange program and frequently send troops down to Venezuela as "radio operators/equipment supervisors". It's the same thing the Soviet Union did in Vietnam when it sent Spetsnaz to teach the VC. Well, I was lucky enough to be on one of those exchanges.

156

We trained with the Venezuelan army which is about as poorly equipped as you would expect a South American dictatorship to be. Russia sent about a company of us and China sent a battalion, maybe a little more

Well the Chinese built this massive satellite dish on this island, call San Margherita I believe. There used to be a resort on the island, this big luxurious building that has marble columns and crystal chandeliers. Well, the Chinese cut it in half and then concreted the cut wall. They then placed the massive satellite on the other side of it where they use it to spy on American Naval fleet movement. The officers and higher enlisted all live inside the resort, it's quite decadent and you can tell they try to keep up with it. The regular enlisted, however, sleep in tents inside a fenced in area around the satellite dish.

It seems fine during normal weather, but this is an island off the coast of South America, so there's plenty of inclement weather and I got to watch hurricane force winds pick up these tents and their soldiers and just hurtle them into the fucking ocean. It was insane. I watched a Chinese soldier hang onto a fence post for dear life, like in a movie, only for him to slip and get blown away into the fence. If they are lucky enough to not get stuck in the middle of a hurricane, they still sleep, eat, and live next to a massive radar dish that I know is just emitting all sorts of nasty radiation.

Overall, I honestly loved Venezuela because all of the women there were gorgeous, they wanted to come back with me because they thought I had money and they would do ANYTHING to leave. The Amazonas is really beautiful and I enjoyed looking around Maracaibo and Caracas even though they were a little too shantytown-ish.

- Anonymous Former Russian Soldier. Beta Company, 218th Battalion, 45th   Independent Guard Brigade, VDV. 2011

"Watching combat unfold"
Russian Soldier: Dagestan

I deployed to Dagestan in 2012. The Caucus Caliphate had decided to rear its ugly head. Instead of funneling weapons and fighters out of the country, they wanted to stand their ground and fight. I remember standing in Kubinka and having both Medvedev and Putin there shaking hands and sending us on our way to go kill ISIS and all of its supporters.

Dagestan is a strange place, because it's almost like Afghanistan environment wise. A largely Islamic population that in some places has gone back in time to tribal/communal settings. There are valleys and sandstone/pumice mountains and there is desert mixed with small dense forests. My unit had a pretty simple job. We were split into small 6 man teams and told to range the mountain tops. We'd go from top to top walking along and observing villages from afar, and sometimes we'd provide over watch for regular ground troops in the valleys below. One particular instance I will always remember.

We were watching a small village in the pocket of a mountain as a motorstrelki (motor rifle) column went thru the winding roads. As they approached the village, we witnessed several firearms open up from a crowd and shoot at the soft skin trucks behind the lead BTR. Well with the amount of civilians that were in the courtyard me and my team couldn't open fire without endangering the locals. So we just had to watch and wait.

The courtyard started to clear but an RPG-7 was fired from a small building and all hell broke loose. All of the motorstrelki disembarked their trucks and opened fire into courtyard, which had that time mostly dispersed. But then this guy with another RPG ran out in front of the lead BTR and no shit DIVES in front of the thing and tries to shoot point blank.

I had a scope on my rifle so I was able to watch the rocket literally leave the barrel and bounce off the BTR which was like a meter away. The BTR then simply rolled over this guy and I watched him exploded from the pressure. The village was cleared out shortly after by my team as the motorstrelki mounted back up.

- Anonymous Former Russian Soldier. Beta Company, 218th Battalion, 45th Independent Guard Brigade. VDV. Dagestan 2012.

"Walking around"
Russian Soldier: Dagestan

We had been walking for like three days when command had authorized us two motorcycles and buggy. These buggy's are seriously cool, they are like a dune buggy with a KORD (50 cal) on a ring on the back. They have three seats but you can sit a fourth guy if you are smart and strap him in using ratchet straps on the back

Anyways, we were super happy to hear that we were going to not have to walk anymore. So we found a flat of land, and called our grid up on the radio, and they sent an MI-8AMTSh, which is like a gunship and a cargo helo all in one. The MI-8 was cable carrying the buggy and had the two bikes in its ass. It lowered the buggy down and we unhooked it and started prepping it. It then landed so that we could push the bikes out of the rear hatch. So I was busy prepping the buggy and getting the gun up and running when I noticed the buggy started to shake violently and tip to one side. I looked over and after my teammates got the motorbikes out of the ramp, the helo was taking off too early. It must've been a rookie pilot who didn't realize this but the downdraft on a MI-8's rotors are powerful enough to flip over regular cars, let alone a buggy optimized for weight and speed.

Well, we all jumped off and watched the buggy we were just given tumble end over end in the desert. By the time we caught up, the machine gun was bent like a paper clip and the buggy's frame was in ruins. Needless to say, me and my guys were pissed, because now the two motorbikes were practically worthless without the rest of the team. We just kept walking.

158

- Anonymous Former Russian Soldier. Beta Company, 218th Battalion, 45th Independent Guard Brigade. VDV. Dagestan 2012.

"Officers? Who needs them?"
Russian Soldier: Dagestan

In Dagestan we were doing a quick drive to, from one camp to another. We were delivering maps and schedules and shit, stuff that wasn't big enough to move by air but also needed to get there by the end of the day.

We were maybe a month into our deployment when we had this absolute dick of a lieutenant. I'm America, officer's act like they are above everyone else. In Russia officers ARE above everyone else. They are practically a different caste of people. But anyways, we were driving a small convoy of one UAZ jeep and one Vodnik and one Tiger. The lieutenant was in the UAZ in the middle and he had our RTO and an engineer in his car.

As we are driving down this small road, all we hear over the radio is "sniper!!! Halt convoy, fan out!" So we get out and make this giant human fan around the vehicles, with all of us pointed in different directions waiting for the next shot. Then our lieutenant shouts "there over at that hill" and he points so we lay covering fire on a hill to the East. There were like six of us just mag dumping at some far away hill as the other six of our team ran over to rush the 'sniper'. When the other team got to the hill, they found no signs of life, not even boot marks or shell casings. We went back to the jeep and the lieutenant was explaining that he was fired upon and pointed at a bullet hole in the window (which was laid down flat against the hood) that had penetrated and gone into the hood

We loaded back up and continued to the other base without incident. When we got back the lieutenant had to explain what happened and an investigation was under way.

About an hour later a captain had asked for the lieutenant's sidearm and when inspected, he found that one round had been fired out of the magazine. The lieutenant then admitted to playing around with his pistol and then firing it into the hood of the UAZ, so he made the RTO and engineer promise not to say anything and he called it up as sniper fire to cover his ass. He was relieved the next week.

- Anonymous Former Russian Soldier. Beta Company, 218th Battalion, 45th Independent Guard Brigade. VDV. Dagestan 2012.

"Target. Maximum firepower"
Russian Soldier: Dagestan

Dagestan, much like Afghanistan, has caves. It has mud huts, regular houses, caves, mountains, forests, and everything in between. It's an odd place. But one time I got to bring something Dagestan didn't have. Massive amounts of explosions. We lost more and more soldiers and federal agents to searching caves and hideouts than ever before. Guys were either getting shot in them, stepping on tripwires and blowing up, or just having whole caves collapse on them Russia had enough and authorized troops on the ground to just seal caves up or knock down entire houses if it was suspected they were trapped. One day we were receiving fire from a village and a small mountain peak to the West.

While having my marksman set up my Observer informed me that not only did I have 2s19 (mobile artillery similar to a paladin) on standby, I also had MI-28 doing a routine patrol and an SU-25T with a five minute window in my area. A sister platoon called us up and told us that nearby was a cave with positive identification on gunfire coming from the inside towards a patrol base.

I simply turned to my observer and said "Bring it down, I want all of it now."

Americans would never have artillery coming down while any type of air is up but Russia just assumes the risk. Within ten minutes I had artillery, rotary gunships, and fixed wing CAS all screaming down on targets within the same grid square. My Observer was jumping up and down like a kid who just saw his Christmas presents.

- Anonymous Former Russian Soldier. Beta Company, 218th Battalion, 45th Independent Guard Brigade. VDV. Dagestan 2012

"We killed all of them"
Philippine Soldier: Marawi

We killed the men who brought war to our homes. I don't feel bad. During the battle I killed several militants. One time, we were crossing a street, and one of our boys was hit by a rifle. He fell and we all ran for cover. Our leader ordered us all to fire at the building the shots came from. At once we all aimed and fired. Slowly we advanced to the building and I saw a man pop his head out of the window. For a moment it appeared that his hands were in the air.

I did not care. I fired and he fell. Two more militants were inside and we killed them also and dragged their bodies into the streets along with their weapons. Three bodies. Three guns. Three killed enemies. Three less in our city. The wounded man was treated and soon returned to battle. I am proud of our military for what we did in Marawi. We fought hard and won against a stubborn enemy. But we fought harder and killed many more of them than they killed of us.

- Anonymous Solider. 1st Infantry Division. Philippine Army. Battle of Marawi, 2017

"Destroyed City"
US Navy: Marawi

I was in Marawi back in 2017, my unit & I were sent to support the Filipino Marines when they retook the city of Marawi from the Maute bros. This basically consisted of us training and working out with the Filipino soldiers & marines,

160

training them in better marksmanship, joining them on patrols sometimes, etc. We were only there for a short while, but I've never seen so much devastation. I was a kid during 9/11, a kid when the images from Fallujah hit the web, and those were intense.

Bodies littering streets, gore and blown up buildings. But Marawi was something else. Less bodies, but more destruction. I don't know if the buildings were made out of glass disguised as concrete, or what, but the sheer reduction of these people's homes to rubble was something that really stuck with me. I feel awful for every family whose lives and livelihoods were ruined during that occupation.

-     Anonymous US Navy Sailor. PO3. Marawi 2017

"Day of Rage"
IDF Soldier: Israel

I personally saw Hamas members dragging kids to the fences, placing them near IEDs against the fence, handing them weapons, etc.... and trying to force them into conflict with our soldiers so the media and record it all on camera. We were involved in a 3 hour ambush near the fence.

Also one time, myself and 3 of my soldiers (4 of us total) fell into a trap were we fell through a made shift platform from Hamas terrorists. About 2-3 stories was the fall. I stepped on this platform first, in full gear, and felt that the floor under me started to give. I tried to stop my soldiers from stepping on but by the time I told them to stop, I fell through right on my back onto jagged rocks, with the other 3 soldiers falling right after me and on top of me.

We were stuck there in that pit for 4 hours. We all believed we would be kidnapped and taken to Gaza by Hamas. We all received significant injuries, unable to move our physically get ourselves out (we had to be air lifted out) so we called in for help, and waited for what seemed like eternity to either be killed or kidnapped. All we could do was wait and have our weapons points up towards the opening we fell through.

-     Shai Gershon. Golani 51. IDF. Israel, 2018.

"Incoming Rockets"
IDF Soldier, Israel

In Gaza when Hamas was shooting missiles, we have an alarm called אדום צבע (red alert) meaning incoming rockets. Israel is such a small country, that a missile can hit anywhere in the country. Hundreds of missiles would be shot into Israel. And every time the red alert went off, depending where you are located, you have anywhere from a few seconds to a few minutes to run and get cover. (Usually bunkers)

We were stationed in Gaza so we had about 10 seconds give or take to run to bunkers. And sometimes you're not always 10 seconds at a full sprint close enough to a bunker. This particular night, we had so many rockets shot in, and myself and my soldiers were exhausted, tired, and hungry, annoyed, etc....every few seconds, rockets, sirens, running to bunkers, clear to leave bunker, then all over again.

Towards midnight-1am we kept getting sirens but no missiles were being shot into Israel. I had a lone soldier from South Africa who was visibly stressed out and agitated. After some back and forth arguments about whether or not we can leave the bunkers, I decided to grab him, myself, and 1 other soldier to just step outside the bunker to smoke a cig. Well we make it outside and keep receiving Red Alerts but no missiles. But for some reason, I had a sick feeling come over me, and decided that all 3 of us need to get back in the bunker. The SA lone soldier was not having it and started to argue with me about how shitty and fucked up the situation was. I understood him, we all felt the same, myself maybe even more so because I was his commanding officer

I didn't let him light his cig, and yelled for him to get inside, he refused to until he got to smoke. So I went to grab him to pull him inside right when a missile fell no more than 20-30m away from us throwing us into the bunker with such force. Immediately saw my SA soldier with blood all over his face and blood all over my chest. I originally thought that blast ripped us apart. After frantically removing my gear, to everyone's surprise we were all ok and the blood that was all over me was from the SA soldier the received shrapnel across his forehead. (A nasty gash/cut)

-    Shai Gershon. Golani 51. IDF. Israel, 2018.

"Jungle Trek"
Indian Anti-Terror Police: Anti-Terror Campaign
The time was around 10am when me, my batch mate Debo (SDPO MRG), I/C Jagun outpost, an Assam Rifles Major and 40 personnel (20 Assam Rifles/ 20 Assam Police Commando battalion) assembled at the entrance of Kothar reserve forest under Lekhapani PS area with the objective of area domination and tackle any ULFA cadres supposedly hiding inside. The men briefed. Password "Buri--Dehing" acknowledged (in case of meeting another patrol party) and off we went into the woods, rifles cocked. Our eyes ahead, left and right, in single file formation. It wasn't long before I found out the forest was not exactly solid ground. As my feet sank beneath the wet soil, with chest-high grasses and ferns, we realised we were crossing a swamp!
(Found out later the swamp path was taken to avoid a herd of elephants, as stated by the local guide)

Upon crossing that we still had lots of jungle in mountainous terrain to cover. I looked down at my feet and realised light bullet-proof vest doesn't provide for suitable neck movement; all I could see were muddy and wet pants up to my hips. The only consolation was this time I was not alone; the entire squad had the same condition. Nevertheless, we marched on. Further up, we were tested by the presence of another muddier water body. Some of the men tried putting up dead logs to cross it. Some of them succeeded too, but those logs couldn't bear 95 kilos of body weight (I fell head first in it). Getting up and being in middle of the line, I crossed it without much difficulty (since you are already covered in mud, filth, leeches, grass, water etc; no point in avoiding them). After reaching solid ground, we stopped to rest (honestly, that was to check how many leeches we could remove from our bodies).

Ten minutes later, we were back to business; adopting to jungle warfare, being able to withstand mosquitoes, leeches, snakes, having skins sticking against uniforms damp and covered with mud, soil, water etc. Icing on the cake would probably be the extra weight of water and mud on jungle boots n uniforms, leaving BP's aside. Darkness started to fall at around 4-30pm and the Assam Rifles Major advised everybody to "speed up". I wondered as to how would that be possible; but as seconds passed, being in the middle of a single line formation, you have to move at the common pace, no matter what! Probably a good thing because it made crossing the jungle less difficult. Water body, thorny plants, vines, elephant grass, elephant dung, leeches etc. whatever the hell the jungle unleashed did not, or could not, reduce our pace! The ones up ahead went about making a path by cutting up the elephant grass, ferns, vines etc. as much as possible (And also to reduce the number of leeches falling off from these upon our heads and necks)

Finally we reached a tea garden and then a village named Kakhoroni (or Nahoroni) where after cordon and house-to-house search, we picked up 2 men supposed to be linkmen. (Normally, in rural areas, people cook food thrice a day and there isn't much in the way of leftovers. Checking a kitchen and garbage dump would indicate if there had been a greater number of people who ate as against the number of family members. Further on-the-spot interrogation and body language gave way to possible suspicion) they allegedly sheltered ULFA cadres at their homes as (As night halts). After that, we rested and checked our clothes n boots for leeches.

At pitch dark night (Cloudy night, no moonlight to speak of), our last obstacle was crossing the Buri Dehing river (no bridge).

Off we went on foot, in pairs, close to each other, marching behind those on our immediate front. Sometimes the water was ankle level n sometimes hip level. Mercifully, this time I didn't fall down. Our guide was well acquainted with the terrain to help crossing the river without any of us getting drowned. The river was kind enough to wash off most of the mud n filth from our uniforms. Upon reaching the other side, after around 4-5km of further walking, there was another village where our vehicles were parked. We went off to Jagun outpost after that.

-   Rahul Protim Das, APS; Deputy Commandant, 13APbn, North Lakhimpur, Assam. Anti-Terrorist Operations

TRAINING, BARRACKS, AND NON-COMBAT OPERATIONS

"Laying the fallen to rest."
US Soldier

I've never been deployed, and only been the field and the range a handful of times. Infantrymen at the Old Guard have it way different than line units, you're lucky if you get to do anything Infantry like. As soon as you get to Myer, you go through ROP, (Regimental Orientation Program) it's basically a 3 week course on house to press, pin, preform rifle manual, and march. It's a base completely centered around D&C, funerals, big wig retirement ceremonies, Cordons, and wreaths at the Tomb. If it requires a dress uniform we probably do it. They put me in a MA company (Memorial Affairs). We escorted caskets from the chapel/transfer site to the grave. My first mission I held back tears, my second it was still hard but it got easier.

A few weeks later we buried a KIA, that one hit harder than any funeral. But now, the only hard part is fighting the wizard. You get numb to seeing crying families. Sometimes I feel awful, because I don't feel anything. You certainly feel bad, the person you're burying is a brother. It's an unexplainable feeling. Guys at the Old Guard don't see combat, they only deploy once a conflict so they can get a streamer on the Reggies. You get NCOs who talk about how chill it is, like it's a vacation. But none of the lower enlisted guys joined for this.

When you get down to it, the job is easy, stand there in a hot uniform. Don't move, squeeze your ass cheeks together, and take deep breaths so you don't smack your face on a head stone or eat grass. After doing this for 3 years, I've grown to hate funerals. I've told my family that if I die before them, don't have a funeral for me.

- Anonymous US Soldier. 3rd Infantry Regiment, The Old Guard.

"Join the Army!"
SADF Soldier: South Africa

Growing up in South Africa in the 1980s every boy was getting groomed to join the SADF. It was an adventure we could not wait to get started. The bush war ended in 1990, conscription went from 2 years to 1 year, but I still got my chance to join the SADF in 1993! I got my call up papers I am going to the Artillery in Potchefstroom. My older brother just looked at me and laughed, you are going to shit he says. Anyway, the big day has arrived. Standing at the show grounds with your parents saying goodbye and yes Mommy crying, what's going to happen to her baby in the army, a friendly Captain walks over and assures her that the army will take care of all these fine boys, nothing to worry about.

So suddenly we are all marched in to this big warehouse with bags and all, wow everyone is so friendly, the guy next to me says thank you corporal, and he gets quietly informed he is a Bombardier not a fucken Corporal, next moment all chaos breaks loose as the MPs arrive with sniffer dogs, this dog is sniffing your bag and up to your ballbag looking for drugs, about 5 guys were put one side as they had MJ on them, next moment we handed a burned Patty and piece of brown bread with a banana and the shittest coffee I ever tasted.

Next moment the Bombardier shouts eat the fuck up and get on the bus! After about 2 hours we reach the military base in Potchefstroom, get a brief introduction by the senior officers at the camp, we were asked politely to go fetch our gear by the stores, so the next two days at the camp is very nice, then suddenly we informed we are going for our medical! How things change when you get your G1K1 that means medically fit to get fucked up, welcome to Basic training in the SADF. Your life has changed forever.

- Anonymous SADF soldier, Bombardier 43 battery, 4 Art regiment Potchefstroom South African defense force. 1993-94

"Pat on the back"
US Marine

My boot year ITX at 29 palms I was a gunner on the 240, before the MWX started (force on force) we were briefed on known assets of each side. We were severely outnumbered in air assets and we knew that it was going to end up being an issue. Right before we stepped off to begin the exercise our BC proposed a challenge to the battalion, any marine who takes out an enemy aircraft would be awarded a 30 rack from the BC himself. As a boot I didn't even really think of it as a possibility and was more concerned with not fucking up, which would in turn obviously piss of my seniors. I'll spare you the monotony of most of the exercise which mostly included sitting in a sardine packed AAV for incredibly stupid amounts of time. One day after 15+ hours nonstop in the AAV we stopped and got out to set up a defense, when we got out, we realized most of us were out of food and water. As good marines do we looted a nearby supply drop that may or may not have been ours.

Our partner unit was postured in and around this natural choke point made by mountains, they had been getting fucked up by enemy air assets the entire exercise and we were sent there to supplement their losses. The cobras were flying in around the same times every day. So we were told what time to basically hide. We didn't really like the idea of hiding but all we had was small arms and 2x 240s. My team leader decided he and I would climb up the nearest mountain and set ourselves up for maximum fields of fire on any approaching enemy, the other machine gun team placed adjacent to us, you know, pairs... Hours go by and many possibly stolen MREs later. We realize what time it is and know the cobras should be coming soon. I was playing with a large bug when I heard the faint sound of rotors. I informed my team leader and at that point we decided fuck it let's get rid of some of this ammo we'd carried up the mountain. When they finally appeared they were much closer than expected and at eye level with us. The mountain blocked a lot of the noise and they arrived faster than we expected. Luckily in our boredom we linked a fuck ton of rounds and lubed her up probably a little too much.

On one knee, holding the vertical grip I attached to the 240s side rail we dumped hundreds of rounds of blanks between a 240 and an M4 lubed with LSA at the two surprised cobras. I've never been able to get a 240 to fire as good as that time with blanks since. The "coyote" (a marine who basically plays referee at these exercises) was amazed and surprised by what we did and called in that those two cobras had been effectively destroyed, in turn earning my team leader and my PFC boot ass two 30 racks from the BC himself. Needless to say I was told "good job marine" by the command and we never received beer from the Battalion Commander.

-    Anonymous US Marine. 1st Battalion 3rd Marines. 2020

"Nothing else like it"
US Soldier

I had a fairly unremarkable Army experience. I joined right out of high school when I was 18, did my 4 years, and got. I went a few cool places, did some cool stuff, met some lifelong friends, and even managed to make Sergeant, but by and large it was nothing too special. I was in a shitty unit towards the end, and by the time I got out I was sick of the pettiness, monotony and general bullshit. I was ready to go. I turned down bonuses and assignments and peaced the fuck out, ready to get on with my life.

The refrain you always hear from the recruiters and the retention people and the salty old timers is how much you're going to miss it when you're gone. "Yeah right," I'd always say, and roll my eyes. No fucking way am I gonna miss this bullshit. You can take your drug tests and motorpool fuck-fuck games and last minute Friday bullshit and stick it up your ass, Army, I'm outta here, and I'm not going to so much as spare you a glance back over my shoulder.
Today, I realized they were right.

Sitting on a bench in South Philly on my lunch break, eating a cheesesteak (American, mayo, ketchup, and fried onions from the original Tony Luke's, I highly recommend it), and enjoying the perfect weather, I realized how much I miss being a young soldier.

I miss my friends, I miss the B's, I miss the Arizona desert, the pines and mountains of the Pacific Northwest. I miss the long weekends, the late nights, and barely making it back for Monday PT, sometimes hungover or still fucked up. I miss the barracks parties, the night shoot qualifiers, and even rolling through the California desert in the gun turret of a sweltering Humvee. I miss Korean nightclubs and smoke pit cigarettes with the boys, beer pong and bonfires, waking up early as shit and running 5 miles on nothing but caffeine and hate.

I miss the sense of community. Of purpose. Of brotherhood. I miss that feeling that no matter how bad it got, I wasn't in it alone. I grew up in the Army. 18 year old me wouldn't recognize present me, and that's a great thing, believe me. I gained a greater appreciation for family, friends, relationships, and the little things in life like "enough water" and "clean underwear." I learned new skills, set myself up for future success with the GI Bill, and made some of the best friends I've ever had. So this is my love letter to the Army. It wasn't perfect. There were some low and dark places, some painful lessons, some people I'd rather not have met, and some memories I'd rather forget about. I wouldn't go back in, and I could never stay for 20.

But I wouldn't trade having done it for the world.

- SGT Will Capuano. US Army. 2016-2020

"Tactical Taco Bell resupply"
US Marine

We were out doing a PB op and my guys brought up how they wanted Taco Bell. Well I reached out to my wife at the time and asked her to give us a supply run. a 250 dollar order later we were trying to figure out how to get the guys the food being that we were in the middle of the woods and my LT was not okay with it. So a squad took the LT out for a patrol while mine went as well. Two different missions in mind and out being time sensitive we somehow silently barreled through the woods to the tree line along the road. Got on the phone with the wife and passed that around every turn she should flash her head lights so I can let her know when she's close.

Upon seeing the two flashes I cracked a string of multi colored chem lights and threw them out she did a quick stop and drop the food off and sped off we loaded our bags and beat feet back before the LT could get back. We passed all the food out and waited for the LT to get back and fall asleep to pass out the rest of the food to the platoon. The LT woke up to the smell of tacos and was about to say something about but our Platoon Sergeant just tells him to stuff his mouth with this taco ,proceeds to push a soft taco into his face, and keep his mouth shut. The rest of the op was a little more upbeat.

- Anonymous US Marine. Camp Lejeune

"Climbing Poop Mountain"
US Marine

If you've ever been to the Infantry Training Battalion, you'd know it's miserable. You're a fresh, new Marine. Still scared of everything, and it's hard to see the light at the end of the tunnel for training. It was the third or fourth week of ITB West in Camp Pendleton. We had just finished a night range and I really needed to make a poopie. I remember the PortaPotties were getting kind of full during the day, so I wanted to unload and show clear my bowels before bed.

We were forbidden to use flashlights at night by our instructors, so I more or less felt my way down to the porta johns to go take a dump. I open the door, lean myself rifle against the side, pull my trousers down and sit down on the seat. Only, I didn't sit on the seat. During the day, so many Marines went to take a dump that it had literally piled BEYOND the seat about 6 inches. Marines before me must have stood up on top of the bowl to shit. And I was the poor fuck who just happened to go take a dump in the dark.

I sat down…and immediately….I felt it...inside of me. Cold, thick, MRE poop. INSIDE of me. Other people's poop. IN. ME. I screamed. I screamed in disgust, in terror…in shame. The instructors and several Marines ran over to the porta John thinking I had been bitten by a rattle snake. They open the door to see me on the ground literally covered in shit. No one laughed. They all knew it could have been them.

This was the first time I had experienced any kindness from an instructor. He felt so bad for me that he let me go back to the barracks. We took his personal truck back, but he made me ride in the bed. Face down. Ass up. I spent 5 hours in the shower that night. Believe it or not, that's still not even close to the shittiest thing I experienced in the Marines.

-    Anonymous US Marine. Delta Company SOI 2012.

"They never forgot"
Canadian Soldier: Netherlands

In 2016 I went to the Netherlands for an international event they call the 4 days March. It's basically a long distance walk with a patrol pack that goes back to the early 1900s, where you cover about 160km over 4 days. Militaries from around the world sent teams & civilians participate as well.

Well, what I saw there really blew my mind. And it's how those people welcomed & treated us in particular. To give some context this event takes place in and around the city of Nijmegen, which is the area that my country (Canada) defeated occupying Germans in WW2 & liberated the Dutch. It was a major operation and although it was successful a lot of blood was spilled there. And even 70 years after that generation of soldiers liberated them, they hadn't forgotten and had the same energy and respect just because of the uniform we were wearing. It's like we were celebrities or something. They were cheering from the rooftops and streets, giving us drinks & snacks etc, there were girls trying to hug & kiss us, this one guy tossed me a 6 pack of beer... I remember we carried these little Canadian flag pins and handed them out, they disappeared quick.

168

It's hard to explain how it felt, but especially at the end of the March it was a surreal & emotional experience to be a part of this & witness the impact made by our forefather's decades ago.

- Cpl A.S. 4th div 32 bde reserve, CAF infantry

"Dazed and confused"
US Marine: Hurricane Katrina

Back in '05, my unit 1/8, was assigned as a quick reaction force that was capable of being boots on the ground anywhere in the world within 24 to 48 hours. Hurricane Katrina had just wreaked havoc to New Orleans so we responded. We hooked up with an AAV company, anyone familiar with these behemoths know they are prone to break down, especially in the water. Let's just say being packed in like sardines, breathing in diesel fumes, and the constant rocking of the ocean is never conducive to a good time.

Our primary mission in New Orleans was going through our designated sectors house by house looking for survivors or bodies. One day after a long hot day of searching through our sector we were headed back to our FOB.

It was my turn to be on over watch while the rest of the squad huddled in the bowels of the AAV trying to stay out of the sun. The combination of the hot day and breathing in diesel fumes was definitely affecting my mental state at this point.

As we are driving down the road I see an elderly man with a backpack pushing his bicycle with two dogs walking at his side. He stops and starts waving at me. My first thought is, 'huh, what a nice man' as I start waving back at him. A couple members of my squad see me waving so they stand up and start waving. Next thing I know the whole AAV of Marines is waving including our Lt. Suddenly I'm snapped back into reality and I start yelling to stop the AAV. The man comes jogging up to us with all his possessions, he is clearly irritated cursing under his breath and commenting how he thought we were going to leave him. After an embarrassing exchange of apologies we load him, his bike and dogs up and take him to the helicopter evacuation site.

To this day I still chuckle when I remember this incident. It must have been pretty comical to see an AAV full of Marines waving at this old man as we drove off. Rescuing people like him was literally our reason of being there.

- Jeff A. CPL USMC, 1/8 B Co. Hurricane Katrina Response.

"I see myself as lucky"
US Marine

So, I was never in combat, but I served in the Marines from 2006-2015. In 2009, I was deployed to Iraq as an Aviation Ordnance man and served in Al Asad and Sahl Sinjar, Iraq. After I got out I found myself in a furniture delivery job for 5 years before taking a job at the VA. Before I got out my life started to spiral out of control and I found myself lost and confused. After a couple of years and close calls I came out on the other side sober, and have stayed that way for 4 1/2 years. This experience caused a deep desire to help others who were battling demons like me.

I work at the VA now, working with Veterans who are battling addictions among other things. I've heard stories of a soldier joining with his childhood friend, only to see him hit by an IED. He is haunted by his friend, standing in different places, mangled body and all. I've heard the screams of Marines in the midst of night terrors. I've heard of veterans having a panic attack as the hospital medevacs come in because the last time they saw their friends, they were being loaded in the medevacs.

I see the anger over the Afghanistan fall since veterans have lost their friends over there. Every time I hear these stories, it puts my own experiences in check. To me, the things I went through and deal with today, at times seem unbearable but it's all put in perspective when I hear their stories. I thank God I didn't go through what they did, so I just try to get in the hole with them and hope one day they can feel some peace.

- Anonymous US Marine. Marine Aviation

"Embracing the suck"
US Marine

I was a lance corporal at the time. Still relatively naive and floating in the "E-3 don't know" mindset on my third annual training in the Marine Corps Reserves. The entire company was digging into the defense in the most miserable place to be in the Midwest during the summer; Fort McCoy Wisconsin. I was hacking away at the rocky soil with my broken E-tool as I watched Corporal Redacted run up and down the line receiving information.   He eventually settled down and finished the fighting hole with me. Hours later we finally looked down at our creation which consisted of a waist deep masterpiece" of a machine gun position. I laughed and said "fuck it, it's good enough" as I jumped in besides the M240 and prepared for a long night.

Not fifteen minutes later a cold breeze rolled in and every grunt on the hill was shook as we all knew what it meant; rain.

The dark grey clouds rolled in unusually fast as we frantically threw all our gear under a tarp and covered the gun. As expected, it pissed rain and we were soaked. Nothing new. But one thing besides our misery and wet socks were absent. We could not find the A-bag. (Bag of goodies for the Machine Gun) I immediately looked under the tarp which contained our gear. It was not there, it was not under the gun tarp either.

In a last ditch halfhearted look I peeked into the hole itself and to my horror the A-bag in question was barely visible under 6-7 inches of water. I swallowed my pride and boldly told Corporal Redacted the bad news. We hauled it out before anyone saw and never spoke of it again. I look back on times like these and only have one regret, I only wish I knew the good times were here before they went.

- Anonymous US Marine. 2/24 Echo Co. Iowa.

"Shit in the wind"
US Marine: Guantanamo Bay

In FAST Company we were in Cuba for a short period of time where we stand watch over Guantanamo Bay. During this time each Marine is assigned to a tower and my unlucky ass was assigned a tower we called HERO. It was around 90 feet in the air and you had to walk a zig-zag form of stairs to reach the top which in all took about 8 mins give or take with all your gear.

One day I was just relieved by our COG (Corporal of the Guard) for lunch chow and I saw him disappear in the distance as he drove off. It was a short time later when I felt the shits in my stomach form and I had to use the restroom immediately.

We could not leave our post without relief without severe punishment so we had a word for such events. Bravo Golf (Bubble Guts). The radio chatter went like this.

Me: Hero to COG.

COG: Go ahead.

Me: Bravo Golf

COG: I'm literally 30 mins away.

ME: BRAVO GOLF! BRAVO GOLF!

It was at that time I knew I was screwed. So I took off my blouse and I had my skivvy shirt on underneath and took it off and laid the skivvy shirt on the ground and proceeded to shit my brains out all in it.

I wrapped it up like a hobo would a bag on his stick and I leaned over the edge to throw it in the water. (Right next to the ocean) Luck was not with me because being so high up the wind caught it and brought it back into the stairway of the post, sending shit everywhere. I then looked up and saw not my COG but my Commanding Officer's vehicle in the short distance.

Once his vehicle came to a stop and he got out to check on me per his daily routine, I'm guessing the scent of shit and the visuals of it all over the stairs was the reason he got back into his truck and left.

- Anonymous US Marine. FAST C Co. 4th Plt. Guantanamo Bay, 2013.

"The Naked Mile"
Australian Soldier

Situation:

I joined the Australian Army at the age of 22 in 1994, I was allocated to the Royal Australian Artillery as a Gunner. The unit I was posted to was the 8/12

Medium Regt 103rd Medium Battery which operated the mighty M198s located in Holsworthy NSW Australia.

Like most of you men at an early age all I ever wanted to do was to be a soldier, my Dad and both brothers were and so now it was my time to shine. As soldier's they require lots of training hard work mostly conducting exercises and raining for war or in some cases just being fucked round.

One of these such exercises was in a place called Shoalwater Bay a Coastal tropical range with huge bush land. It was mostly a dry and dusty place until the wet season came and torrential rains turned it all into a complete shit fight.

It was about October-November 1995 And After 5 weeks of digging in shell scrapes constantly moving bringing our guns into and out of action, we were dirty wet tired and exhausted men really utterly morale-less.
Yes, you know that kind of feeling.

Our gun which was called 'Echo' and had unfortunately bore the brunt of this cunt ass fuckery as our bombardier had just been promoted and so he was hell bent on completing he's class act in bastardy…to the point that he's own lance bombardier tried to impale him with a star picket (by accident of course)..??

Anyway I too had enough of his shit and the whole fucking exercise, so thus began scheming mostly during picket on how to get square with all this fuckery.
AKA let off some steam bombardier Bennett?
Anyway during the last few days of the Ex one of our subbys (junior officers) Let's call him Lieutenant Dan, a fucken top bloke by the way had came up with the idea to streak right across the gun position's.
We all started laughing at the idea because we were fully tactical and in a live fire gun position.

Mission:

Nobody thought anyone let alone me would accept this challenge. We all sat there laughing like a bunch of 5 years olds at a puppet show. I imagined what if I could make the whole gun battery feel as happy as we were! Now you see just a minute ago we all looked as if we had eaten a bowl of cat shit, in fact it was kind of like that for the whole ex.
Now everyone was so happy!

The LT smiled, 'Hey Northey, if you do it I'll be your defending officer at your charge!'He snickered. Well how could I refuse? We all knew that's what would most likely happen, I mean a live gun position we only finished firing 5 mins ago.

Then I imagined the glory! Streaking though a battery during a fire mission! The accolades, oh the accolades?! Mmm? People would tell stories about me to their grandchildren…and great grandchildren! But was it really worth going

172

to the cells, stoppage of pay and possibly all of the extras in the world!? Well I thought about that for half a second.

'Sir you're on.'

Execution:

The fellas started pissing themselves laughing uncontrollably. I calmly and slowly disrobed and prepared for battle stripping away my webbing, Cams and rifle to just boots and a Bush hat!

"Fuck off he's really doing it!" they muttered giggling like little school girls. I'm not lying when I say that these men were laughing so hard absolutely crying with anticipation! It was drunken silly stewpot one bloke actually pissed himself and with all that idiot-like banter going on.

I'd lost surprise as the command post went off at the noise due to the tactical nature of our position. Noise disturbance! Pfft that would be the last thing on the BC's

(Battery Commander) mind after this bloody stunt!

I would have no more of tactics or green shit, because I was on a mission a mission of morale primed and ready to go over the top!

I was totally naked but armed to the teeth with a wicked sense of Aussie humour, and thus didn't need anything more.

I began my attack at dusk during stand-to for added reality. My cock spinning around like around like a rotor blade on an attack helicopter. I felt totally invincible. By all accounts it was quite a hot day.

Sprinting from gun to gun I thought about assault the Command Post and even a secondary mission to hit the forward observer elements but unfortunately they were miles away. Disaster struck early on after passing the 3rd gun 'Bravo'. A group of men commenced a flanking attack at first about 3 blokes then 7 or 8. Thus being massively outnumbered almost 10-1. I had to abort my attack, and make for a tactical withdrawal.

However it was far too late for me…

"Kill him!' Kill that cunt!" they yelled. I then reassured myself that Bravo gun weren't taking prisoners and so turned back heading for home. Bravo were closing fast full of mockery and furious anger.

It was unknown to me but the good old Bravo gun Sgt had told this gun crew that a crazed homosexual had attacked an infantryman in our AO a few nights ago.

It was just a dumb BS story for the new guys, but guess it had a lasting effect on them, because they currently weren't happy campers!

After running through the lime green with my cock spinning out of control' one of these boys crash tackled me. Like he was conducting a match saving tackle…at a grand finale. And so I hit the ground like a 1000 pound bomb! I bravely tried to escape his clutches with only one leg fully operational. Gravely wounded I failed to escape as the whole battery swarmed. Enveloping me like bees on honey! I mean I felt like that guy in the movie Platoon trying to run for that chopper it was so tragic! The man that tackled me and rearranged my leg was Jordo the regiments No 1 prop forward for our rugby side and possibly the last guy I wanted to run into.

The kangaroo court commenced like Comanche's on General George Custer. Flurries of punches kicks, knees and even some wicked laugher… was brought to bear!
Bastards.

After much hard heart ache, covered in dirt, blood and many bruises plus a dick hole full of gravel, I was finally recognised by someone eye gouging me. 'It's Bully!' Everyone started pissing themselves with laughter. I was released from the onslaught. "You mad cunt Northey, what the fuc*k* are you doing mate?!" "Trying to make you cunts happy!" I said.
Administrations and Logistics:
My pride undiminished I was then marched off to see the Battery commander in the CP. Walking up to face the boss like a war criminal at the Haig and with the whole gun battery in stitches.
Some prick had the gall to yell out to me, "Where's your rifle, cunt?"
And with that the whole CP started laughing. The boss was still angry but much to my surprise let me go! The fact was after it was over they were all laughing.

Command and Signal:

Mission accomplished! I know many a soldier has given his life for his mates, buddy's and comrades, Queen and country. But a dick full off gravel? That has got to be just as good if not better. The motto is this: Morale is always worth a dick full of gravel…So don't ever forget that! Now every Anzac Day my beloved mates remind me of that act of valour back in 95 with a whoop whoop whoop and few cold beers.

- Greg Northy. Australian Army. 8/12 Medium Regt 103 Medium Battery. 1995

"Shit head"
Anonymous

I served for a few years in a peace time military in the south pacific, and did my basic in a frozen hellhole in the middle of winter. Just like every basic, you had your popular recruits, physically able recruits, terrible recruits and those who didn't make it through because of bullshit injuries.
Any which way, we were in a foxhole at our platoon position in the winter, snow all around. Recruit A and B were on Stag/Sentry at about 0300.
Recruit B decides she needs to go relieve herself, an emergency of the MRE related nature.
Recruit B disappears for about 25 minutes.
She comes back, and gets back in the foxhole.
Recruit A exclaims, "Can you smell that?"

Recruit B, who hadn't taken notice of the smell, suddenly realizes the worst and takes off her helmet.

Turns out, she'd had a bit of a mishap, and completely missed the hole she'd dug. Que the shit on the night watch cap, which was then hurrily discarded, and Recruit B had a cold head for the remainder of the FTX.

- Anonymous Soldier. New Zealand Defense Force.

"Why I hate the army"
Romanian Soldier

I served in the Romanian army in the 1980's. We did field exercises most times and especially during the summer. We had to dig holes and sometimes in gas masks. My partner helped me dig the hole with our shovels. The sun was going down so we could not see so well. The hole was about 3/4 my height so we were almost done. I start to pat the sides to make them hard so it doesn't cave in when we sit in it.

I'm patting the side of the hole with my shovel when I feel a soft patch. I stabbed it with the shovel and it felt very soft. I stabbed it again and I see dirt all up my arm. The gas mask makes it hard to see so I put my face to my arm. I said to my friend, 'This dirt is moving.' He looks closer at me and then starts to hit me with his shovel. I said, "What the fuck are you hitting me for!?" Then I felt the dirt move on my neck. It wasn't dirt.
It was hundreds of baby spiders.

I started to scream and scream but it was muffled because of the mask. Other soldiers came over to see what was happening and they all started hitting me with their shovels too to get them off. By the time I get naked and all of the spiders off I'm all bloody and bruised. I put my clothes back on and kill the rest of the spiders. "I fucking hate the army." is what I said all night long.

- Private Apostol Stoian. Romanian Army. 1980's

"I cried for all of them"
US Soldier

I served 23 years in the Army. I fought in the Gulf War, the Iraq war and in Afghanistan. I didn't realize how greatly it affected me until I retired and went on a battlefield tour of Europe.

Being a military history enthusiast I had saved money for years to visit battlefields from Russia to France. While I was visiting the memorial at the Somme, something hit me. I don't know what it was, but it was like…realizing…and I mean really realizing the amount of blood that was spilled there.

I looked across the fields where the British advanced and I just fell to my knees and wept. I saw the faces of so many soldiers in my head. The anonymous faces of British soldiers. German soldiers. French soldiers…and then my soldiers.

I couldn't control myself. I was on my hands and knees crying like a small child. My wife was with me, and she hadn't seen me cry in almost 15 years. She was concerned and knelt beside me. "What's wrong, babe? Are you okay?" "I'm crying for them." I said. "For who?" My wife asked.

"All of them."…I could tell she couldn't understand, but it was clear as day to me.

I cried for every man who has ever held a sword, spear, musket or a rifle. I cried for the men whose lives were taken. For the ones who's souls were shaken by the savagery and barbarism of war. For the men who would forever be empty shells.

I cried for them because visiting that place was the final realization of what war takes from all of us. It was the most vulnerable and therapeutic moment of my life and I shall never forget it. God bless all those men. Of all wars.

- Anonymous US Army. Colonel. 1991-2014

"We almost died and had no idea"
US Marine: Guantanamo Bay

Cuba is mostly a waste of time for infantry Marines. I was in FAST (Fleet Anti-Terrorism Security Team) and for some reason the Marine Corps likes to send us to Cuba to be glorified border patrol to catch Cubans who sneak over or under the fence.

Other than that, it's not a bad place to get some good training in to refine your infantry skills such as patrolling and land navigation. It's not a rare thing to see a whole squad of boot rifleman learning to patrol in the hills and salt flats of the eastern side of Guantanamo Bay.

Anyway, there's lots of old relics around the area that are left over from the Cold War. Machine gun bunkers, mortar pits and trenches. We were out patrolling one day when we come to this open field. We started walking through it when we noticed all these odd extremely rusted, distorted, circular disks on the ground.

None of us had ever seen anything like them before so we started picking them up and tossing them at each other. I tapped on one and felt that it wasn't hollow and I tried to find a way to open it, including bashing it on a rock. Nothing.

Once we reached the edge of the field my buddy came across this super old wire fence with a metal sign face down on the ground. He picked the sign up, turned it around so he could read it and said, "Uh guys. Don't fucking move." "What why?" He turned and held the sign up so we could read it. "DANGER: MINEFIELD"…we were playing with old Cold War mines. Somehow we had wandered into an old minefield. It took us probably two minutes to walk into that field, and another 90 to walk out.

- Anonymous US Marine. Charlie Co FAST. 2009

"Ghosts haunt them"
US Marine

I never served in combat, but a lot of my senior Marines did. I joined a battalion of fresh boots who had never seen combat, and a drop of Marines from a different battalion that was being disbanded joined us. They were all combat veterans fresh off of a deployment from Afghanistan. I was lucky enough to be one of their roommates. We all looked up to them. They were tough, knowledgeable, but also kind of mean and sad. Frankly, I was jealous. They got to experience the litmus test of combat.

My roommate was a nice enough guy, but he had anger issues. He would come back to the room late at night super drunk and just fuck with me. He's throw some of my stuff around, call me names, and I felt like he just tried to scare me. I grew to hate him.

One night, he came back especially drunk. He stumbled into the room and pissed in his pants. He was just obliterated. I helped him into bed. He could barely keep his eyes open. I sat down in a chair next to his bed because I was afraid he might have alcohol poisoning and I was going to keep an eye on him. He started moaning and crying. He kept saying a name. "Chris. Chris. Chris." He wept, in his drunken stupor. I didn't know why he was saying that name. I slipped out of the room onto the catwalk and saw some Marines down at the smoke pit. It was late, and they were all drunk. Some of them were the veterans I mentioned. I explained what was going on and asked who Chris was. They told me he was killed on their last deployment and that it hit everyone pretty hard. In that moment, I ceased to hate my roommate. Instead, I felt sorry for him. I respected him, but I could tell this would affect him his whole life. After that, nothing he did bothered me.

- Anonymous US Marine. 2nd Marine Division. 2014.

"Blood for the Blood God"
US Marine

As Marines in Camp Lejeune, we sometimes trained in Fort Pickett, Virginia. It sucks. We hate it there. We were bivouacked out in the woods and had been out in the alternating rain and extreme summer heat. We had been out there by ourselves for days. Slowly going insane. I was sitting on my pack one day smoking a cigarette when I heard faint chanting in the woods. I put out my smoke and walked in the direction of the noise. I went through the woods and came to a small clearing where I saw the strangest shit of my life.

A group of Marines had gathered in a half circle, and were chanting in musical tones, 'Blood for the blood god! Give us libo! Give us salvation! Blood for the blood god!' I walked closer, and saw that the Marines had found a dead squirrel, made a small crown of twigs for it, tied it with 550 chord to a homemade cross and placed it on a podium.

The chanting stopped and a Marine wearing a headband made from a skivvy shirt and a cape from a woobie blanket held up a field notebook and gave a sermon to the Marines who had gone insane.

"Ooga booga. Oh glorious blood God. Grant us freedom from this shitty army base! Grant us unlimited tobacco and Rip Its. In your name we slay. Amen".

Then, he held the dead squirrel above his head and the Marines all began chanting again.

Before long, I was also on my knees before our Squirrel Blood God praying and chanting. If you can't beat em', join em.

- Anonymous US Marine. 2nd Battalion 6th Marines. 2015.

"Not So Special Forces"
US Marine

If you've done the Mountain Warfare Training in Bridgeport California, you know it SUCKS. It's 30 days of getting your peepee smashed by the mountain and sucking for air. We had some "Special Forces" from a certain Middle Eastern country training with us. They think they're high speed, but basically they're a bunch of rich boys playing soldier.

We were hiking up the mountain, hour 4 or 5 into a 10 hour hike. One of the foreign dudes asked if he could help carry one of our machine guns. We reluctantly gave up a 240 for the sake of international relations. He had the gun over his shoulders for probably ten minutes before you could visibly see him struggle to move up the trail. When we came to a bend in the mountain, on the left side of the trail was a straight up incline, and to the right was a drop off of about 50 feet. A straight cliff. The sPeCiAl fOrCeS dude looked right at us, said, "No no. This is too heavy." And no shit just tossed it off the side of the cliff.

We just stood there wide eyed with open mouths looking at him. "What? My country buy you another. No problem. No problem." So a few minutes later me and a few other Marines were climbing down that straight cliff to go retrieve our machine gun that this idiot just tossed off the side of a cliff. We were so pissed that in the middle of the night one of my guys peed a little bit in that guys Camelback hydration source.

Don't throw our guns. And you won't drink our pee.

- Anonymous US Marine. 2017. Bridgeport MWTC

"Off with his leg"
US Marine

Bridgeport Mountain Warfare School sucks. And sometimes there are civilians everywhere. There are public roads that go right through training areas. Sometimes the civilians like to take pictures of us like we are wild animals. So one day, we decided to freak some of them out. Morale was low, and being a Squad Leader I decided to raise some morale.

178

So, naturally, we did what Marines do. We decided to see if we could end up on CNN so we staged a fake amputation. My friends held me on the ground, and found a large stick that resembled an axe and I laid down next to a road. Two Marines held me down and shoved a rolled up boonie cover in my mouth, while the third Marine held the "Axe" in his hands. We waited for cars to drive by and then "Amputated" my leg by swinging the branch down.

Another Marine stood by with a piece of paper in hands presiding over us like a judge. He would give a speech loud enough for cars to hear of their windows were down. "YOU HAVE BEEN FOUND GUILTY OF WITCHCRAFT AND TREASON. THE PUNISHMENT IS AMPUTATION" Every time a car drove by, we performed this little skit. One car was so freaked out they almost drove straight into the forest.

Our fun ended when Gunny found out and made us break the axe in half and broke up our little play.
- Sgt Nicholas Laidlaw. 2/24 Echo Co. Bridgeport 2017.

"Broken Compass"
US Marine

So during our work Up for deployment went through a series of training events called FEX (Field Exercises). Well we just got our new platoon commanders and one night he set a recon patrol out. Nothing too crazy ya know. Patrol belt, NODS, dip and water. We're going really slick is what I'm saying and we conducted PCC's and PCI's etc. We step off and it's only a fire team plus one on this patrol and everything seems like we're all good. I'm on point with my navigator. Wales only a few meters behind me with the Now this patrol was only supposed to be an hour long tops and I start to notice that it's taken quite a while to get to the next checkpoint so I told the patrol to hold and I got him up to me. I asked him how far until we got to the next checkpoint and I kid you not in those shitty ass NVG's the Marine Corps gave us I saw this man's hand shaking like and earthquake was happening. His first words to me were "I don't know man this compass needle keeps moving back and forth".

My first thoughts are "Fuck…god knows how far we've walked though these woods with no actual sense of direction". I call the Lt. up to me to tell him the situation and I could of swore he shit himself cause he had no answer what to do. I suggested we radio the COC and tell them what's up and try and a ballpark reverse azimuth.

So after 4 hours of walking through the swamp, spider webs, creeks and Michael j fox for a Nav man we get back to the PB and this butter bar absolutely bashes me for getting the patrol lost. At this point I was already tired and pissed from everything that happened that my smart ass mouth said "Well sir, I didn't exactly see you leading out there" and I have never been throat punched harder in my life from a man smaller than me.. And I'm 5'7.

"Born wrong place, wrong time"
US Soldier

My name is Brady Atherton and my story is very different from most that you will read throughout this book, but one that should be heard nonetheless as many younger soldiers share the same demons as I.

I will start by saying that I only ever made it as far as Kuwait. The date was May 18, 2014 when I signed my papers at the MEPS station down in Sioux Falls, South Dakota. It was the day after my 17th birthday. I was a small town farm kid full of piss and vinegar and ready to lay my life down for my country. Basic training and A.I.T. went by like a flash, I arrived at my first unit. The 235th MP Company had just returned from a 9 month deployment to Bagram Prison, Afghanistan. I was devastated to find out that it could be another 5 years before the 235th could deploy again.

As a young man growing up in South Dakota I was raised to believe that there is no greater sacrifice than to lay down your life for your country and I was prepared to do so. I went on with the Army for 6 years in total, across three separate units and offered myself up for 4 different combat deployments. But I was NEVER the right rank or M.O.S. for what they needed. I was NEVER ENOUGH. After 3 M.O.S. changes and B.L.C. I still wasn't ENOUGH. Stories from the men and women that have been in combat would horrify any human being or at least should. Not me. It only intrigued me and made me want it more. I wanted to be a part of making a difference in the Middle East. But I was NEVER ENOUGH. I've always been the person who wants to help and would give the shirt off of my back but how can I help someone deal with issues that I myself couldn't understand. The feeling of being, you guessed it, NEVER ENOUGH.

The DEMONS whispered to me every time I would watch the news and the faces of soldiers who weren't coming home would pop up. That could have been me, that should have been me. Why does his family have to bear the folded flag? Can they handle that? I know my family would be fine. They would be proud. I wish I could take their place. The Demons whispered. They STILL do to this day. UNDERSTAND that it is not my fault that I cannot wear a patch. UNDERSTAND that it is not my choice that I don't. UNDERSTAND that I have my own internal battles every day. I was robbed. I was Uncle Sam's waste of space, air, and money for 6 years and not by choice. I will never know whether or not I would have made a difference. It is not my fault that I am young, I was born into the wrong generation. Just know, I WISH I had been there. I WISH I could have saved and taken the place of just one of those faces I saw on the news.

Just know that I am BATTLING DEMONS of my own and I never even stepped foot into a warzone. I was lied to and robbed. As I grow older and have been reading "Battles and Beers" for some time (maybe even since Nick started it)

I'm not sure I understand the war as many of you probably don't, and I NEVER WILL. I have made my permanent separation from NEVER being good ENOUGH and have learned to be "down" with the DEMONS.

- Brady E Atherton. 235th MP Company/ 147th Transportation/ 644th MP Company United States Army/ South Dakota Army National Guard

"High Speed, Low Drag"
US SOF

I'm very well aware that Navy SEALs, Green Berets, Recon, MARSOC, and any other high speed cool guy unit is vastly over represented in pop culture. Kids these days in high school want to be a cool-guy high-speed operator when in my opinion, the REAL cool guy work is done by the grunts.

Plenty of times we'd go out on missions, be out for a few hours, and then come back to our Wi-Fi and Pizza Hut. I remember seeing grunts come back onto base and just seeing how fucked up their uniforms and equipment was. Like they'd just chewed and pounded some major dirt for weeks, because they had.

I'm proud to be an 'operator', I know lots of guys are TOO proud. But from my perspective, it's your riflemen, machine gunners, arty, and other infantry-type dudes that win wars. They're the dudes on the ground day in, day out, in close proximity to the enemy. They do it all with a fraction of our training and budget. They're legit, hardcore warfighters with varsity level balls who get almost no media recognition unless they die in large numbers. Here's to the ground pounders!

- Anonymous Special Operator. Unit and branch redacted due to current service.

TO BE CONTINUED IN VOLUME TWO
Please consider submitting your experiences in war, or experiences of a loved one to be added to my latest book. Reach out through either Facebook or Instagram at Battles and Beers: War Stories or Battles and Beers: Military History

I would like to extend a special "Thank You" to every single person who helped to make this book possible. From all the veterans who consented to sharing their stories, and their family members who submitted one on their behalf; you are amazing. I thank all of you for your service, and for your work in ensuring that generations of stories don't get told for the very last time.

As a reminder, it is impossible to verify any war story 100%. I have tried my best to document as many stories as I could. Take each of these stories with a "grain of salt". I believe this work is important and have tried to present it the best I can. I will remind you, I am no author but just a dumb grunt who had the time to sit and document all of these. I receive more and more stories from veterans all over the world every day. There will be more books coming in the future, so if you would like to contribute, please reach out to me at **Battles and Beers** on Facebook or Instagram.

A special thank you to the following Marines for being good dudes during my time in uniform:

Dustin Peters	Dalton Henning	Logan Henning
Captain "O"	Ryan Trantham	Cody Wynn
Anthony Palmer	Aaron Reep	"Petey"
David Packer	Tyler Frederick	Hunter Adrian
Nate Campbell	Ryan Whitbeck	Criss Cornelison
Marco Beachley	Andrew Herring	Frederick Mannhardt
Norman Renfro	Blake Mitchell	Doc Bishop
"Black Jones"	Landon McCabe	Deivy Sanchez
Sean O'Neill	"Pit Viper" Pittman	Jake Stotts
Mike Pullen	Doc Vliet	Jake Gunderson
Jeff Gilliard	Nathan Rudolph	Austin Conklin
Dan Daly	Jachin Adams	Asa Floyd
Gage Trevino	Jake Hammons	Preston Ross
Jon Cavazos	Brandon Ward	Aidan Price
"Robocop"Robinson	David Reeves	TJ Conway
Omar Carlos	Ronald Walsh	Nick Lacey
John Sadler	Alex Cline	Arata Young
Austin Newell	Shaun Keene	Hunter Merkel
Micah Cole	Zach Simkins	Josh Reynolds

Austin Reynolds

Joshua Brown

Michael Albright

Anthony Russo

Anthony Zazzaro

Darwin Peralta

Justin Lewis

Gray Dellinger

Nathan Derr

Austin Smith

Rolando Ramirez

Earnest Haggard

Jacob Royer

Blake Richardson

and many, many

more.

Made in the USA
Monee, IL
06 January 2025

76108473R00105